D1809663

European Glocalization in Global Context

Europe in a Global Context

Series Editor: **Anne Sophie Krossa**, University of Giessen, Germany

Titles in the series include:

Nicole Falkenhayner
MAKING THE BRITISH MUSLIM

Roland Robertson (*editor*)
EUROPEAN GLOCALIZATION IN GLOBAL CONTEXT

Roland Robertson and Sophie Krossa (*editors*)
EUROPEAN COSMOPOLITANISM IN QUESTION

Sophie Krossa
EUROPE IN A GLOBAL CONTEXT

Forthcoming titles:

Chris Grocott and Jo Grady
CAPITALIST IDEOLOGIES IN EUROPE AND BEYOND

Europe in a Global Context
Series Standing Order: HBK: 978–1–137–00313–3 PBK: 978–1–137–00314–0
(*outside North America only*)

You can receive future titles in this series as they are published by placing a standing order. Please contact your bookseller or, in case of difficulty, write to us at the address below with your name and address, the title of the series and one of the ISBNs quoted above.

Customer Services Department, Macmillan Distribution Ltd, Houndmills, Basingstoke, Hampshire RG21 6XS, England

---

European Glocalization in Global Context

Edited by

Roland Robertson

Distinguished Service Professor of Sociology Emeritus, University of Pittsburgh, US and Emeritus Professor of Sociology and Global Society, University of Aberdeen, UK

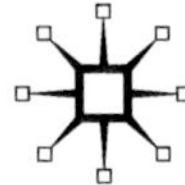

First published 2014 by
PALGRAVE MACMILLAN

Palgrave Macmillan in the UK is an imprint of Macmillan Publishers Limited, registered in England, company number 785998, of Houndmills, Basingstoke, Hampshire RG21 6XS.

Palgrave Macmillan in the US is a division of St Martin's Press LLC, 175 Fifth Avenue, New York, NY 10010.

Palgrave Macmillan is the global academic imprint of the above companies and has companies and representatives throughout the world.

Palgrave® and Macmillan® are registered trademarks in the United States, the United Kingdom, Europe and other countries.

ISBN 978–0–230–39079–9

This book is printed on paper suitable for recycling and made from fully managed and sustained forest sources. Logging, pulping and manufacturing processes are expected to conform to the environmental regulations of the country of origin.

A catalogue record for this book is available from the British Library.

A catalog record for this book is available from the Library of Congress.

For Judy

Contents

Tables and Figures

Tables

Figures

Acknowledgements

I owe much to Anne Sophie Krossa, the editor of the Palgrave series Europe in a Global Context. I am especially indebted to Sophie for her encouragement and practical assistance in helping me to finish this book. She has been much more than a series editor – not only a great help but also a great friend, as well as a very congenial co-editor of *European Cosmopolitanism in Question* (2012), which was published in the same series. I am also greatly indebted to Didem Buhari Gulmez, who has done much editorial work in other publishing ventures with which I have been involved. I wish to thank both Sophie and Dido.

Richard Giulianotti has co-authored with me quite a large number of publications in the field of sports studies. Indeed, it was Richard who took the initiative in this collaboration. Victor Roudometof, undoubtedly one of the best graduate students that I have ever had, has been in the forefront of exploring and promoting the helpfulness of the concept of glocalization, largely independently.

I am very grateful to Victor and Richard for keeping the glocalization flag flying.

Contributors

Paolo Demuru is a post-doctoral researcher at the Pontíficia Universidade Católica de São Paulo, Brazil. He received a PhD in Semiotics from the University of Bologna and a PhD in Linguistics from the University of São Paulo. His work aims at developing a dialogue among Semiotics, Sociology of Culture and Anthropology. His research interests include football culture in Brazil and Europe, stadia, urban conflicts, historical and political discourses, and media. His publications include the book *Essere in gioco: Calcio e cultura tra Brasile e Italia* (2014).

Andrea Esser is Principal Lecturer in Media and Communications at Roehampton University (London) and founder of the AHRC-funded Media across Borders network (www.mediaacrossborders.com). Her research interests centre on media internationalization and cultural globalization. Recent work focuses on the growth of the TV format trade, patterns of flow, and the local–global nexus of format adaptation. Publications include "Television Formats: Primetime Staple, Global Market" in *Popular Communication* (2010) and "The Format Business: Franchising Television Content" in *International Journal of Digital Television* (2013). In 2013 she also edited a special issue on TV formats for *Critical Studies in Television* (8:2).

Debra Gimlin is Professor in Sociology at the University of Aberdeen. She is the author of *Body Work: Beauty and Self-Image in American Culture* (2002). Her most recent book, *Cosmetic Surgery Narratives* (2012) focuses on cross-national differences in women's accounts of aesthetic procedures.

Christopher Kollmeyer is a Senior Lecturer of sociology at the University of Aberdeen. He received a doctorate in sociology from the University of California, Santa Barbara, where he was subsequently a faculty fellow in the Global and International Studies Program from 2003 to 2005. His interdisciplinary research focuses on the economic and political consequences of globalization and the changing nature of contemporary work and labour markets. His research has appeared in leading social science journals, including the *American*

Journal of Sociology, European Sociological Review, Social Forces, and *Social Problems.*

Ewa Morawska is Professor of Sociology at the University of Essex. She specializes in comparative-historical sociology of past and present international migration and ground-level multiculturalism in Europe and the United States. She is currently working on a project comparing multicultural orientations and everyday practices in Cairo under the Fatimid caliphate in the late 10th–mid-11th centuries; Venice in the 15th century, St Petersburg in the late 18th century, and Berlin at the turn of the 19th and 20th centuries.

Roland Robertson is Distinguished Service Professor of Sociology Emeritus at the University of Pittsburgh and Emeritus Professor of Sociology and Global Society at the University of Aberdeen. Among books that he has authored or co-authored are: *International Systems and the Modernization of Societies,* 1968; *The Sociological Interpretation of Religion,* 1970; *Meaning and Change: Explorations in the Cultural Sociology of Modern Societies,* 1978; *Globalization: Social Theory and Global Culture,*1992; and *Globalization and Football,* 2011. Among books he has edited or co-edited are: *Identity and Authority: Explorations in the Theory of Society,* 1980; *Church–State Relations: Tensions and Transitions,* 1986; *Religion and Global Order,* 1991; *Talcott Parsons: Theorist of Modernity,* 1991; *Global Modernities,* 1995; and *European Cosmopolitanism in Question,* 2012. His work has been translated into more than 20 languages.

Victor Roudometof is an Associate Professor of Sociology at the University of Cyprus. He is the author of three monographs, editor or co-editor of several volumes, and author of over 30 journal articles. His main interests include globalization, glocalization, culture, transnational relations, diaspora, and religion. His latest book is *Globalization and Orthodox Christianity: The Transformations of a Religious Tradition* (2014). Currently, he is working on a manuscript about glocalization. For a full profile see www.roudometof.com.

Franciscu Sedda is Research Professor of Semiotics at "Tor Vergata" University of Rome. He previously held the position of vice-president in the Italian Association of Semiotic Studies (2007–2009). His main fields of research are semiotics of cultures, the development of a general semiotic theory and a theory of glocalization, the history of Sardinian culture and consciousness. Professor Sedda was awarded the "Sandra Cavicchioli" prize, chaired by Umberto Eco, for the best MA thesis in semiotics in 2000–2001. The work is published under the title *Tradurre la tradizione* [*Translating Tradition*] (2003). Among his edited volumes is *Glocal: Sul presente a venire* [*Glocal: On the Present to Come*] (2005). His most recent book is entitled *Imperfette traduzioni: Semiopolitica delle culture* [*Imperfect Translations: Semiopolitics of Cultures*] (2012).

Prologue

Roland Robertson

1

My work on the theme of globalization began as long ago as the mid-1960s although I did not explicitly use that precise concept until a few years later. My own first, very brief, use of the concept of glocalization was in my book *Globalization: Social Theory and Global Culture* (1992). Since then I have published a great deal on glocalization, quite often with other colleagues. In fact, the themes of globalization and glocalization have been, in one way or another, central to most of my published work in the last three decades. It should be noted, however, that this has been continuously combined with my very long-standing concern with culture, religion, and theory. In contrast, my strong interest and publications in the field of European studies have been of a significantly shorter duration. In fact, while I was working in England in my earliest full-time academic positions (at the Universities of Leeds and Essex), culture, religion, and theory were my major preoccupations and I wrote exceedingly little about Europe.

I did, nevertheless, develop strong feelings about the European Economic Community and its subsequent development and geographical expansion, but, somewhat ironically, it was not until I migrated to the USA in 1967 that I began to think seriously and academically about Europe. This definite interest in Europe arose on a number of bases. In the first place the University of Pittsburgh had a large and fast-growing centre for international studies, part of which consisted of a distinct programme in (West) European studies; although I was also attached to other area-studies programmes, including ones dealing with Latin America and Asia. I can now recognize fully that my comings and goings between the USA and Europe, from 1967 onwards, were of enormous significance in my obtaining a fairly comprehensive appreciation of Europe and its shifting adjacent countries. Moreover, my frequent visits to Europe from the USA in the late 1970s, the 1980s, and the 1990s enabled me to "cover" intellectually much of the European continent. It should also be said that I was at the University of York, England, from 1970 until 1973, and the University of Aberdeen, Scotland, from 1999 until 2010. In addition I have occupied visiting positions in Sweden, Japan, Brazil, Turkey, Austria, Thailand, and Czechoslovakia (before the Czech Republic was separated from Slovakia).

I now recognize that the frequency of my travels, not only between the USA and Europe, but also within the latter and other countries, sensitized me considerably to processes of glocalization. More specifically, they sharpened my sense of diversity and discontinuity, on the one hand, and recognition of sameness and continuity, on the other.

Having accounted, at least in part, for my orientation to matters European, it should also be said that my political attitudes, as they developed from an early age, greatly shaped my thinking. Of particular importance were my early contacts with the USA in the form of encounters with American servicemen, owing to my living in the 1940s in a small village in rural Norfolk, and subsequently in the 1950s in the city of Norwich, in close proximity to a number of American and Canadian airbases. These features of my early childhood contrasted very significantly with what I could only perceive as a dark, forbidding, and turbulent continent just over the North Sea. I was acutely aware of the latter because I lived only few miles from the coast of East Anglia. This meant that, to the east I discerned "darkness", threat, and confusion, while to the west (Canada and the USA) there seemed to be brightness, hope, and simple clarity.

As I became increasingly interested in British domestic politics, as well as world politics in general, I began to form specific attitudes towards Europe and the USA. Those were years in which there was not inconsiderable debate about whether, on the one hand, Britain should join Europe, and, on the other, the widespread sense that Britain was being overwhelmed economically and politically by the USA. For example, there was talk at that time of the UK possibly becoming, in effect, the 51st state of America. Britain's orientation towards Europe was also much affected by the demise of the British Empire in the years following the end of the Second World War. During that period I was rather swayed by the idea that, from the ashes of the old British Empire there could be established a genuine commonwealth of nations. Like many young people of that period I was very active in the movements for colonial freedom and was a participant in many demonstrations about freeing British and other colonies from imperial rule. Concomitantly, however, I became very sceptical about the value and viability of the move towards European integration. However, after more or less fully returning to Britain, at least for residential purposes, in late 1999, I have become convinced that Britain should be an enthusiastic, but ever-vigilant, member of the (much enlarged) European Union.

2

It was in part as a result of my visit to Japan in 1986 that I came to see the value of the concept of glocalization. Specifically, I was to learn that the Japanese term *dochakuka* was common in that country. Literally this word means to indigenize; but by the late 1980s it had become fairly common as a term in business studies in the USA and elsewhere: a term that involved calculated synthesis of the local and the global. (Much later I learned that geographers had also been using the term glocalization, adapting it primarily from the same Japanese source.) Very briefly put, glocalization involves the diffusion of ideas and practices from one "place" to another. The intention in this book as a whole is to approach Europe – more specifically Europeanization – as a site and a form of glocalization. Also, in its opening chapter and its epilogue, the question is intermittently raised as to the viability of institutionalized Europe in its present form.

In my own first chapter I attend to Europe as a particularly unique site of glocalization; at the same time dealing with some of the more triumphant views of Europe in the global arena. I promote the idea of Europeanization as the institutionalization of the idea of Europe. In addition, I consider the manner in which processes of glocalization work and its advantages over the much more frequently used concept of globalization.

In the second chapter Franciscu Sedda attends to what he calls the theme of the world of worlds; this being the starting point for his semiotic discussion of unity-within-multiplicity. Also central to this chapter is the thesis that Europe consists of a history of constant and plural glocalizations. He concludes by advancing the proposition that we can speak of the globality of meaning in relation to local globalities. Much of Sedda's chapter is framed in reference to the very influential work of Braudel.

In the third chapter Victor Roudometof discusses the glocalizations of Christianity in Europe and Eurasia, with particular attention to Europe "itself". Apart from its direct concern with religion and globalization/glocalizations, Roudometof's chapter is particularly important in its dealing with boundary issues; since Christian Orthodoxy extends considerably beyond the boundaries of Europe as conventionally understood (as of mid-2014). The tension between Christian universalism and ethnic nationalism is given particular emphasis.

In the chapter that follows, Andrea Esser outlines the ways in which TV formats are sold internationally, or globally, for local adaptation. As with most chapters in this volume she focuses on the simultaneity of homogenization and heterogenization. In so doing she critically considers the notions of delocalization and deculturalization. Esser's is an innovative contribution to both European and media studies as well as to the theory of glocalization.

In the fifth chapter Ewa Morawska, one of the world's leading scholars of migration, takes critical but constructive issue with the formulations of Giulianotti and Robertson; rendering their types of glocalization as *phases* of the latter. She emphasizes the neglect in studies of migration of the immigrants' inputs to their host societies. She concludes with the important observation that it is much easier to incorporate cultural traditions in contrast to their human carriers.

Paolo Demuru considers, in Chapter 6, the interpenetration of Brazilian and European forms of football, with particular emphasis upon the dance-like quality of "the beautiful game" in Brazil. Like Sedda he also uses semiotic ideas, with particular emphasis on the way in which the Brazilian form has been influenced by football in Europe.

In the chapter that follows, Debra Gimlin, a leading world figure in the study of the human body, explores the flow of conceptions of primarily female physical beauty from Europe and America, on the one hand, to the world in general, on the other. Central to her investigation is the phenomenon of beauty contests and the different ways in which Euro-American "standards" have affected other regions of the world.

In chapter eight Chris Kollmeyer attends to the simultaneous rise and fall of democracy around the end of the 20th century, with particular attention to the glocalization of the democratic ideal. This is a particularly important topic given the widespread doubts about, and declining lack of trust in, "normal" democratic politics. Specifically, Kollmeyer tackles the arguments concerning globalization's capacity to democratize authoritarian countries. Drawing upon world-polity theory, Kollmeyer concludes, with a considerable amount of empirical evidence, that increasing connectivity across the globe both enhances democratic propensity and, at the same time, decreases it.

In the epilogue that concludes this volume I assess the overall analytic value of considering Europeanization in the frame of glocalization. This epilogue also takes stock of contemporary views concerning the place of Europe in the world as a whole in relation to its imperial past.

In one way or another, most of the chapters deal with Europe in what I would call a non-provincial way. Even though other regional areas are not discussed in any detail, a major concern is to illustrate the connections between different aspects of Europe with the "outside world". In other words, this is not a book about Europe per se, but rather about the application of a particular analytical approach to Europe, this approach demonstrating that Europe cannot, nor should not, be treated in an island-like manner.

1
Europeanization as Glocalization

Roland Robertson

Introduction

Carol Gluck (2009: 3) has aptly insisted that as "words change, the world changes...but the world...also has the power to change words". She goes on to say that "words are always in motion, and as they move across space and time, they inscribe the arcs of our past and present" (Gluck, 2009: 3). Furthermore, as scholars, "what we have in common is the injunction to follow our word to where it does its work" (Gluck, 2009: 3).

In this chapter I will follow Outhwaite (2008: 137) in attempting to do justice to a theory of European society by considering "the interpenetration of the local, the national and the global, in Europe and elsewhere". At least implicitly Outhwaite is, I think, critical of those who *have* claimed to consider Europe globally. In any case, in spite of such pronouncements as "Europe in the Global Age" (Giddens, 2007), the actual, comprehensive analysis of Europe *globally* has barely begun. My tack is to consider Europe in the frame of glocalization – hence the title of this chapter (cf. Delanty and Rumford, 2005). However, I do depart from Outhwaite's highly impressive *European Society* (2008), by decoupling the themes of Europe and modernity. In so doing I follow the increasing number of writers – notably anthropologists – who have come to regard the concept of modernity with some suspicion (e.g. Latour, 1993, 2013). To put this another way, a number of very important anthropologists have applied the methods and perspectives of anthropology – both cultural and social – to the so-called modern world. I contend that associating modernity with Europe is a classic example of Eurocentricity (Bhambra, 2007).

Eurocentricity and its offshoots

Bhambra is, however, only one of an increasing number of academics who have adopted anthropological methods – or, at least, an anthropological stance, to approach the so-called modern world. I think, for example, of Ulf Hannerz, Pnina Werbner (2008), Marshall Sahlins, Arjun Appadurai (2013), John and Jean Comaroff, among others. The binary that opposes modernity to "the primal" or pre-modern is steadily being eroded, as demonstrated by the increasing use of the concept of the in-between society (Robertson, 2014a). It is, however, not only anthropologists who have undone the all too easy distinction between the pre-modern and the modern (leaving out altogether the fast-fading notion of the postmodern) and contributed greatly to the abolition of the simple binary or overdone distinctions between regions and civilizations. A good example of this is the way in which our thinking about the Renaissance has been changed in the recent past, notably by Lisa Jardine (1998) and Jerry Brotton (1997) – the latter having made major contributions to the entire issue of the history of the mapping of the world in his work on cartography.

In addition I feel obliged to supplement Outhwaite's plea regarding a global focus on Europe with my claim that this cannot be accomplished without giving due attention to the increasingly important issue of glocality and glocalization. It is my contention that the idea of the glocal enables us to focus more satisfactorily on Europe – or, for that matter, any other worldly unit, as opposed to the relatively simple plea for a "global approach". In fact, this is what I seek to justify more fully during the course of this chapter.

In her review of a recent book on the French Revolution in global perspective (Desan et al., 2013), the British historian Linda Colley (2014) has remarked that the discipline of history is clearly a participant in the global turn. She has been particularly concerned to make the claim that North American historians are much more cosmopolitan than their European counterparts. Her main point is that European historians do not take a genuinely cosmopolitan approach to their studies, particularly studies of Europe itself.[1] One might also say that the same kind of contention is applicable to that which Edwards and Gaonkar display in their edited book *Globalizing American Studies* (2010), which is as glocal as it is global: the contributors illustrate well the ways in which the USA is treated differently by analysts in different countries, even though they approach their specific topics under a general rubric of American studies. This is clearly an example of glocalization (see also Pease, 2010).

Colley's mention of cosmopolitanism is somewhat ironic in the context of the present volume when one considers that, in the last few years, such authors as Ulrich Beck and Anthony Giddens have made cosmopolitanism the major characteristic of Europe as a whole (Robertson and Krossa, 2012). Beck's claim that we are experiencing, on a worldwide basis, what he calls a "cosmopolitanisation of reality" (Beck and Sznaider, 2006) raises very serious problems in this regard. The numerous contributions of Ulf Hannerz (e.g. Hannerz, 1992, 1996: 17–55 and 102–126) to the topic of cosmopolitanism have the great advantages of being truly global but not triumphantly so (see also Moyn and Sartori, 2013; Pollock, 2013).

It should be made clear that, in what follows, the concept of the global is firm but flexible, in the sense that, on occasion, global refers to the world as a whole; although sometimes it refers to Europe as a continent. The same flexibility applies to the concept of the local. In other words, that which is indicated as being local may well be a very large "unit" within an even wider context. Globality and locality are relative terms.

This chapter is largely concerned with the applicability and fruitfulness of applying the concept of glocalization to Europe. My argument in this respect is that Europe is particularly suitable for such. This is principally because, throughout its history, Europe has been clearly marked by many fragmentations and shifting territorial boundaries. Because the territorial mosaic of Europe has been so fluid – often violently so – this makes it a particularly suitable site for the application of a concept that seeks to overcome the strong – but, I maintain, meaningless – contrast between the global and the local. Of course, the fissures within Europe have not merely been territorial they have also frequently been ethnocultural. The expansion of the European Union since the fall of the Berlin Wall at the end of 1989; more specifically, the issue of East, Central, and South-Eastern European countries, as well as those in the Baltic area, have to be considered. The inclusion of ex-Soviet countries, including the former East Germany, has given a particular gloss to the overall consideration of Europe, not least its susceptibility to analyses deriving from the theme of glocalization. Moreover, the eastern limits of Europe have been in continuous dispute or uncertainty for hundreds of years, and at this time of writing the uncertainty about the limits of Europe are of particular relevance in terms of the geopolitics and geoculture (Hannerz, 2009) of the border regions. In addition, this has not merely been an empirical, historical issue, but one that is also of great analytic and theoretical concern. For example, one has only to refer to the great and growing controversy concerning Orientalism (Irwin, 2006).

At the present time of writing, summer 2014, the European scene is particularly complex and volatile, although these features of contemporary Europe should not be exaggerated within the context of the overall history of the continent. There is much continuing controversy about the EU's Eurozone, the fallout from its crisis of 2008–2012, the largely subsequent rise of anti-immigrant, right-wing movements across the continent, and a significant number of national controversies concerning membership in the European Union.[2] The present "turbulence" in Europe (Giddens, 2014) is being greatly exacerbated by Russia's annexation of the Crimea and the closely related problem of the boundaries of Europe centred upon the crisis in Ukraine. At various points in recent years many European nations have expressed their doubts about the viability of the European Union. In fact, support for the European Union is at an all-time low. At the present time much of the external threat to the EU arises from the seemingly aggressive (or, perhaps, defensive) behaviour of Russia; including the European and US fear that Putin is on the verge of annexing other previously Soviet states, particularly those in the Baltic area (as well as Transnistria, the Russian-speaking portion of Moldova, and even Moldova itself). As will be seen in the Epilogue, Putin's apparent Eurasian ambitions further complicate the overall situation. As of late July 2014, the ability of Ukraine to maintain its territorial integrity seems to be fading, with the apparent possibility that the eastern part of that country will separate.

It is against this backdrop that this introductory chapter – as well as the Epilogue – is being composed. It should also be said that this is a period when there are a number of potential breakaway movements or territorial entities within the states of the European Union. A few examples may suffice. Perhaps most visibly, the cases of Scotland and Catalonia are evident, with a referendum pending in September 2014 within Scotland concerning its claim for independence from the London-dominated United Kingdom, but certainly not from the EU. In the somewhat parallel case of Catalonia there has been a long-standing desire to gain independence from Spain, the same being true, again within Spain, of the Basque people; although the aspirations of the latter crossover into France. In the case of both Spain and the UK there are quite a large number of less conspicuous moves in a similar direction. Indeed, the same kind of development has been happening in most parts of Europe, with some movements inside particular nation-states being linked to parallel movements in other EU countries. For example, there have been some actual or putative alliances between the Celtic components of Britain, Spain, and France.

To a significant extent these phenomena are linked to a long-standing concern with regionalization within Europe (Buttner, 2012). In fact, Buttner has connected the issue of "mobilizing regions" specifically to the theme of glocalization. At the same time, we are now witnesses to considerable "official" concern with what some political elites call localization, this being but part of a more or less globewide valorization of "the local", more specifically the local *community* (Robertson, 1997). This concern with the local has – at least in the case of Europe – arisen largely because of the sense that far too much legislation has been unilaterally imposed from the EU centre in Brussels. This proclaimed eagerness to localize has been a prominent feature of the current British Coalition government's programme. There is some irony in this, particularly at the nation-state level, in that the very ideology of localization (Hines, 2000) is, for the most part, being imposed upon localities by national governments, most clearly in the UK. This way of combining the "global" and the local might well be called imposed glocalization. Ritzer's (2004; Andrews and Ritzer, 2007) concept of grobalization might well be relevant in this case, although I have reservations about his general approach to globalization.

Other regions, such as the island of Corsica (long a part of France), have had much older claims to independence; while there have been long-standing and conspicuous right-wing political parties such as the Front National in France, the Freedom Party (FPO) in Austria, and others elsewhere that have agitated for the same. Much more recently we have witnessed the rise of the overtly neo-Nazi Golden Dawn Party in Greece; the racist, authoritarian Jobbik Party in Hungary, as well as the latter's dominant governmental party, Fidesz; the Our Slovakia Party (whose members wear Nazi-style uniforms); the Freedom Party in Ukraine; the Alternative für Deutschland; the Vlaams Belang Party in Belgium (that has Nazi roots); the Five Star Movement and the Northern League, both in Italy; the Danish Peoples' Party; the Finns Party in Finland; the Swedish Democrats; and the Freedom Party in the Netherlands. We should also include the Right Sector Movement in Ukraine that certainly has very authoritarian tendencies, even, possibly, Nazi tendencies. This has been a major target of Putinists in Russia and Eastern Ukraine. There are also the British National Party, the English Defence League, and, of course, the United Kingdom Independence Party (UKIP). The latter is particularly significant because, by the early summer of 2014, it had controversially and ambiguously more or less entered the mainstream of the British political scene.

One must also mention the relatively left-wing Eurosceptics, the Dutch Socialist Party also being anti-immigration. A few of the anti-EU movements on both the left and the right have joined forces to create transnational, anti-EU alliances. However, it should be emphasized that those on the left of this tendency are strongly opposed to discrimination on the basis of race or religion. In effect, these groups are forming a kind of European Tea Party "paralyzing the European parliament in much the same way as ultra-conservative Republicans have paralyzed Washington" (*The Guardian,* 2014: 8–9). Much of this extremism has been intensified by what is regarded in some quarters as the problematic and threatening presence of many thousands of Muslims in a number of European countries. In fact anti-Muslim sentiment has been amplified by a number of "terrorist" incidents in the UK, Spain, and elsewhere. Generally there has been a spurt of authoritarian right-wing movements all over Europe as well as in countries and other continents, such as the election of the Bharatiya Janata Party (BJP) in India.

It should be emphasized, however, that there has been a worldwide crystallization of left-wing movements, notably the Occupy Movement that strongly opposes contemporary capitalism, increasing inequality, the growing strength of large corporations, and the global financial system. This movement, as with most other contemporary movements (cf. McDonald, 2006), began in the USA as the Occupy Wall Street Movement, using the slogan "We are the 99%." This has spread to virtually every region of the world. However, as with most such movements the programmes or policies have varied from country to country – and with greatly varying degrees of success. Apparently the Occupy Movement was inspired in part by movements in the Iberian Peninsula as well as the Tea Party and the fast-fading Arab Spring. Here again we find a great deal of variation under the global umbrella of Occupy, with these local variations constituting examples of glocalization.

Much of the contemporary radical, right-wing tendency can be viewed in the frame of the theme of *populism*. In fact, Kennedy (2010: 182–184) deals briefly with this issue in the context of his discussion of "working-class cosmopolitan urbanism". The mere demand in a number of countries for referenda is one indicator of the rise of populism. The latter is, of course, difficult to separate from racist, anti-immigrant, and nativist movements – at least in the contemporary period. A great deal has been written about populism but I will not dwell on this debate here. Suffice it to say that populism involves actual or putative political leaders appealing to what might well be called the lowest common denominator; seizing upon, fusing, and aggregating widespread complaints and grudges concerning the threat to, or demise of, what are conceived of as traditional and/or local values and identities. Such values and identities are often regarded as being a consequence of the actions of the "political establishment" – a favourite phrase of UKIP in Britain.

In fact, populist movements draw upon and strategically amalgamate grudges, grievances, and complaints from all across the political–ideological spectrum. For example, UKIP draws much of its support from disaffected and disillusioned working-class, traditionally Labour Party, citizens, and even from "despised" ethnic minorities. In the case of the latter there is the "drawbridge" phenomenon that involves scrambling to demonstrate allegiance to the host country and keep potential or actual newcomers out. Undoubtedly, many of the controversies about immigration derive from the Schengen Agreement that was initially signed in 1985 by (a mere) five nations well before the European Union formally existed. The Maastricht Treaty in a sense consummated the principles that were indicated by the original Schengen Agreement. This latter agreement involved the abolition of internal European border controls so that individuals or groups could move freely without having to show passports. Schengen has been substantially extended and is now at the centre of numerous disputes concerning migration within the EU. The Maastricht Treaty accelerated the move towards the goal of making the EU an "ever closer union".

One salient feature of the presence and rise of racist and/or populist movements has been the scapegoat phenomenon. As in many other parts of the world – including China, France, Australia, the USA, and yet others – at any point in time particular peoples have been blamed for the stresses and strains in a particular society, the most prominent – not to say tragic and egregious case – being the European Jews in the 1930s and 1940s (Robertson, 2014b). Of course, the European Holocaust was not concerned solely with the extermination of the Jews. It included, as other victims, Gypsies and Roma, as well as left-ideological opponents. In any case, Gypsies and Roma have frequently been conflated into one category of scapegoat and often further collapsed into or combined with the category of Travellers. Antagonism towards the Turks in Germany has not been confined to their Muslimism. In fact, the fusion of Turkishness and Muslimism in itself indicates the ways in which religion, ethnicity, and cultural tradition have been conflated Soysal (1995, 1998) has characterized this kind of societal presence as a form of post-national membership across much of Europe.

Even though I am particularly concerned with Europe – or specifically at this point with respect to the European Union, or what I call here institutionalized Europe – it should not be forgotten that the history of Europe has been replete with fissures, secessions, and utopian expectations. These phenomena have, of course, been the cause of numerous wars. In fact, institutionalized Europe, mainly in the form of the European Union, was largely inspired by the desire to overcome these, but particularly the rise of the Nazis and the horrors of the Holocaust perpetuated by them as part of the Second World War.

However, it may be rather controversial to state that some strong supporters of the EU have had one thing (only) in common with those who have thought that the control of Europe has meant control of the world as a whole. In any case, the chequered history of Europe (e.g. Simms, 2013; Wallerstein, 2006) makes it a particularly fruitful site for the application of the concept of glocalization. As Knill and Tosun (2014: 266) have argued *"Europeanization can be conceived as a special case of glocalization, since both concepts challenge the assumption that international pressures lead to a homogenization of national practices and structures"* [emphasis added]. This statement does, indeed, provide the principal rationale for the present chapter and its remaining pages.

Of crucial importance in the fluidity of communal, ethnic, and other collective claims within Europe, has been the theme of *self-determination*. Having become increasingly prominent during the 19th century, particularly in terms of the rise of nationalism – or what is sometimes called ethnonationalism – the idea of self-determination became widespread across much of Europe. This acceptance occurred during the period leading up to, and during the discussions concerning, as well as the years following, the Treaty of Versailles (1919), which was designed to conclude the First World War.

The most forceful leader of the self-determination movement at the deliberations in Versailles was the American President Woodrow Wilson (Manela, 2007), who subscribed to the principle that each "nation" should have its own covenant with God. This was in spite of the fact that Wilson did not agree with Mexico's achievement of independence during the Mexican Revolution of 1910. He also offended Japan by his refusal to recognize non-Western ethnic claims to recognition. Controversy concerning the wisdom and consequences of the Treaty of Versailles continues to the present day, primarily because of its precipitating significance with respect to the rise of Nazism and the breakout of the Second World War in 1939. However, a more relevant consideration is the point made by Delanty in his argument that post-First World War reconstruction was closely "linked to the attempt to forcibly create nation-states in the territories of the former central European empire" (Delanty, 1995: 100). As he (Delanty, 1995: 101) says, "the sheer impossibility of creating a peaceful European order based on ethnically defined nation-states ultimately led to the failure of the European idea". The carving-up of Europe in this manner has made it particularly susceptible to processes of glocalization and, at the same time, consolidated the very principle of self-determination. In particular respects the latter consequence has been disastrous, since it has more than encouraged many subsequent nativistic movements, notably the break-up of the former Yugoslavia, which, rather ironically, had *itself* largely been the result of the implementation of the self-determination principle along Wilsonian lines. It should be also noted that the Bolsheviks had their own conception of self-determination and currently, under Putin, there is a "post-Soviet" version of this that is of considerable significance (Robertson, 1995a; Zizek, 2014).

Since glocalization (as well as hybridization) involves the problem of the fitting or adaptation of an idea to a "place" (Burke, 2009; Canclini, 1995) then Europe's susceptibility to such processes should be very apparent (Robertson, 2014a). Indeed, this is, perhaps, one of the most important European features so central to the present book (Tilly, 1975, 1992). Peter Beyer (2007) has persuasively argued that globalization actually involves *multiple glocalizations*; and Victor Roudometof (2014) has applied this thesis very effectively to Orthodox Christianity. The basic idea involved in this respect is that something that is promoted and regarded as being universal (in the present context, Europe) is thematized along local particularizations. Leaving the specific theme of Orthodoxy to one side, one can readily see that Europe has simultaneously undergone a process of universalization with respect to the ongoing formation and reformulation of the European Union, as well as having to deal with the relationship between its national components. In fact, many of the controversies within Europe have involved precisely this issue.

Much resentment has occurred in particular countries concerning the applicability and, particularly, the desirability of European laws, protocols, and conventions being applied to their specific cases. The complexities of both the UK case and comparable ones are beautifully articulated by Linda Colley (2014) in her *Acts of Union and Disunion: What has held the UK together – and what is dividing it?* (See also Nairn, 2003).

Glocalization and the case of language in the EU

The issue of language provides a particularly good site upon which to consider the great relevance of glocalization to the theme of Europeanization within the EU. De Swaan's work is of particular importance in dealing with what he calls the EU as "a subsystem of the global language system, but one with a multitude of strongly anchored national traditions. From the outset the official language of every member state was recognized as an official language of the European community and, later, of the European Union" (De Swaan, 2013: 69). In tracing the relationship between language and the expansion of the European community up to the formation of the European Union, De Swaan notes that, in 1956, the six founding members of the original European Community (the EEC) contributed four languages – Dutch, French, German, and Italian – clearly a manageable number.

Over a number of years the addition of various other languages, including English, Greek, Portuguese, Spanish, Finnish, and Swedish meant that, by 1995, the official languages of the EU numbered eleven and that was, to again quote De Swaan (2013: 69) "increasingly difficult to cope with for the translation and interpretation services". By the beginning of 2007 the total population of the EU was around 486 million and the number of official languages numbered twenty-three. There are four levels of communication within the European Union: the first level concerns the sessions of the European Parliament and of the external dealings of the European Commission; the second level has to do with the affairs of the EU Commission bureaucracy, with the officials more or less informally using a few working languages. At the third level, involving transnational communication, there is what De Swaan (2013: 70) calls "the 'civic' level of the citizens of Europe, where several languages compete for predominance...". The fourth level has to do with the functioning of national languages *within* each member country. As De Swaan (2013: 70) puts it,

> As long as each state continues to act as the protector of its national language, there is no immediate threat from the supercentral language, not even when a large majority of citizens has learned it as a foreign language. A state of diglossia, a precarious equilibrium between two languages in one society, will prevail.

In spite of De Swaan's insightful account of the complexities of linguistic use and its relationship with English as the hub of the world-language system, it is noteworthy, however, that the issue of language plays no part in the Council of Europe's publication *Interculturalism and Multiculturalism* (Barrett, 2013), even though language is claimed in the same publication to be a critical problem in the debate concerning cultural plurality (Garcia and Byram, 2013). Moreover, discussion of language should surely involve the ways in which meanings change from place to place and over time. For example, the meaning of the word Hijab (in English, Headscarf) varies a great deal in Europe and has much to do with attitudes towards Muslims (Koonz, 2009). Many of the ramifications of such a variation are thoroughly considered in the book edited by Gluck and Tsing, *Words in Motion* (2009). Although very little is said in the latter about European languages as such, there is an extremely relevant chapter on the Hijab/Headscarf by Koonz (2009).

On the concept of glocalization

Glocalization is a cross-disciplinary – better, transdisciplinary – concept. The major disciplinary initiators of the use of glocalization as a concept were geographers, sociologists, and anthropologists (Drori et al. 2014; Giulianotti and Robertson, 2002, 2004, 2007, 2012; Robertson, 1993, 2007a, 2007b, 2014a). Glocalization has also been rather prominent in the field of business studies, where the practical problem of advertising and selling goods and services to heterogeneous sets of buyers and purchasers has been of great importance. In fact, the most prominent social-scientific users of the concept of glocalization were much inspired by Japanese business practice concerning precisely this problem. Indeed, Japanese business endeavours of the 1980s provided much of the inspiration for the adoption of the glocalization perspective (Swyngedouw, 1997, 2004; Robertson, 2007a, 2014a).

There is considerable overlap between such concepts as glocalization, vernacularization, indigenization, and hybridization, to name but a few related and, perhaps, overlapping themes. Roudometof (2014: 155–172) has taken promising strides in dealing with this issue. The theme of cosmopolitanism has also to be considered in this context (Robertson and Krossa, 2012). Bhabha's discussion of V. S. Naipaul's "Trinadadian cosmopolitan" – an idea that Bhabha (1994) himself characterizes as vernacular cosmopolitanism – is an example of the ways in which the concept of cosmopolitanism cannot by any means be limited to Europe. The same can be said about the observation that much Asian cosmopolitanism involves people imbibing new ideas and participating in long-distance connections "without leaving the places of their birth" (Amrith, 2011: 195). (See also Bose and Manjapra, 2010; Slate, 2012.) Cosmopolitanism has been triumphantly claimed to be an overriding characteristic of Europe, particularly by Beck (e.g. 2000, 2002, 2006, 2013), as if cosmopolitanism was not to be found outside Europe – or at least not to the same extent. Much of this celebration of the idea of cosmopolitan Europe is highly and uncritically normative and removed from much of the reality of everyday life in Europe and other parts of the world; although Beck himself speaks of the cosmopolitanization of reality. Cosmopolitanism as a hegemonic motif of European origin is, I should emphasize, strongly rejected here. One very important reason for this rejection is the "eternal" persistence of strong, if uneven, nationalism in Europe. In fact, nationalism is one of the more prominent characteristics of contemporary Europe.

In the early years of the 21st century nationalism has become increasingly significant. This is not at all surprising for, somewhat paradoxically, attempts to unify previously deeply fragmented regions has led, in the case of the USSR, not so much to the obliteration of national sentiment, but quite the opposite. A number of analysts have shown that the break-up of the old Soviet Union in the early 1990s led to the re-emergence of old, somewhat primordial sentiments – often with disastrous results. This has meant that the so-called national question that greatly troubled the Bolsheviks in the Soviet Union, as well as other more moderate socialists across Europe, was not solved or overcome by the Soviet elite. In fact, if anything, the attempt to institutionalize and put "nations" in their ethnic spaces (cf. Massey, 2005) only encouraged the persistence of these emotional attachments (cf. Robertson, 1995b; Halikiopoulou and Vasilopoulou, 2011). We might call this the institutionalization of national nostalgia; what in a rather different manner Brubaker (1996: 107–147) has called homeland nationalism. It is clear that contemporary Europe cannot be adequately analysed without attention to the entire issue of *nostalgia* (Robertson, 1992: 146–163), this having much to do with the themes of *home* and *belonging* (Duyvendak, 2011).

In comparing "the politics of home" in Western Europe and the USA Duyvendak (2011: 2) observes that "the often desperate quest for the nation as nation-home has unintended consequences: instead of reaffirming 'Dutchness' or 'Danishness', the cultivation of citizenship has led to endless bickering over identities, loyalties and meanings of the national 'home' ". He goes on to say that "nostalgic nations feel a loss of unity...; even the most progressive among them look backwards to find a way out of their national crises". This has much to do with the present authoritarian protectionism. Duyvendak argues that, at first sight the US situation seems to be similar, particularly since the notion of homeland has been so conspicuous since 9/11. However, the idea of a national home has been much more ambiguous than it has in Western Europe. Patriotism in America is "rarely based on thick descriptions of place.... In fact, there is a great deal of tension between the old ideals of rootlessness and restlessness ('Go West young man'!) and the new notion of homeland (security)" (Duyvendak, 2011: 2).

The idea of glocalization has been applied to many facets of human society across the entire world. Indeed the spread, the flow, or the diffusion of facets is, by definition, a process of glocalization. These include migration; health and medicine; restaurants, food and cuisine (Laudan, 2013); exhibitions, festivals, and expositions; theme parks and heritage sites; music and dance; art genres; academic and professional disciplines; sports; tourism; beauty, fashion and cosmetics; bureaucracy and administration; and yet other spheres or facets of life. It should, however, be said that in some countries within Europe the theme of the relationship between the global and the local has received more attention than in others. Among those in which it has been taken most seriously are Italy, the UK, Germany, Sweden, while Central Europe (Mitteleuropa) has often been considered the centre of modern cosmopolitanism. Needless to say, the term "rootless cosmopolitanism" as used in Soviet Russia was thoroughly opposed to this. In fact, the very theme of cosmopolitanism can and has taken a variety of different regional or societal forms – another case of glocalization in Europe.

It is important at this juncture to state that one strong feature of glocalization is that it is – or at least can be seen as – a self-limiting aspect of globalization. In other words, there is a sense in which globalization is self-defeating. This proposition can be supported by pointing out that much of the relatively early work on globalization gave a strong impression that globalization equalled homogenization; so much so that differences were obliterated as globalization "proceeded". However, in recent years this triumph of "the homogenous" has been heavily criticized and "difference" has become much more apparent in the work of most, if by no means all, students of globalization. Most observers and analysts have come to realize that globalization has, for the most part, encouraged difference. Indeed, this theme has much to do with Sigmund Freud's notion of the narcissism of minor differences. In this connection it might well be said that there is something like a European ideal of cultivating difference-within-limits.

One might go further and suggest that the cultivation of difference is necessary for the very survival of the EU itself. This, one might speculate, has much to do with the problem of EU cohesion (Rumford, 2000). In fact, cohesion has been one of the more significant general problems of the European Union, particularly since the publication of the *First Cohesion Report* in 1996. In fact, the European Commission was required by its Article 130B to issue a cohesion report every three years (Rumford, 2000: 53ff, 181–182). An excellent discussion of cohesion as it obtains in the EU is to be found in Rumford's *European Cohesion?*, particularly when he speaks of metaphors of cohesion (Rumford, 2000: 163–178). Subsequently, the issue of cohesion has become closely bound up with the controversy concerning the rival merits of interculturalism and multiculturalism as descriptors of cultural plurality (cf. Baumann, 1999; Cantle, 2012, 2013; Barrett, 2013).

The major break from the old-style conception of globalization came with the slow but steady widespread recognition that globalization involved more than economic or politico-economic considerations. Obviously, the politico-economic kind of definition is still used in many quarters, but the anti-WTO (World Trade Organization) demonstrations in Seattle in late 1999 demonstrated that globalization involved much more than the economic factor. Even though the events in Seattle involved protests against an economic institution, the fact that a large number of people were brought together to protest against what was then called globalization, in the narrow sense, inevitably led to acknowledgment that there were social, cultural, and obviously political aspects to globalization. This quickly and widely became known as globalization from below. The Seattle events confirmed the belief held by a few academics at that time, including the present author, in the clearly multidimensional nature of globalization. Indeed, since the early 2000s the economistic conception of globalization has greatly, but by no means completely, faded – this, in spite of its remaining a key point of reference for many political leaders in Europe.

In parallel with the development of recognition of the much more comprehensive characterization of globalization there also arose much opposition to ideas concerning that the world was "flat" and increasingly homogenous (Friedman, 2005). The subtitle of the book by Friedman, *The World is Flat: A Brief History of the Globalized World in the Twenty-First Century*, claiming that the world was flat, claimed also that the world had become *globalized*. Clearly, if this were true there would be no world; for a flat world, in Friedman's sense, would be a world without any dynamism or "spirit" at all. In fact, somewhat ironically, it was the recognition that there was a great intimacy between capitalistic and cultural factors that gave rise to the modification of globalization so as to render it increasingly as glocalization; although this by no means involved the elimination of the social and political factors.

The concept of glocalization came into fully fledged existence by virtue of the explicit acknowledgment of its connotation of spatiality (Robertson, 1994, 1995, 2014; Roudometof, 2003, 2005). This was, of course, where the work of geographers and anthropologists had become very relevant – beginning, perhaps, with the work of Lefebvre (e.g. 1991; Brenner, 1997, 2004). Whereas globalization normally had a temporal connotation, glocalization had a much more spatial one. Having said this, the theme of localization should by no means be overlooked. Throughout the 1990s, the issue of the relationship between the local and the global became of increasing, if primarily, theoretical significance, quite apart from its deployment in business studies and the concrete work of businessmen and businesswomen. It was in the mid-1990s that there was growing recognition that the only solution to the seemingly attendant conundrum involved was to fuse or conflate the two, although this has required – indeed demanded – sophisticated analysis.

Sophistication was required mainly in respect of the multidimensionality of the concept of globalization. It was also the case that the cultural aspect or dimension should be given much more attention than had normally been done with respect to globalization (Robertson and Chirico, 1985). This emphasis on culture arose largely from the necessity of relating the cultural to the economic (Bielby and Harrington, 2008).

More generally, the interpenetration of the cultural and the economic is a hallmark of the current transdisciplinary study of globalization. Moreover, it is the functioning of early 20th-century capitalism(s) in Europe and elsewhere that has heightened the interest in, and visibility of, culture in general. Put simply, modern capitalism in all of its forms has involved increasing sensitivity to the variety of cultures and culture in general, including the concept of world culture (Robertson, 2002; Lechner and Boli, 2005). At the same time, capitalism has promoted and facilitated vested interests in the advocacy of cultural difference. In short, the connection between the economic and the cultural has become of pivotal significance in Europe – indeed in the world as a whole. In fact, this culture-promoting outcome of contemporary capitalism may well be leading to the latter's thorough transformation in Europe and probably elsewhere.

In the perspective of William McNeill (1986), polyethnicity and multiculturality are the human norm, with homogeneity being historically and anthropologically *unusual*, indeed aberrational. In this respect, the situation that has led to the current interest in glocalization and associated concepts and processes is the result of a break in the norm of plurality and difference by the standardizing processes of the period, that has lasted from the mid-18th century to the near present. When the EEC was founded in 1956, and in all subsequent years, the process of standardization has proceeded inexorably and become more intense and of wider scope; particularly since the signing of the Maastricht Treaty in 1993. Maastricht was supposed to be the foundation for the completion of the European Union. It should also be said, however, that some considered Maastricht to be leading quickly to a United States of Europe. (It is to this very possibility that so many current Eurosceptics take great exception.)

Thinking in terms of glocalization analysis, it is relatively clear that there would be some kind of crisis if standardization continued unabated. By now it should be clear that the EU's standardizing processes have been insufficiently sensitive to – and might well have learned much from – glocalization theory.

Glocalization refers to the process in which phenomena that spread, flow, or are diffused, from one "place" to another, have to be, and indeed are, adapted to the new locality at which they arrive. This process of adaptation constitutes the pivotal motif of the very idea of glocalization. In fact, it stands largely in a tradition concerning diffusion as an anthropological idea and also one that was developed in the field of rural sociology. In the latter, diffusion was intimately related to the theme of innovation. Specifically, in American rural sociology (e.g. Rogers, 2003; Robertson, 2007a; cf. Meyer, 2009: 136–155) practitioners were mainly concerned with the ways in and the degrees to which new ideas were adopted and transferred from one context to another. It would not be too much to say that the diffusion of innovations literature was the indirect foundation for much of the contemporary, and more empirically wide-ranging, theme of glocalization.

It has already been stated that Japanese business practices greatly inspired Robertson and Swyngedouw with respect to their introduction of the concept of glocalization; the nearest Japanese equivalent to this term being *dochakuka*, a word that literally means to indigenize. This tradition of the Japanese conception of production generally was undoubtedly how Japanese business practices became so prominent in the 1980s and early 1990s. During that period, when Japan seemed to be in the vanguard of modernization (Vogel, 1979), and there was much fear of rapid Japanese success among Americans, it became increasingly clear that Japanese elites had acquired very sophisticated skills with respect to American tastes. In contrast, it was quite common during this period for American business journals and newspapers to complain about Japanese culture being unreceptive to American exports; thus, arguing that Japanese people were too short; houses and cars were too small; Japanese streets were too narrow and their car parks too limited in space. Of course, the "exotic" nature of Japan was greatly admired – an exoticism that Japan itself strongly promoted (Hendry, 2000). In a nutshell, in that period Japan had a particular ability, or so it seemed, to be hypersensitive to the demands of glocalization, whereas US elites were more demanding with respect to the problem of adaptation. From the American standpoint Japan had to change its culture and social practices in order to play its part in world society and, in particular, to facilitate the import of American goods and services.

It should be emphasized that Japan has, for many centuries, had a great capacity to selectively incorporate features of other countries and civilizations. It did this in the first place with China and, more pertinently to the present chapter, only allowed European ideas, largely from the Netherlands, to enter Japan via a small enclave in the Nagasaki area. For about two and a half centuries Japan was, to all intents and purposes, shut off from the rest of the world. When it was opened, in the mid-19th century, the political elite took the decision to select the most useful beliefs and institutions from West European markets and (to some extent American) sources. It was in this sense that Europe had a great impact on Japan from the mid-19th century onwards (Westney, 1987; Kunitake, 2009). In fact, Kunitake and his colleagues have illustrated very well the ways in which Japanese individuals were selected carefully and sent to Europe and the USA, particularly in the early 1870s.

Needless to say, it is China, rather than Japan, that is now the principal rival to the USA (Mishra, 2012), but China is much less concerned with the issue of being sensitive to the sociocultural characteristics of the Other. China seeks to override the glocalization trend and this may well be a case of what Ritzer (2003) has called grobalization. Moreover, as China is rapidly becoming a major imperial power the question is raised as to the ways in which different imperial projects have involved different styles of glocalization (or, even, grobalization). Such relatively recent imperial projects – including those within Europe, for example, the British, the French, the Portuguese, and the Dutch – have displayed their own distinctive modes of "coping" with "native" cultures and practices. Indeed, the study of imperialism could well be one of the most useful sites for the application of what should be called *methodological glocalism* (Holton, 2005, 2009).

Advocacy of methodological glocalism stands in sharp contrast to the procedure advocated by Ulrich Beck and his colleagues, namely methodological cosmopolitanism. Axford (2013: 42ff.) has cogently displayed the variety of different methodologies. He compares methodological glocalism with other isms, including methodological globalism, methodological nationalism, and methodological territorialism.

As has been emphasized, the invocation of the concept of place does not have a specific, essentialistic geographical connotation. In modern geography the notion of place is much more fluid and socially constructed than many "outsiders" would recognize. Nevertheless, in a sociological or anthropological, as well as a geographical, framework, the idea of place can have a very constructivist connotation. Specifically, sociologists and anthropologists have drawn increasing attention to the construction of potential consumer niches, clients for particular products or services. The promotion and advertisement of goods and services increasingly involves the "invention" and calibration of new or latent markets. For example, it is not easy to see whether the increasing recognition of gays, lesbians, bisexuals, and transsexuals as consumers is actually based upon the recognition of already existing, "natural" characteristics or whether, at the other extreme, gayness and related characteristics are, in part, promoted for financial gain or personal power. Of course, between these extremes there lies the possibility of choice with respect to sexual preference. In any case, the current concern with gender fluidity or gender bending greatly enlarges the space for the production of clienteles for various products and services. The same could well be said of numerous other constructed needs or desires. In this sense, when we speak of glocalization involving adaptation to a "place" we should not, as I have previously said, be misled into attributing to adaptation an essentialistic meaning. The ideas of both adaptation and place are much more fluid than this. Indeed, it would probably be more appropriate to say that "the place" has to adapt to the phenomena that flow or are diffused into it. In fact, contemporary consumerism plays into the theme of glocalization and frequently involves the mobilization of potential consumers. Consumers are not simply, so to speak, passively "out there". An example from (an American) best-selling "how to" book may make this point clear:

> Logic would seem to suggest that if the world were becoming flatter, then brands would succeed by developing a global image tailored to

> that flat world. The thinking in many corporations is that a brand needs to find its place around the globe by targeting its message to a particular market (in essence, redefining itself in every region of the world) or by creating a one-size-fits-all global stance that appeals to everyone.
>
> (Rapaille, 2006 : 201)

There have been scores, if not hundreds, of interrogations of the so-called problems of the relationship between the local and the global. However, such deliberation has little or no effect on the *actual* management of corporations, big or small. The latter have taken it for granted that they have to deal with the issue of a product that they wish to sell widely. Inevitably, or at least in most cases, this involves a variety of cultures and social contexts. Therefore, it is not surprising at all that many well-known global products are advertised and sold in different forms and with different recipes. To take but a few European and/or American examples, there is a great variety of ways in which such products as Starbucks coffee, Coca-Cola and Pepsi-Cola drinks, McDonalds food, and Heineken beer are produced, distributed, and consumed. Of particular significance is the Italian corporation United Colors of Benetton, whose magazine, *Colors*, is proudly dedicated to global diversity; for in this case a seemingly homogenous global brand proclaims that it is heterogeneous. Manufacturers and distributors simply take it for granted that they must cater to a variety of markets and, moreover, widen those markets as part of the same process.

As the drift towards a multidimensional conception of globalization gained strength in the late 1980s and early 1990s the question arose as to the degree to which globalization inevitably involved standardization. Indeed, in some circles – both academic and political – the idea of globalization as standardization still prevails; as it does in much of European Union legislation. Moreover, until very recently globalization was conceived as not merely a form of standardization but even more narrowly as Westernization.

In recent years, there has been an increasing stress on and valorization of locality. Indeed, one could well argue that locality has been globalized – and that the very idea of the local has been intensified by so-called globalization (Wilson and Dissanayake, 1996; Robertson, 1997). This apparent paradox is pivotal to the present discussion. The globalization of the local has gone hand in hand with the idea of globalization from below.

Reflexive glocalization

As various institutional leaders have become increasingly aware of the issue of diffusion and flows, and the relative advantages of some kinds of glocalization over others, there has developed a much greater awareness of the importance of adaptability and which forms adaptability can take. This can usefully be labelled reflexive glocalization, meaning that glocalization increasingly becomes a way of outdoing other "glocalizers". As practitioners become increasingly conscious of the apparent success of glocalization projects it becomes the norm, in contrast to the kind of standardization that has been so common in the European Union. Moreover, contrary to the emphasis on standardization and routinization that has been central to the McDonaldization thesis (Ritzer, 2002), people become increasingly aware of the value of difference. In fact, it would not be too much to say that "being different" is one of the major motifs of our time, in spite of what is known as ethnic cleansing. From a different perspective, glocalization, as has been stated in the section "On the concept of glocalization", can be seen to be in the tradition of Freud's idea concerning the narcissism of minor differences. Freud emphasized, in effect, that the greater the standardization the greater the need for difference. This can be clearly seen in the case of fashion. On the surface most "fashionistas" (men and women) appear to be clones, whereas the perceptive observer will notice slight but crucial differences. The latter are particularly significant for the wearer and are meant to be observed by the discerning. The intention is to be simultaneously different and the same – different within the in-group, but the same to outsiders.

Cohesion and integration

Ever since the foundation of the European Economic Community in 1957 there has been a succession of increasingly ambitious projects to bring together and expand the number of countries in institutionalized Europe; an overall attempt which is now being severely resisted – indeed challenged – by Russia, as well as by a number of "extremists". In this concluding section I attempt to connect the concept of glocalization to these developments. I will do this with particular attention to the current fashionability of the concepts of interculturalism and multiculturalism. While the notion of multiculturalism has a lengthy genealogy, the idea of interculturalism is much younger in modern discourse about Europe (Pym, 1998). In fact, the most persistent and influential advocate of this has been Ted Cantle (e.g. Cantle, 2012, 2013). Cantle has developed his ideas concerning this in terms of his contention that the interconnectedness – or what I myself would prefer to call the connectivity – of the world as a whole, has been the basis upon which interculturalism has become both necessary and desirable. This need was brought into particularly sharp relief a few years ago by Huntington's *The Clash of Civilizations* (1996). On the other hand, one should not be led into thinking that the general idea of interculturalism, or intercivilizationalism, is by any means new. To take a relatively recent example, Dahlen (1997), a Swedish social anthropologist, labelled interculturalists as members of what was called the prevention of the culture shock industry, in his book *The Interculturalists*. It should be added that intellectual attempts to deal with the problem of miscommunication, or the inability to communicate at all, have been on the academic agenda, both in the West and the East, for many years (Yoshino, 1992).

Regardless of questions of originality, Cantle and likeminded people have much overlooked the issue of global – in our present case, European – consciousness. In other words, they are guilty of the same analytic omission as are many contemporary theorists of *globalization*. The link that is missing is global consciousness. The latter is particularly important for the simple reason that speaking of interconnectedness or connectivity surely cannot be a phenomenon that occurs, or has occurred, without there having been some sort of imaginary, or ideational, aspiration to make such connectivity possible or viable. The concept of the imaginary (Castoriadis, 1987; Taylor, 2007; Steger, 2008; cf. Ballantyne and Burton, 2012; Rosenberg, 2012a, 2012b, 2012c) surely precedes the discourse of connectivity (Robertson, 2011). Also, various "myths" of Europe have been constructed over the years (Delanty, 1995), these also having a bearing on the subject at hand.

It should be noted that both the issues of multiculturalism and interculturalism are somewhat misleading, in that, over recent years, the relationship between such motifs as culture, tradition, religion, ethnicity, and others have become increasingly blurred, a blurring that has plagued much of Europe in the recent past. This trend has run in parallel with the phenomenon of gender bending – or, generally speaking, the apparent liquidity of modern life. In fact, this characteristic makes contemporary attempts to split life into separate spheres extremely problematic. Indeed, this is the very subject of the highly innovative, but somewhat mistitled book by Olivier Roy, *Holy Ignorance: When Religion and Culture Part Ways* (Roy, 2010); although Roy's volume cannot be comprehensively discussed here.

While interculturalism seems, on the surface, to mitigate the segregational features of multiculturalism (better, multiculturality), it has, on the other hand, the disadvantage of running the danger of "accentuating" the uniqueness of different cultures or of each culture. Kymlicka (2000) persuasively argues that interculturalism requires individuals to exercise local interculturality even more than global interculturality. However, as Barrett (2013: 31) argues, "Local interculturality is especially difficult and challenging as it can involve breaking down peoples' preconceptions, prejudices, misinterpretations, sense of threat and anxieties about others within the ambit of their everyday lives...."

Conclusion

As was said at the outset, my intention here has been to follow Outhwaite's plea to do more to situate Europe globally, but to do so via the concept of glocalization. In one way or another much of this chapter has been precisely about this. Nonetheless, it can be said more precisely that, in my view, the obsession with interconnectedness, or what I prefer to call connectivity, has been a particular failure of analysts as well as of leading participants in "the European project". As I have been completing this chapter yet another book lands on my desk, so to speak, *The Butterfly Defect* by Goldin and Mariathasan (2014), the starting point of which is precisely the interconnectedness of the world, including the EU, with no mention at all of global consciousness, global imaginaries, or similar concepts. Moreover, there is a great tendency, both within and without the European Union, to conceive of interconnectedness as identical with, or the equivalent of, integration; when in fact, on many occasions, connectivity is the exact opposite in its effects and, indeed, undermines integration.

Notes

1. Colley, L. (2013); see also Colley (1992, 2007, 2010).
2. Legrain (2014: 9) has appropriately spoken of Eurozone fiscal colonialism in reference to what he calls the reckless lending of German and French banks to Spanish and Irish homeowners, Portuguese consumers, and the Greek government. "European Union institutions have become instruments for creditors to impose their will on debtors, subordinating Europe's southern 'periphery' to the northern 'core' in a quasi-relationship" (Legrain, 2014: 9).

References

Amrith, S. F. (2011) *Migration and Diaspora in Modern Asia*, Cambridge: Cambridge University Press.

Andrews, D. L. and G. Ritzer. (2007) "The Global in the Sporting Local", in R. Giulianotti and R. Robertson (eds.) *Globalization and Sport*, Oxford: Blackwell, pp. 28–45.
Appadurai, A. (2013) *The Future as Cultural Fact: Essays on the Global Condition*, London: Verso.
Axford, B. (2013) *Theories of Globalization*, Cambridge: Polity.
Ballantyne, T. and A. Burton. (2012) "Empires and the Reach of the Global", in E. S. Rosenberg (ed.) *A World Connecting 1870–1945*, Cambridge, MA: Belknap Press of Harvard University Press, pp. 285–347.
Barrett, M. (2013) "Introduction – Interculturalism and Multiculturalism: Concepts and Controversies", in M. Barrett (ed.) *Interculturalism and Multiculturalism: Similarities and Differences*, Strasbourg: Council of Europe, pp. 15–42.
Baumann, G. (1999) *The Multicultural Riddle: Rethinking National, Ethnic, and Religious Identities*, New York: Routledge.
Beck, U. (2000) "The Cosmopolitan Perspective: Sociology in the Second Age of Modernity", *British Journal of Sociology*, 51 (1): 79–105.
Beck, U. (2002) "The Cosmopolitan Society and Its Enemies", *Theory Culture & Society*, 19 (1–2): 17–44.
Beck, U. (2006) *The Cosmopolitan Vision*, Cambridge: Polity.
Beck, U. (2013) *German Europe*, Cambridge: Polity.
Beck, U. and N. Sznaider (2006) "Unpacking Cosmopolitanism for the Social Sciences: A Research Agenda", *British Journal of Sociology*, 57 (1): 1–23.
Beyer, P. (2007) "Globalization and Glocalization", in J. A. Beckford and N. J. Demerath (eds.) *The Sage Handbook of the Sociology of Religion*, London: Sage, pp. 55–73.
Bhabha, H. K. (1994) *The Location of Culture*, London: Routledge.
Bhambra, G. K. (2007) *Rethinking Modernity: Postcolonialism and the Sociological Imagination*, Basingstoke: Palgrave Macmillan.
Bielby, D. D. and C. L. Harrington. (2008) *Global TV: Exporting Television and Culture in the World Market*, New York: New York University Press.
Bose, S. and K. Manjapra. (eds.) (2010) *Cosmopolitan Thought Zones: South Asia and the Global Circulation of Ideas*, Houndsmills: Palgrave Macmillan.
Brenner, N. (1997) "Global, Fragmented, Hierarchical: Henri Lefevbre's Geographies of Globalization", *Public Culture*, 10: 135–167.
Brenner, N. (2004) *New State Spaces: Urban Governance and the Rescaling of Statehood*, Oxford: Oxford University Press.
Brotton, J. (1997) *Trading Territories: Mapping the Early Modern World*, London: Reaktion Books.
Brubaker, R. (1996) *Nationalism Reframed: Nationhood and the National Question in the New Europe*, Cambridge: Cambridge University Press.
Burke, P. (2009) *Cultural Hybridity*, Cambridge: Polity.
Buttner, S. B. (2012) *Mobilizing Regions, Mobilizing Europe: Expert knowledge and Scientific Planning in European Regional Development*, Abingdon: Routledge.
Canclini, N. G. (1995) *Hybrid Cultures: Strategies for Entering and Leaving Modernity*, Minneapolis, MI: University of Minnesota Press.
Cantle, T. (2012) *Interculturalism: The New Era of Cohesion and Diversity*, Basingstoke: Palgrave Macmillan.

Cantle, T. (2013) "Interculturalism as a New Narrative for the Era of Globalisation and Super-Diversity", in M. Barrett (ed.) *Interculturalism and Multiculturalism: Similarities and Differences,* Strasbourg: Council of Europe, pp. 69–92.

Castoriadis, C. (1987) *The Imaginary Institution of Society*, Cambridge: Cambridge University Press.

Colley, L. (1992) *Britons: Forging the Nation, 1707–1837*, New Haven, CT: Yale University Press.

Colley, L. (2007) *The Ordeal of Elizabeth Marsh: A Woman in World History*, New York: Knopf.

Colley, L. (2010) *Captives: Britain, Empire and the World, 1600–1850*, New York: Random House.

Colley, L. (2013) "Wide-Angled" [Review of Desan, Hunt and Nelson (2013)], *London Review of Books,* 35 (18): 18–19.

Colley, L. (2014) *Acts of Union and Disunion: What has Held the UK Together – and What is Dividing it?* London: Profile Books.

Dahlen, T. (1997) *Among the Interculturalists: An Emergent Profession and its Packaging of Knowledge*, Stockholm: Stockhom University.

Delanty, G. (1995) *Inventing Europe: Idea, Identity, Reality*, Basingstoke: Palgrave Macmillan.

Delanty, G. and C. Rumford. (2005) *Rethinking Europe: Social Theory and the Implications of Europeanization*, Abingdon: Routledge.

Desan, L. Hunt and W. M. Nelson. (eds.) (2013) *The French Revolution in Global Perspective*, Ithaca, NY: Cornell University Press.

De Swaan, A. (2013) "Language Systems", in N. Coupland (ed.) *the Handbook of Language and Globalization*, Oxford: Wiley-Blackwell, pp. 56–76.

Drori, G. S. and M. A. Hollerer, and P. Walgenbach. (eds.) (2014) *Global Themes and Local Variations in Organization and Management: Perspectives on Glocalization,* New York: Routledge, pp. 25–36.

Duyvendak, W. J. (2011) *The Politics of Home: Belonging and Nostalgia in Western Europe and the United States*, Basingstoke: Palgrave Macmillan.

Edwards, B. T. and D. P. Gaonkar. (eds.) (2010) *Globalizing American Studies*, Chicago: University of Chicago Press.

Friedman, T. (2005) *The World is Flat: A Brief History of the Globalized World in the Twenty-First Century*, London: Allen Lane.

Garcia, M. del C. M. and M. Byram. (2013) "Interculturalism, Multiculturalism and Language Issues", in M. Barrett (ed.) *Interculturalism and Multiculturalism: Similarities and Differences*, Strasbourg: Council of Europe, pp. 133–146.

Giddens, A. (2007) *Europe in the Global Age*, Cambridge: Polity.

Giddens, A. (2014) *Turbulent and Mighty Continent: What Future for Europe?* Cambridge: Polity.

Giulianotti, R. and R. Robertson. (2002) "Die Globalisierung des Futballs: 'Glokalisierung', transnationale Konzerne und demokratische Regulierung", *Futballwelten*, Leske: Budrich, Opladen, pp. 219–251.

Giulianotti, R. and R. Robertson. (2004) "The Globalization of Football: A Study in the Glocalization of the 'serious life' ", *The British Journal of Sociology*, 55 (4): 545–568.

Giulianotti, R. and R. Robertson. (2006) "Globalization, Glocalization and Popular Culture: A Fresh Analysis", *European Journal of Cultural Studies*, 47–64.

Giulianotti, R. and R. Robertson. (2007) "Recovering the Social: Globalization, Football and Transnationalism", in R. Giulianotti and R. Robertson (eds.) *Globalization and Sport*, Oxford: Blackwell, pp. 58–78.

Giulianotti, R. and R. Robertson. (2012) "Glocalization and Sport in Asia: Diverse Perspectives and Future Possibilities," *Sociology of Sport Journal*, 29 (4): 433–454.

Gluck, C. (2009) "Words in Motion", in C. Gluck and A. L. Tsing (eds.) *Words in Motion: Toward a Global Lexicon*, Durham, NC: Duke University Press, pp. 3–10.

Gluck, C. and A. L. Tsing. (eds.) (2009) *Words in Motion: Toward a Global Lexicon*, Durham, NC: Duke University Press.

Goldin, I. and M. Mariathasan. (2014) *The Butterfly Defect: How Globalization Creates Systemic Risks, and What to Do about it*, Princeton, NJ: Princeton University Press.

The Guardian (2014) "EU's Enemies from Left and Right Ride High on Wave of Discontent", 29 April: 8–9.

Halikiopoulou, D. and S. Vasilopoulou. (eds.) (2011) *Nationalism and Globalisation: Conflicting or Complementary*, London: Routledge.

Hannerz, U. (1992) *Cultural Complexity*, New York: Columbia University Press.

Hannerz, U. (1996) *Transnational Connections: Culture, People, Places*, London: Routledge.

Hannerz, U. (2009) "Geocultural Scenarios", in P. Headstrom and B. Wittrock (eds.) *Frontiers of Sociology*, Leiden: Brill, pp. 267–288.

Hendry, J. (2000) *The Orient Strikes Back: A Global View of Cultural Display*, Oxford: Berg.

Hines, C. (2000) *Localization: A Global Manifesto*, London: Earthscan.

Holton, R. (2005) *Making Globalization*, Basingstoke: Palgrave Macmillan.

Holton, R. (2009) *Cosmopolitanisms: New Thinking and New Directions*, Basingstoke: Palgrave Macmillan.

Huntington, S. (1996) *The Clash of Civilizations and the Remaking of World Order*, New York: Simon Schuster.

Irwin, R. (2006) *The Lust of Knowing: The Orientalists and Their Enemies*, London: Allen Lane.

Jardine, L. (1998) *Worldly Goods: A History of the Renaissance*, New York: Norton.

Kennedy, P. (2010) *Local Lives and Global Transformations: Towards World Society*, Basingstoke: Palgrave Macmillan.

Kymlicka, W. (2000) *Multicultural Citizenship: A Liberal Theory of Minority Rights*, Oxford: Oxford University Press.

Knill, C. and J. Tosun. (2014) "Europeanization of National Administrations in the Czech Republic and Poland: Assessing the Extent of Institutional Change", in G. S. Drori, M. A. Hollerer and P. Walgenbach (eds.) *Global Themes and Local Variations in Organization and Management: Perspectives on Glocalization*, New York: Routledge, pp. 264–277.

Koonz, C. (2009) "*Hijab* /Headscarf: A Political Journey", in C. Gluck and A. L. Tsing (eds.) *Words in Motion: Toward a Global Lexicon*, Durham, NC: Duke University Press, pp. 174–198.

Kunitake, K., C. Tsuziki and R. J. Young. (eds.) (2009) *Japan Rising:The Iwakura Embassy to the USA and Europe 1871–1873*, Cambridge: Cambridge University Press.

Latour, B. (1993) *We Have Never Been Modern*, Cambridge, MA: Harvard University Press.

Latour, B. (2013) *An Inquiry Into Modes of Existence: An Anthropology of the Moderns*, Cambridge, MA: Harvard University Press.

Laudan, R. (2013) *Cuisine and Empire: Cooking in World History*, Berkeley: University of California Press.

Lechner, F. J. and J. Boli. (2005) *World Culture: Origins and Consequences*, Oxford: Blackwell.

Lefebvre, H. (1991) *The Production of Space*, Oxford: Blackwell.

Legrain, P. (2014) "Eurozones Fiscal Colonialism", *International New York Times*, April 22: 9.

McDonald, K. (2006) *Global Movements: Action and Culture*, Oxford: Blackwell.

McNeill, W. H. (1986) *Polyethnicity and National Unity in World History*, Toronto: University of Toronto Press.

Manela, E. (2007) *The Wilsonian Moment:Self-Determination and the International Origins of Anticolonial Nationalism*, Oxford: Oxford University Press.

Massey, D. B. (2005) *For Space*, London: Sage.

Meyer, J. W. (2009) "Diffusion: Institutional Conditions for Diffusion", in G. Krucken and G. S. Drori (eds.) *World Society: The Writings of John W. Meyer*, Oxford: Oxford University Press, pp. 136–155.

Mishra, P. (2012) *From the Ruins of Empire: The Revolt Against the West and the Remaking of* Asia, London: Allen Lane.

Moyn, S. and A. Sartori, "Approaches to Global Intellectual History" in S. Moyn and A. Sartori (eds.) *Global Intellectual History*, New York: Columbia University Press, pp. 3–32.

Nairn, T. (2003) *The Break-Up of Britain: Crisis and Neo-Nationalism*, Edinburgh: Common Ground.

Outhwaite, W. (2008) *European Society*, Cambridge: Polity.

Pease, D. E. (2010) "American Studies after American Exceptionalism? Toward a Comparative Analysis of Imperial State Exceptionalism", in E. T. Edwards and D. P. Gaonkar (eds.) *Globalizing American Studies*, Chicago: University of Chicago Press, pp. 47–83.

Pollock, S. (2013) "Cosmopolitanism, Vernacularism, and Premodernity", in S. Moyn and A. Sartori (eds.) *Global Intellectual History*, New York: Columbia University Press, pp. 59–80.

Pym, A. (1998) *Method in Translation History*, London: Taylor and Francis.

Rapaille, C. (2006) *The Culture Code: An Ingenious Way to Understand Why People Around the World Live and Buy as They Do*, New York: Broadway Books.

Ritzer, G. (ed.) (2002) *McDonaldization: The Reader*, Thousand Oaks, CA: Pine Forge Press.

Ritzer, G. (2004) *The Globalization of Nothing*, Thousand Oaks, CA: Pine Forge Press.

Robertson, R. (1992) *Globalization: Social Theory and Global Culture*, London: Sage.

Robertson, R. (1993) "Globaliseringens Problem", *GRUS [Denmark]*, December, pp. 6–31.

Robertson, R. (1994) "Globalisation or Glocalisation?", *Journal of International Communication*, 1: 33–52.

Robertson, R. (1995a) "Glocalization: Time-Space and Homogeneity-Heterogeneity", in M. Featherstone, S. Lash, and R. Robertson (eds.) *Global Modernities*, London: Sage, pp. 25–44.

Robertson, R. (1995b) "Theory, Specificity, Change: Emulation, Selective Incorporation and Modernization", in B. Grancelli (ed.) *Social Change and Modernization: Lessons from Eastern Europe*, Berlin: Walter de Gruyter, pp. 213–231.

Robertson, R. (1997) "Values and Globalization: Communitarianism and Globality", in L. E. Soares (ed.) *Identity, Culture and Globalization*, Rio de Janeiro: UNESCO, pp. 33–97.

Robertson, R. (2002) "Le Dimensioni Della Cultura Globale", in E. Batini and R. Ragionieri (eds.) *Culture e Conflitti Nella Globalizzazione*, Florence: Leo S. Olschki, pp. 17–30.

Robertson, R. (2007a) "Diffusion", in R. Robertson and J. A Scholte (eds.) *Encyclopedia of Globalization*, New York: MTM/Routledge, pp. 318–320.

Robertson, R. (2007b) "Glocalization", in R. Robertson and J. A. Scholte (eds.) *Encyclopedia of Glocalization*, New York: MTM/Routledge, pp. 402–410.

Robertson, R. (2011) "Global Connectivity and Global Consciousness", *American Behavioral Science*, 55 (10): 1336–1345.

Robertson, R. (2014a) "Situating Glocalization: A Relatively Autobiographical Intervention", in G. S. Drori, M. A. Hollerer and P. Wagenbach (eds.) (2014) *Global Themes and Local Variations in Organization and Management: Perspectives on Glocalization*, New York: Routledge.

Robertson, R. (2014b) "Civilization(s), Ethnoracism, Antisemitism, Sociology", in M. Stoeltzler (ed.) *Antisemitism and the Constitution of Sociology*, London: University of Nebraska Press, pp. 206–245.

Robertson, R. and J. A. Chirico. (1985) "Humanity, Globalization and World Wide Religious Resurgence: A Theoretical Exploration", *Sociological Analysis*, 46: 219–242.

Robertson, R. and R. Giulianotti. (2001) "Glocalization, Transnational Corporations and Democratic Governance: An Analysis of the Globalization of Football", in P. Losche, U. Ruge and K. Stolz (eds) *Yearbook of European and North American Studies*, pp. 219–251.

Robertson, R. and R. Giulianotti. (2006) "Futbol, Globalizacion Y Glocalizacion", *Revista Internacional de Sociologia*, 64 (45): 9–35.

Robertson, R. and A. S. Krossa. (eds.) (2012) *European Cosmopolitanism in Question*, Basingstoke: Palgrave Macmillan.

Rogers, E. (2003) *The Diffusion of Innovations*, 5th edn. New York: Simon and Schuster.

Rosenberg, E. S. (ed.) (2012a) *A World Connecting 1870–1945*, Cambridge, MA: Belknap Press of Harvard University Press.

Rosenberg, E. S. (2012b) "Introduction", in E. S. Rosenberg (ed.) *A World Connecting 1870–1945*, Cambridge, MA: Belknap Press of Harvard University, pp. 3–28.

Rosenberg, E. S. (2012c) "Transnational Currents in a Shrinking World", in E. S. Rosenberg (ed.) *A World Connecting 1870–1945*, Cambridge, MA: Belknap Press of Harvard University, pp. 815–996.
Roudometof, V. (2003) "Glocalization, Space and Modernity", *The European Legacy*, 8: 37–60.
Roudometof, V. (2005) "Transnationalism, Cosmopolitanism and Glocalization", *Current Sociology*, 53: 113–135.
Roudometof, V. (2014) *Globalization and Orthodox Christianity: The Transformations of a Religious Tradition*, Abingdon: Routledge.
Roy, O. (2010) *Holy Ignorance: When Religion and Culture Part Ways*, New York: Columbia University Press.
Rumford, C. (2000) *European Cohesion? Contradictions in EU Integration*, London: Routledge.
Simms, B. (2013) *Europe: The Struggle for Supremacy, 1453 to the Present*, London: Penguin Books.
Slate, N. (2012) *Colored Cosmopolitanism: The Shared Struggle for Freedom in India and the United States*, Cambridge, MA: Harvard University Press.
Soysal, Y. N. (1995) *Limits of Citizenship: Migrants and Postnational Membership in Europe*, Chicago: Chicago University Press.
Soysal, Y. N. (1998) "Toward a Postnational Model of Membership", in G. Shafir (ed.) *The Citizenship Debates: A Reader*, Minneapolis: University of Minnesota Press, pp. 189–220.
Steger, M. F. (2008) *The Rise of the Global Imaginary*, New York: Oxford University Press.
Swyngedouw, E. (1992) "The Mammon Quest: 'Glocalization,' Interstate Competition and the Monetary Order: The Construction of New Scales", in M. Dunford and G. Kafkalis (eds.) *Cities and Regions in the New Europe: The Global-Local Interplay and Spatial Development Strategies*, New York: Wiley, pp. 39–67.
Swyngedouw, E. (1997) "Neither Global nor Local: 'Glocalization' and the Politics of Scale", in K. Cox (ed.) *Spaces of Globalization: Reasserting the Power of the Local*. New York: Guilford, pp. 137–166.
Swyngedouw, E. (2004) "Globalisation or 'Glocalisation'? Networks, Territories and Rescaling", *Cambridge Review of International Affairs*, 17 (1): 25–48.
Taylor, C. (2007) *Modern Social Imaginaries*, Durham, NC: Duke University Press.
Tilly, C. (ed.) (1975) *The Formation of National States in Western Europe*, Princeton, NJ: Princeton University Press.
Tilly, C. (1992) *Coercion, Capital, and European States, AD990–1990*, Oxford: Basil Blackwell.
Vogel, E. (1979) *Japan as Number One: Lessons for America*, Cambridge, MA: Harvard University Press.
Wallerstein, I. (2006) *European Universalism: The Rhetoric of Power*, New York: New Press.
Werbner, P. (2008) *Anthropology and the New Cosmopolitanism: Rooted, Feminist and Vernacular Perspectives*, Oxford: Berg.
Westney, D. E. (1987) *Imitation and Innovation: The Transfer of Western Organizational Patterns to Meiji Japan*, Cambridge, MA: Harvard University Press.

Wilson, R. and W. Dissanayake. (eds.) (1996) *Global/Local*, Durham, NC: Duke University Press.

Yoshino, K. (1992) *Cultural Nationalism in Contemporary Japan: A Sociological Enquiry*, London: Routledge.

Zizek, S. (2014) "Barbarism with a Human Face", *London Review of Books,* 36 (9): 36–37.

2

Forms of the World

Roots, Histories, and Horizons of the Glocal

Franciscu Sedda

What kind of world is this?

A world of worlds

What kind of world is the world we live in?[1] Or better, what is its form? And is there maybe more than one? Let us consider the idea of "forms of the world" in the simplest of its senses. The very idea compels us from the start to accept an inevitable plurality. Consider the following immediate and ordinary examples. In today's common sense the earth is *spherical*; in scientific discourse it is slightly flattened at the poles, so it is *elliptical*; photographs showing us planet earth from space, beautiful and solitary, make us perceive it as *circular*; children, without too much concern, draw it as an *irregular ball*; for a long time many peoples and cultures have believed the earth to be *flat*, just as in the geographic maps that we all study in school growing up. In the latter, Europe is always at the centre and the sizes of the continents are distorted. Could it be that only one of such forms is correct? Certainly, they all *make sense* and *have meaning* for someone.

But if the world has many forms, do we not find ourselves in many different worlds?

The most advanced theories of physics tell us about one reality that contained in itself a potentially infinite number of universes.[2] In the same way, our semiotic cosmos, the cultural space that we humans inhabit, increasingly appears to us as containing a variety of worlds that mutually interpenetrate, overlap, intersect, contest, translate. But let us not run too fast. Let us first observe that, in any attempt to understand our world, and, within it, the position that Europe occupies, the best thing to do is to consider it in its multiple forms, by exploring the relations of sense and power that shape it. And to do so, in all probability, nothing is better than to begin from a new complex and revelatory sign, one which has been populating and at the same time defining the world: *glocal*.

The emergence of "glocal"

> According to *The Oxford Dictionary of New Words* (1991: 134) the term "glocal" and the process noun "glocalization" are "formed by telescoping *global* and *local* to make a blend". Also according to the *Dictionary*, that idea has been "modeled on the Japanese *dochakuka* (deriving from *dochaku* 'living on one's own land'), originally the agricultural principle of adapting one's farming techniques to local conditions, but also adopted in Japanese for *global localization*, a global outlook adapted to local conditions". More specifically, the terms "glocal" and "glocalization" became aspects of business jargon during the 1980s. By now it has become, again in the words of *The Oxford Dictionary of New Words*, "one of the main marketing buzzwords of the beginning of the nineties".
>
> (Robertson, 1995: 28)

The emergence and the assimilation of a new word in a specialized lexicon and in common speech is always a meaningful event. Its entrance in the academic discourse, as in the collective imagery, helps us sense a certain spirit of the times in which we live. For example, we could think about the appearance of *glocal* in international bestsellers, such as Thomas L. Friedman's essay *The World is Flat: A Brief History of the Twenty-First Century* (2005), or as the "protagonist" in Jason Reitman's recent film *Up in the Air* (2009), starring George Clooney. Moreover, the new word may provide us with a glimpse into the future that we may inhabit.

At the same time, we can regard the arising of a new sign on the surface of the sea of social life as the tip of an iceberg, that invites us to see into the depths, that is, to explore and gain insight into the political and cultural systems and processes that it underlies, and that, in some way, push it and keep it afloat.

The appearance of a new concept can induce a fruitful doubt, a curiosity. It can raise new questions, both with regard to ourselves and to the histories that led us to our present. Shedding new light on what now surrounds us and on what preceded the emergence of a new concept can drive us towards a new perception, one that simultaneously implies a reinterpretation of the world and of the categories through which we make the world meaningful.

Thus, the emergence of a new sign is a cause and an effect of the act of reopening the meaning of our becoming. Therefore, if it is true that each generation creates its predecessors – to paraphrase Borges – the arising of *glocal* offers us a chance to rethink some of the "roots" – be they *physical, anthropological,* or *phenomenological* – of our world, that is, of those structural devices that shaped our existence in the past and still shape it today. A rediscovery of these roots will direct us towards novel ways, new "stories" – *natural, dominant, imagined* – telling us about the systems and processes that led us to the current configuration of the globe. This reflection will help us focus on some of the possible "horizons" – *ecological, plural, shared* – of our glocal world. Along this re-elaboration we will seek to individuate those devices and concepts that allow us to gain a deeper insight into the idea of *glocality* itself.

The coherence of the world, the plurality of the human

Physical roots

How is it that we came to be what we are? And, most of all, what is it that we really are? In other words, what is the quality that is most peculiar to our contemporary world?

Let's start answering with a quotation:

> The possibility of a physical coherence of the world and of the generalization of a certain biological history on a universal basis would give the globe its first unity, well before the great discoveries, before the industrial revolution, before the interpenetration of the economies.
>
> (Braudel, 1979: 22)

This statement of Fernand Braudel – which is part of a complex reasoning that the French historian develops in *Material Civilization, Economy and Capitalism* (1979) – is not unrelated to our questions. On the contrary, it will help us undo the complex tangle that these questions form, until they reveal their glocal essence. As a matter of fact, Braudel underscores the "physical coherence of the world" and refers to a "biological history on a universal scale" precisely by asking in what ways late 19th-century society evolved.

Braudel's point of departure is connected to the problem of the figures of world population. This structuring and structural factor of the planet's life, obviously not only of human life, places us at the outset before an enigma: that of its sudden increase, during the 18th century, after long periods of continuous and yet tendentially stable fluxes and refluxes. The world population, which until then was under half a billion people, of whom the majority were peasants (between 80 and 90%), explodes at once. This unprecedented explosion of world population reconfigures the globe and its assets: in particular, it builds the material bases for a type of life – so interconnected and interdependent – that, if we agree with this "sedentary" view of the configuration of humanity, had been until then practically impossible.

What, then, propelled this leap? Braudel's response places us before two well-known factors that are taken into consideration in current discourses on globalization: *economy* and *space*. What the historian remarks is that, in the 18th century, a general economical restoration corresponds to a "multiplication of the spaces offered to men": "All the countries of the world then colonized themselves, occupying their territories that were empty or semi-empty of inhabitants" (Braudel, 1979: 20).

In any event, this response, which interlaces economy, spaces, and movement, does not leave Braudel satisfied. First of all, because the "empty space" that is available to man has always been there and it still is today (forests, steppes, arctic regions, deserts...), even in an age in which the world appears as "finite". Second and foremost, this interlacement fails to explain the very "globality" of such change. As Braudel notes:

> The true question remains the following: why is it that, in the same moment, the "geographic conjuncture" enters into play, although the supply of space has been permanent in any case? The problem is posed by synchronism. International economy, effective yet still very fragile, cannot be deemed responsible, by itself alone, of such a general and powerful movement. It is itself a cause, as much as it is a consequence.
>
> (p. ivi)

The solution to the enigma that Braudel advances is interesting in two respects. On the one hand, it invites us to reflect on what we could call the *synchronizing factor*, which begins to operate to bring about the world's becoming-global. On the other, the factor that he thus individuated shows us that this apparent *becoming-global* is indebted to a more fundamental *being-glocal*.

According to Braudel, in fact, what functions as an instrument of correlation between actors, times, and spaces, is, in this case, the *climate*, that is, to be more precise, its rhythm, the series of climatic variations that, following one another, relate to daily life and consequently transform it.

Although there is not the space here to venture into Braudel's complex reconstructions of the causal chain that transformed the world, it should be noted that, between the 16th and the 17th centuries, the globe experienced a general cooling – a "small ice age" (p. 22) – and that the effects of the 18th-century life reflux, intended by Braudel as the expansion of life, along with economical mechanisms such as the "enormous price fluctuation" to which this climatic change gives rise, generate a biological leap. "With the eighteenth century, in China so as in Europe, an ancient biological regime and an ensemble of constrictions, obstacles, structures, relations and numerical games that had been until then the rule, breaks", so that from then on the rule of the equilibrium between the number of deaths and the number of births is invalidated, and "life would win over death, ever since overtaking her adversary" (p. 45). It implies, in fact, a double glance that grasps elements on two different scales: the regular and equilibrated cycle of life and death in the very short term, and the overall effect of the victory of the compensations in the long term (p. 62) once the "fluctuations of material life" enter into a particular relation with the "climatic fluctuations" (p. 22).

What interests us here is that, while, on the one hand, this temporary and yet decisive "climatic unification" of the globe makes us foresee the first globalizing factor of the world in its physical coherence, on the other hand, it invites us at once to go beyond Braudel's analysis. Braudel himself is immediately aware of this:

> If this climatic explanation contains, as I think, some truth to it, we should in any case prevent ourselves from oversimplifying it. Each climate is a rather complex system and its impact on the life of plants, animals and men can only be fulfilled by means of winding ways that depend upon the places, the cultures and the seasons.
>
> (p. 22)

It is then clear that we are locked inside a *glocal device* within which the climate, only just evoked as a singular and synchronizing factor, reveals itself in its plurality and multiplicity. In other words, upon mentioning "climate", its plural "climates" immediately appears: globality appears as the overall effect – one that may be principally located by way of a speculative and generalizing view – of a series of infinitely minute phenomena that are *at the very same time independent and interdependent*. The glacial age, the Gulf Stream, the monsoon, the natural disasters in

China between the 16th and the 17th centuries, can probably be traced back to a single "logic", as part of a complex systemic network. And yet, like the sun, the clouds, and the rains, they continue to distribute themselves locally, to the extent that they almost seem to take shape as mutually separated processes.

To understand this, let us return, one last time, to Braudel's reasoning:

> [The] equality of death and life lightens up its grasp beginning with the eighteenth century, naturally with different modes according to the regions. Only a certain Europe, and not even all of western Europe, begins to free itself from the grip of the equality of life and death. In the long run, compensations insensibly come forth, but eventually end up having the last word. The reflux never carries away entirely that which the previous tide has brought. Such ascendancy in the long run, difficult and marvelous, is the triumph of the number, upon which many things would depend.
>
> (Braudel, 1979: 61–62)

The triumph of the number – a number which is related to the power of climate and to the diversity of climates – is, on that occasion, Europe's triumph, or better, that of "a certain Europe, and not even all western Europe". And yet it is not an eternal triumph.

Natural histories

When we depart from this root to look at our world, what appears is a long history that several scholars have recently defined as the *natural history of globalization*. From the point of view of human beings, it is a history made "of migrations, of colonizations, of drifts, and of hybridizations" (Pievani, 2002: 25, 29), that is, governed in a subterranean fashion yet by a strange, non-human protagonist that is precisely the climate: "We will see that climatic alterations will be a constant in the natural history of our biological family. The span of geological time occupied by hominid evolution will always be characterized by a climatic and environmental turbulence, a crucial (and often underestimated) factor for the structure of our evolutionary path" (p. 58).

In other words, well before the modern planetarization of European make – a recent, contingent, and principally socio-economic event – there would be a million-years-long history made of subsequent "planetarizations". A history based on the complex *coevolution* between populations, natural habitats, and climatic variations.

Telmo Pievani, one of the foremost Italian philosophers of science, has set forth, through a retelling of the studies of Niles Eldredge, Stephen J. Gould, and Ian Tattersall, to classify this history into three major phases – the first spanning from 1 million to 150,000 years ago; the second from 150,000 to 30,000 years ago; the fourth extending from 30,000 years ago to the present (p. 208 – that would correspond to the three waves of diffusion of three kinds of *Homo* from Africa throughout the world: first, the spread of the *Homo ergaster* and of the *Homo erectus*, then a first wave of the *Homo sapiens*, and lastly a second wave of *Homo sapiens* (pp. 205–207).[3]

What is most striking to our common sense, and most decisive from the point of view of a glocal history of the world and of humans, is that, underlying these three planetarizations can be found "the pluralistic character of human evolution" since its origins (p. 205). In other words, according to the current results of paleoanthropological studies, a plurality of hominid species has simultaneously populated the world (at least twenty in total, and at certain times at least five simultaneously). The contemporary solitude of the *Homo sapiens* would then be the temporary outcome of a "declining diversity" (Gould, in Pievani, 2002: 246).

This outcome is also a rather recent one (considering the 6 million years of homination). As Pievani notes:

> If an unaware extraterrestrial fell on planet Earth 30,000 years ago, there, spread across the old world, she would have found three contemporaneous forms of hominids: the *Homo neanderthalensis* in Europe, the *Homo erectus* in Asia, and the *Homo sapiens* who cohabited with both in the course of its relentless expansion toward the most recondite corners of the inhabitable world. [...] What today we call "humanity" has always been represented, in the past, by a multiplicity of cohabiting species.
>
> (2002: 206)

In other words, our history would be saturated, since its origins, with *different forms of the human* that *planetarize* and at the same time *relativize* the world, *giving it shape through myriad formations*.

While, on the one hand, the global diffusion of the *Homo sapiens* confirms the common origin and the deep communality of human beings (that thus deprives all racist discourses of any meaning), on the other hand it does not exclude human diversity: "The diaspora of the peoples on earth reveals in fact a genetic and anthropological unity even within the noticeable diversity of human cultures and morphologies." So it is for languages (p. 203), that, as Pievani reminds us, are "in the smallest part of biological origin (the few genes that regulate the color of the skin and some anatomical traits adapted to climate)" and in the greater part "fruit of different and contingent histories" (p. 211). From here, once again, although within a single species, the necessity – according to Pievani – of recurring to the (evidently glocal) metaphor of the *unitas multiplex* represents itself.

Once more, the history of globalization reveals itself as the history of a constant and plural glocalization.

Ecological horizons

What are the – practical and theoretical – horizons of this first, mainly local, root?

It is impossible to summarize all of them. But a first point that we find interesting to notice is that this becoming of the world sees man – and his cultural universe at large – as the *conditioned,* and not as the *conditioning*: that is, it sees man as the object that undergoes the effects of "global" processes, and not as the agent who causes them, rules them, or is, by all means, at its centre. This reflection invites us, especially considering the view of a very long period, to avoid tracing all explanations back to a single anthropocentric dimension. Furthermore, it leads us back, on the contrary, to the complex play between ensembles of possibility and constraints that interlace, overlap, link up, and articulate in history: from genetic to climatic variations, up to environmental niches and, further, to the latitudinal–longitudinal structuring of the continents – all able to favour the domestication and the consequent development of the different immune systems among the populations of the globe (Diamond, 1997) – we then find ourselves among a complexity of interacting and structuring factors. This complexity conditions the stability and the mutations of the forms of our existence, of our worlds, creating, in the long run, interdependencies that are not easily sensed between cultural and extra-cultural factors to which, in general, the studies on globalization primarily point.

Second, such apparently *global* processes have been, since their beginning, *glocal* processes. Talking once more about climate and its impact on the lives of all beings, one could attempt to summarize the argument by saying that a *change* in the *global economy of climate* is, *locally,* the fortune of some and the misfortune of others. What emerges, then, is the problem of the continuous *correlation* between different series: the correlation between genetic, climatic, environmental, demographic variations in relation to social, cultural, economic, and technological variations. In this sense "globalization" is given as the *apparent and temporary synchronization* between the various series that simultaneously underlay a constant *plurality of rhythms that are,* in turn, *necessarily mutually asynchronous.*[4]

Third, one should not forget that the nearer one approaches the present time the more the socio-cultural aspects – due, also, to the deepening of scientific knowledge and of technological skills – begin to retroact on the "ecological" aspects that were initially regarded to be the conditioning aspects. What appeared to be conditioned now becomes conditioning: men, acting upon the world in an increasingly intensive and extensive way, become, at least potentially, the cause of changes in the physical coherence of the world and in the biological history of humans.

Finally, the awareness of possible collapses on an increasingly global scale, linked with the knowledge not only of past collapses but also of past experiences of positive responses and of local management of ecological problems (Diamond, 2005: 14–17), leads towards more accentuated forms of *reflexivity*. A reflexivity that is simultaneously inextricably local and global.

The transformation of the climatic (or, more generally, ecological) question in a sort of common discourse of contemporary society – a kind of "global common sense" – emphasizes the local perception of the *world-as-a-whole* (Robertson, 1992; Robertson and White, 2004). At the same time, the planetary environmental risk, the daily perception of the fragility of our world – increasingly emphasized, for that matter, by its centrality in the mediatic and political discourses – seem to be creating the conditions for a cosmopolitan awareness, that is, the almost automatic perception of a "common destiny" (Beck, 1997: 58) or the instinctive belonging to a single earth/motherland (Morin, 1993). To conclude, the concrete processes of desertification, or the simple destruction of the environment caused by savage exploitation of the territory and of natural resources, by putting into motion the relative chains of illnesses, famines, wars, migrations, and by relating to the demographic growth of the world population, once again shuffle the cards of planetarization. While the political response to environmental issues remains entrusted to difficult forms of *global coordination* of local, unanimous, and plural interests, the daily and concrete commitment on a small scale seems left to confront global processes and forces that are hard to manage. Within the daily perception of the *world-as-a-whole,* then, there is clear evidence for multiple glocal conflicts and disorders.

Imagining oneself human in a different way

Human roots

Our biological history led us to ascertain the *unitas multiplex* of the *Homo sapiens*. On the threshold of our contemporary world, once we confront with the first verbal documentary evidence of our ancestors, we find, once again, confirmation of this unity within the multiplicity:

> When peoples give themselves names, make exception for denominations of a geographical character, they differentiate, as far as we can judge, in two categories: the ethnic appellative either consists in a laudatory epithet "the Brave, the Strong, the Excellent, the Eminent", or, in most cases, they simply call themselves "the Men". Beginning with the Germanic *Ala-manni* and, regardless of their origin and of their language, following the parade of peoples up to the Kamčatka or to the southernmost end of South America, one encounters dozens of peoples that designate themselves as "the men;" all of these set themselves up as a community that has the same language and the same origin, and implicitly pose against the neighboring peoples.
>
> (Benveniste, 1969: 284)

As we can see, the traces of the *self-denominations* of peoples ooze with glocality and immediately give insight into the *imaginative* and, at the same time, *differential* character of cultural identities.[5]

In other words, while historical data testifies the pervasiveness of the self-description of various peoples as simple and pure "men", to such a degree that it leads us towards the hypothesis of a global "innate" consciousness of the humankind, on the other it appears to indicate that this tension towards the *universal* inextricably matches with an apparently opposed tension, a tension towards the *particular*. Thus, history at its beginnings seems to hand over to us a scene made of as many humanities as were the collectivities that comprised it. Or better still, a scenery made of many *local* collectivities that self-defined as "human", that is, representing *globality*, at the very time when they distinguished themselves from and were opposed to other collectivities that, in turn, probably in another language, self-defined as "men". Imagining oneself human by defining oneself different; defining oneself human by imagining oneself different.

Let us pause for a moment to note that the scenery of self-denominations outlined by Benveniste is actually further stratified. To the side of the simple definition "the Men" one also finds again another series of definitions: "the Brave, the Strong, the Excellent, the Eminent". In our view, such apparent dyscrasia links up in a very clear way with a distinction highlighted by Jurij M. Lotman and Boris A. Uspenskij, two of the foremost scholars of the semiotics of culture, leading us to identify two *forms or effects of glocality*.

Lotman and Uspenskij (1973) remind us that, from a typological point of view, the self-definition of a "culture" in terms of *globality of meaning* generally takes place either in opposition to a "non-culture" or in antithesis to an "anti-culture". The history of cultures teems with collectivities that, albeit recognizing the existence of otherness, viewed it as the space of a *non-culture*. They thus moulded their own world on the opposition *orderly vs non orderly, organized vs non organized, cosmos vs chaos*, or, considering otherness to be an *anti-culture*, as the place of a different order, an opposed sign, a negative sign: therefore the structuring of the relation departs from the pair *correct vs erroneous*, or, even more radically, from *true vs false*.

The two types of self-denominations that we have considered are essentially traceable to these two typological forms. The denomination in terms of "Brave, Strong, Excellent, Eminent", presupposes the existence of an otherness deprived of value: weak, wrong in some way, and marked by a trait of cultural negativity or inferiority. The denomination in terms of "Men", on the contrary, presupposes the existence of a collectivity whose culturality appears inexistent or so unrecognizable that these "other men" are often marked as "savages" with the trait of animality or barbarity.

The practical consequence of such a distinction is, according to the Russian authors, that the cultures that conceive themselves as order struggling against chaos regard themselves as the potential carriers of organization in the space that, for them, is dominated by disorder. On the contrary, cultures that conceive themselves struggling against a different culture of a negative sign would have the opposite tendency: rather than aiming to spread their own principles, they rather tend to shut themselves away to defend and preserve them. Hence, there are two cultural–political logics: the one "expansionist", and in some way inadvertently "hybridist", the other "protectionist", with apparently "purist" effects.

If we further elaborate such prototypical stances we can then say that they suggest *two basic (but not exclusive) ways for articulating glocality*.

Cultures that perceive and describe themselves as representative of the human in its entirety, and that may consequently have a tendency to expand, can be considered as *global localities*: even though they are partial (and perhaps they even sense it), they feel their locality to be potentially valid on a global scale, exactly because what surrounds them appears to them lacking organization, coherence, values.

On the contrary, cultures that base themselves on the antithesis between their own positive values and the other's negative values, and, as such, are able to develop forms of protectionism, would behave as *local globalities*: that is, as spheres of meaning that, exactly because they perceive and describe themselves as complete, tend to shut themselves away in a space that is best impermeable to alterity.

Such attitudes clearly indicate extreme polarities, and the complexification of the contemporary world should, in theory, render extremely difficult their reactualization in such forms that, looking back into the past, appear to us as more clear-cut. In any event, on the one hand it is not difficult to bring to the mind numerous contemporary discourses based on the exportation, at times violent, of one's own principles and values on the part of collectivities that attribute to themselves a civilizing mission. On the other hand, it is not difficult to think about the construction and the maintenance of walls and barriers, real or imaginary, in defence of one's own territory and of one's own culture on the part of collectivities that perceive their supposed coherence (if not their very existence) under the threats of alterity. Notwithstanding appearances, resorting to narratives based upon the struggle between the civilized and the barbarous or between good and evil, the missionary work of values or the defence of an owned space that is imagined as uncontaminated, still seems present, pervasive, and very often politically effective.

Dominant histories

Regardless of how such typologies may be applicable to the complexity of the contemporary world, it is evident that defining the human leads us into an unsettled and, at the same time, slippery territory. We say unsettled because the human appears to be the root and the horizon of our discourses and of our actions; we say slippery because the necessity that collectivities have to recognize themselves as humans – or as declinations of the human – matches with a tendency to transform one's own peculiar humanity in humanity *tout court*.

We could say that the recent history of humanity has very often been motivated and put into motion by such confusion of *one's own peculiar humanity* with *humanity as such*. As a consequence, the world changed into the product of subsequent or competing *histories of dominations*.

Lotman, in his important work *The Semiosphere* (1985), has adapted the concept of *dominant*, as developed by the Russian formalists and by Roman Jakobson within the field of analysis of artistic texts, exactly to the dynamic of cultural systems. By readapting, in turn, Lotman's elaboration, we could say that the dominant is a *local structure* that seeks, in the first place, to subject all others to its organization (to its rules, to its system of values); second, that it appropriates the right to speak and act "in the name" of globality (or of some idea of globality); third, in this journey of domination, the local structure produces its own self-description that legitimizes as globally valid only its own specific (and initially local) structuring of the world, while seeking to relegate other local forms of organization of sociocultural reality to non-existence or to insignificance.

The history of the past 500 years, as many have already implicitly or explicitly maintained, could be read as a series of attempts of subsequent or competing dominations: Ibero-Catholic mondialization, Dutch commercial rule, British globalization based on sea control and on industrialization, the United States' hegemony of financial capitalism, and so on up to the post-1989 tale of the "end of the history" (the birth of "the Empire", in the terms of the counter narratives that, while contesting this new and further globalization, actually risk emphasizing its omnipervasiveness).[6]

Even if we were to pause at this radical simplification of recent world history, it would be impossible to deny the overlapping of (governmental, national, ethnic, continental, civilizational, confessional ...) subjectivities and of (economic, religious, political, linguistic, territorial ...) logics that are not isomorphic, that are not completely and perfectly correlated: subjectivities and languages that are continually created and redefined at the very moment of their coming into relation. Moreover, it would be equally consequential to recall that, for each domination, not only were there alternative ones in evident competition, but also that, before the advancement of each hypothesis of domination, there were, as well, forms of open resistance, of ambiguous compromise, of refined and yet impossible impermeability, of partial and perhaps involuntary foreignness to the dominant logics due to the imperfect finitude of the world.

The transformation of the dominated alterity into a mere local position within the discourses and the practices of the dominant, or an authentic "construction of the barbaric" (Lotman, 1985) – that is, the ability to deprive a collectivity at once of the possibility of self-defining and of reproducing itself culturally, up to the point where it becomes a destructured mass of individuals apparently ready to adhere to an identity and to a universe of values that are imposed – are games whose stake has always proved complex and inexhaustible. But such games are, above all, unpredictable – and even sardonic – in their outcomes. So, as the dominant never recognized themselves when they looked at their image in the eyes of the dominated, even in those of the most docile, likewise the dominated, even the most belligerent, at the time when they attempted to achieve liberation, were never able to return to what they were before. The relation had changed both, making the tangle of the world again more intricate.

Plural horizons

The very long history of dominations – one into which we cannot enter here – appears interesting to us for it helps us gain insight into a further *glocal device*: one in which a *globality* and a *locality* are not given as ontological entities but as *relative and relational meaningful effects* departing from strategies and tactics of *incorporation* that are played through specific *force and power relations*. In other words, we are dealing with systems and processes (more or less) *englobing* or (more or less) *englobed*, where, by all means, the meaningful effect is always given through the generated and adopted *positions* within the relation, and *from the point of view* from which we look at the relation itself (that is, from the position from which we relate with the relation).

Let us provide a single example by reporting an apparently shocking statement of Jean-Marie Tjibaou, a former priest who later became the leader of the Kanak Independence Movement. According to Tjibaou, the Bible did not belong to white men but was reinvented by the Kanak people: with this statement, the New Caledonian politician drew attention to the selective and transformative appropriation of an object that originally did not belong to the Kanak (Bensa, 1998; Clifford, 2001, 2003: 86) and that later became, in a distant Pacific island, different from itself and simultaneously part of an ancient and, at the same time very new, culture. One should note the paradox: here Christianity both plays the role of a parameter discourse, of a language of "global" translation that is dominating in its own way, and exists concretely, at the same time, only as a part of the life world, of the imagined world of a situated (and apparently dominated) collectivity that, making it its own, "localizes" it, not only in the sense that it introduces the object into a territorial locality (New Caledonia), but especially in the sense that makes it a "local" piece within a cultural system that is "global" in itself (what we could call "contemporary Kanak culture").

It is as if we first defined the plane of those who adhere to Christianity and then said, with no fear of contradiction, that: "They have the same religion, but it is not the same anywhere: it does not have the same *value* and the same *form* everywhere." To complicate this already complex question we should also take into account the fact that the religious discourse that arrived in New Caledonia is that of Protestantism, a specific form of Christianity. Furthermore, when Tjibaou declared a semiotic sovereignty – if we can so call it – of the Kanak, he did so within a severe conflict with the French state that incorporates his island, his land, into the European political space within a long colonial history. How many globalities and how many localities come into play in this cross-section of the world? What, then, is "global" and what is "local" in this net of plural relations? Probably, in order to try to provide an answer, the questions to ask are others: Who englobes who? How? Within what type of relations of force and meaning? From what point of view and from what position?

When we widen our view and interlace the theme of the *plurality of non-isomorphic logics* (or "disjunctive" logics, as Appadurai (1996) would put it) with the *glocal device of englobement*, what we obtain is a sort of a "crossed-eye sight" (Sedda, 2006, 2012) that is capable of analytically keeping in simultaneous presence several planes that are apparently contradictory: that is, various *levels of homogenization and heterogenization* that are commonly regarded to be mutually exclusive. We think, in this respect, about the observations of Sahlins (2000) on the coexistence of a generally "capitalistic" logic (a language) and of its local overthrows (or else simply of its own adaptations and misunderstandings). We also think about the endless reasonings on "westernization" (Tomlinson, 1999) in terms of a unified and unifying dynamic that, in all respects, clashes with the impression, when descending to a lower level, if not of its disappearance, but, to say the least, of its turning into dust within other logics, other sights, other narratives that are more composite and heterogeneous, or globally coherent but from another point of view, from another position.

Ultimately, the games are always more complex than we like to think. It is not only *the global* that can be (and in fact often is) only a locality, a substructure, dominating (only temporally and only from some points of view), but the same *local*, if we observe it well, reveals itself to be construed through global languages and *recipes* (Robertson and White, 2004) or through *neighbouring relations*, at the same time translocal and differential, that have correctly suggested a "production of locality" (Appadurai, 1996). Once again, the definition of locality and globality is worked through complex semiotic devices. It produces itself through effects of meaning and power that are contingent and unstable, if not completely aleatory or imponderable.

For such reasons the horizon of our glocal world that is made of distant proximities seems to be exposed to continual processes of *fragmegration* (Rosenau, 2003), that is, to a continual play of fragmentations and aggregations on several levels and by means of plural logics. This concept, developed in the field of study of international relations, seems to match with the idea that our cultural identities are the cause and the effect of repeated *linkings* and *delinkings*, of repeated spatial and historical *(re)articulations* that make subjectivities and identifications what is at stake in identity politics (Clifford, 2002, 2003). In other words – more consonantly with Greimasian lexicon (Greimas, 1970, 1983) – we are those who produce the figures of identity and alterity, one's own and the other's, that populate the world; we are those who, time after time, for tactical or strategic needs, thematize "the local" and "the global" as dimensions that are given and natural, and place ourselves in relation to them; we are those who define the values that guide our own existences; we are those who tell the stories of those authorities that should legitimize our loyalties, our attachments, our belongings, that is, the things for which is worth to live or even to die.

My body, the world

Corporeal roots

Let's start the final part of our work quoting Merleau-Ponty's *The Visible and the Invisible*:

> Rather than saying that I am in time and in space, or that I am in no place, why not say better that I am everywhere, always, being in this moment and in this place?
>
> (Merleau-Ponty, 1964: 132)

Merleau-Ponty's question leads us to inquire into a further root of the glocal, a phenomenological root inscribed into our very corporeality and in its relation with the world. It is worth trying to follow, for a moment, the reasoning of the French philosopher, who poses this question in an attempt to weave together the split between fact and essence, between things and ideas.

Now, according to Merleau-Ponty, the divarication between fact and essence only occurs under a particular condition: that is to say a condition that presupposes or that relies upon "a thought that looks at being from another place, and in front, one might say" (p. 132). Given this postulate, the subject presents itself as a *kosmotheoros*, a person who is able to preside over the cosmos with a "sovereign sight" but who grasps things in a fixed and total order that is manifold and yet flat. This means that, according to this theory, things gain an absolute givenness, for the determination of their placement in space–time is absolute, which, in turn, signifies that the same meanings that relate to this world of things become frozen and form "a system of meanings with neither locality nor temporality" (p. ibid, vi).

This possibility of *abstraction*, of *generalization*, the possibility that the subject has to "enthrone" herself into a sort of "zero point of Being" in order to exercise a sort of "bird's-eye view", matches, however, with the perception that "tomorrow, in a short time" these same imaginative and globalizing operations are destined to "fall" towards that from which they detached, to reveal their rootedness in a situation, in a space–time – "a certain point of apparition on earth and in my life" (p. ivi).

The question Merleau-Ponty poses above comes into play at this juncture. If the subject can constantly produce globalizing generalizations without giving up rooting herself in a specific space–time and without giving up the ability to translate – in the double meaning of transporting and at the same time transforming – this background within the semiotic formations that she produces, why should we not think that, in the end, she may not be "*everywhere, always, being in this moment and in this place*?" In other words, are we not able to reach out with our imagination, moving among different places and cultures, going back to the past, anticipating the future, building the present, inventing worlds? Moreover, are we not able to inscribe these worlds into manifold semiotic formations that, by realizing imagination, make imagination accessible, shareable? Are, then, our located, fragile, and perishable bodies not able to build a globality of meaning, a sort of "worldmaking"?[7]

If this inextricability between global and local is possible, if the subject can produce the world that contains it, it is exactly because the world – the "visible" in the words of Merleau-Ponty – detects the subject, dominates it by filling it and occupying it, "because, I who see it, I don't see it from the bottom of nothing, but from the heart of the visible itself: I, the seer, am also the visible . . . " (ibid., p. 133).

We thus see that, at the apex of its localization, the subject discovers her greater universalizing power: in her co-inherence with the world, at the time when the world roots itself in the body, the subject discovers the power of opening her own thought to the universal, that is to say to a thought that is dense with *unthought*, that is capable of a "general distortion" of things and of discovering their deep nerve while – we say – translating them semiotically.

Then, what keeps together the two poles, facts and essences, is this profound *glocality* of the body–world relationship and of the *statements* that structure it. The imagination of the world branches out from our body, and yet there is no other life chance for the single body other than exiting from itself towards a generality that is not within, in the "In Self". On the contrary, it is exactly a "crossing point" with and on the world: "[...] we do not live and know on the road amidst opaque facts and clear ideas, but at the point of encounter and of crossing in which families of facts inscribe their generality, their relation, grouping around the dimensions and the place of our own existence" (ibid., p. 135).

Our *situated statements* – producers of *global statements* by way of carrying a globality of meaning and by way of being able to journey through the world to be appropriated by other bodies – are the crossing place between world and body. Owing to an eidetic variation, a manipulation of forms that is simultaneously a production of *semiotic formations*, the body is the very producer of the "systems of meaning" that produce it, and by means of which it locates itself within some generality.[8]

That which Merleau-Ponty calls *interworld* is, in our reading, the space that semiotic formations open, regardless whether they are actions or words, routes or discourses, institutions or narratives. Semiotic formations allow the subjects to articulate shared forms of subjectivity, spatiality, and temporality, so as to define the figures and the themes, the authorities and the values that, time after time, give structure to our worlds.

Imagined stories

If viewed as originating from this root, our story may appear to be the history of the multifarious ways by means of which we have imagined ourselves and our world: how we have recounted ourselves and how we have acted consequently. However, it is impossible to trace here a history of *glocal imagination* and of its continuous rearticulation[9]. What we can do here is try to sketch one of the many possible journeys.

Let us start again from some interesting historico-cultural data, as highlighted by Lotman and Uspenskij. According to these authors, "in ancient and in medieval literary texts so as in fourteenth-century novels one encounters with unusual rarity the theme of *incomprehension*" (in Lotman, 2006: 79). Communication becomes a problem only with the texts of Romanticism. Now, the legitimate coexistence of different points of view on the world, the constant conflict between different discursive universes, between competing systems of truth, causes incomprehension to become established as the rule – from which follows the happening of "tragic" communicative and cultural "collisions" (ibid.).

The consequence is that, while before Romanticism, for example in the epic plot, communication was regarded as an "ideal act, instantaneously realizable and without loss" (ibid.) now the problem of translation imposes itself in a dominant way.

We find a clear example of the way in which it begins to define the field of culture in the early 20th century in James Joyce's *Finnegans Wake*. As Umberto Eco (2003) wrote, *Finnegans Wake* is a plurilingual text, "already translated" in some way; or, we could say, that it reveals within itself the question and the very centrality of translation. But *Finnegans Wake*'s own plurilingualism, one that tries to give shape to the global complexity of the world within a single text, is such by way of its originating from a certain *fold* of the world. As noted by Eco, *Finnegans Wake* is plurilingual "but from the point of view of the English language. It is a plurilingual text as an Anglophone may have thought it" (ibid., p. 304). And, we should add, an Irish Anglophone. It is not a case that, when Joyce had to translate both the text and himself, he had to rethink such plurilingualism, such *world-in-translation*, beginning from another fold of the world: "It thus seems to me that the choice of Joyce-translator-of-himself has been to think about the destination text (French or Italian) as a plurilingual text such as it could be thought by a Francophone or an Italophone" (ibid., pp. 304–305).

The example of *Finnegans Wake* helps us focus upon the entrance into a world that is so global to be *twice glocal*. A babelic world (Fabbri, 2000) made of a myriad languages that mix together and translate constantly; a world in which this mixture, this self-translation, gives different results depending on the space in which it realizes itself and on the position from which this *world-in-translation* is grasped (and in turn translated again). In other words, the mechanism of translation becomes exponential. Consequently, the boxings, the crossings, and the interdefinitions between globality and locality become infinitely complex.

The tragic glocal paradox of the early 20th century, which translation tries to answer, can be summarized as follows: *the world shrinks, incomprehension increases* (Sedda, 2004b). Precisely at the time when the world "ends" and becomes fully interdependent – as noted by Valery (1945) between 1931 and 1938: "There begins the age of the finite world" (ibid., p. 23), "nothing will be done again that does not involve the entire world" (ibid., p. 37) – there begins the period of the most tragic, "great", "world" wars. The very redefinition of the "Great War" into "World War I" seems to indicate this reflexive and imaginative leap towards a unity of the world that fully reveals itself in the tragic, collective inability to live together on the planet.

The world, forcedly and ambiguously interconnected by means of mass communication as well as by European colonialism, then found itself caught in an explosive tension between naked bodies and impossible imaginaries. As Walter Benjamin would say about the traumatic historic turning point that the "world war" brought about: "... nothing had remained unchanged besides the clouds, and below them, in a magnetic field of deadly currents and explosions, the minute and fragile body of man" (1936, in Benjamin, 1966: 248). And to this return upon naked and fragile, minute and hyper-localized bodies corresponded the very setback of human imagination at the end of World War II. The end of humanity prospected with the Holocaust, inscribed within the very same unimaginability and unrepresentability of such inhumane event. The end of humanity and of its future – the end of the future of the species, that is, the realization of the very possibility of imagining ourselves as physically extinguished – was given real life with the atomic bomb.

Such is the bloody caesura between located bodies and global imagination that, in the history of the global, imagery will seem to begin healing only towards the late 1960s. Two emblematic examples: the Beatles, who in 1967, right in the middle of the *Summer of Love*, sing *All You Need is Love* in the first satellite programme in world-vision in all history, which was significantly called *Our World*; humanity, that in 1969 remains breathless when a tiny human body places his own foot "live" on the Moon, a collective imagination that becomes true, with the possibility of looking at oneself from another place and of actually imagining oneself "as one" ... ("as one", just like, as if by coincidence, a year later, John Lennon would sing in his *Imagine*).

Furthermore, at the time when all this was happening, the 20th century was offering us, from within the "west" – a label that is as generic and slippery as that of "orient" – as well as from its colonial space, a new explosion of voices and bodies and englobed peoples, apparently mute and in any event once again ready to gain speech, willing to tell their own story and to imagine themselves differently.

As a matter of fact, while the world became apparently globalized (and "globalization" itself became, for many, a "mythology", "a great narrative"), the west – as the privileged actor of this history of "unification" – had to come to terms with the fact that her "others" had always told their own story and wanted to keep doing so. This story was "different", or more precisely, *differently located* within the common plot of stories and spaces of which our world is made. Those others, those minute bodies apparently divided, broken, deprived of their own possibility to imagine the world and its transformations, had already foreseen a place for alterity inside *their own* cultural system. They were ready to *reinvent themselves*. They were once again ready to "reinvent" what had been imposed onto them;[10] but they also generated new contradictions, bringing about new conflicts and new dominations, ambiguous or incomplete "liberations".

Let us provide a single, brief example. It is an example that, despite its limits, is well known and paradigmatic of the relationship between the bodily phenomenological dimension and the potential invention of worlds. Moreover, it is an example from a socio-political field that helps us ponder the ways in which the possibility of imagination and agency, whether individual or communal, artistic or scientific, political or technical, can intervene in the historical structures of domination (see *Dominant histories, Plural horizons*) as it does in the natural structuring of the world over a very long period (see *Natural histories, Ecological horizons*). The example is Mohandas K. Gandhi. Involved in great collective movements made up of numerous governmental, religious, cultural, and linguistic aggregations (and disintegrations); tester of unpredictable truths and translations, of unthought actions and ideas; he was a small, fragile, and contradictory man who believed that each body can and should provide *world examples*: "We must be the change we wish to see in the world."[11]

Aside from the concrete historical events of the case, and beyond the (contested) reliability of such citations as Gandhi's own statement, the actions and words of the "Mahatma" aid us in underscoring the practical and explicit assumption of the body in quality of both the semiotic-discursive matrix and support. It is a device *within everybody's reach* for the experimentation, the exemplifying, and the opening of worlds. It is a potency that becomes more striking and evident when it turns into a means of *empowerment* in the struggles of self-affirmation of the oppressed, of the emarginated, of the weak, of those who are excluded and persecuted for their diversity.[12]

And yet, as the examples we took into consideration remind us, nothing and nobody is left this *relation of forces* intact and unchanged – independence and interdependence, clash and collaboration, homologation and differentiation, translation and incomprehension – that today continues in each corner of the earth, each time more or less tense and asymmetrical, productive and destructive. And yet the many "others" of the west left for a long time at the margins stirred, by way of very different strategies and objectives, an apparently globalized world. Making it, time and again, glocal.

Shared horizons

What, then, is the world that we have inherited and that is now before us, if not a *shared world*? The idea of sharing – of *con*-dividing (dividing together[13]), the "being *between us*", the inexhaustible tension of being together while dividing ourselves, or of dividing something while being together – appears as one of the key concepts aiding us to view our glocal horizons, our *being singular-plural*.

As the philosopher Jean-Luc Nancy wrote:

> The world, each time, keeps arising from an exclusive, local-instantaneous fold. Its unity, its uniqueness and totality, consist in the combination of this networked multiplicity, which has no resultants.
>
> (Nancy, 1996: 15)

Here, what is offered to us is the possibility to think and inhabit a *world of worlds*. On the one hand, the world is taken as known and as the goal of our action, as the beginning and as the end of our being in it, but on the other hand it keeps opening itself: *the world* opens itself to itself through plural singularities, *the worlds*, that constitute it. It is a proliferation from the inside, similar to an explosion of lava that falls back again to return perpetually onto what created it, that in turn flows back to the origin, to the earth – to what it already is and what it continually becomes – modifying it with no interruption.

The interesting thing that, perhaps is not immediately perceivable, is that the idea of *sharing* (Nancy, 1990) connects and relates to that of *border* (Lotman, 1985, 1993). Here, border understood as the place of contact and communication between *semiospheres*, the place that simultaneously unites and divides, the place of the encounter with the other, understood as the mechanism activating reflexivity, self-definition, and self-awareness. Is it not, then, the encounter with the other that changes us and simultaneously makes us who we are, creating us anew and simultaneously making us believe we have recovered our memory, our past, and our conscience?

But if the border is the *locus classicus* of the translating relation,[14] and if it is true that there is a (semiotic) border wherever there is an attempt or a need for translation, then borders, in our glocal world, are omnipervasive. Furthermore, as much as it may sound paradoxical, it is their excess that makes difficult, if not impossible, any definitive asphyxia and total impermeabilities, though it forces us into a wearing, imperfect, and at times even traumatic, work of mutual cultural translation. We must constantly face the other's alterity and the very alterity that we ourselves are. For this, we are repeatedly called to *translate alterity* but also to *translate the tradition*,[15] to constantly redefine what we believe is "ours".

From the immemorial depths of our biological life to the languages that we inhabit, and from our most profound ethical choices to the stories that we share to define ourselves, we are continually called to translate one another, overcoming limits, giving shape to our existences, living between spaces, places, languages: "we are beings who are born to overcome limits. We know this thanks to the stories that we tell each other [...] the changing of language makes us change" (Rushdie, 2002: 434).

In conclusion, at the time in which the space of the world ended, what was being realized was not its flat homogeneity but the plurality of its internal, overlapping, interconnected spaces; what was emerging was the network of its cross-stratified histories, of its manifold borders, of the various languages and points of view, of the many logics and narratives that structure it and constitute it while they fringe it and make it complex it at the same time.[16]

Our glocal horizon seems to place us in this space of interplay between the heterogeneity of the real and the (social, historical, cultural, or, in a wider sense, semiotic) formations that, by articulating borders, conflicts, contradictions, do create possibilities – albeit imperfect and contingent ones – of sharing and identification. As do new borders, new conflicts, new contradictions, new translations.

Notes

1. I would like to express my gratitude to Martino Dibeltulo and to Harjeet Grewal for translating this chapter from Italian into English, and for providing valuable comments on earlier drafts of the work.
2. See, for example, Greene (2011).
3. Pievani finally reaches a model in five phases that comprises the first phase of emergence of hominids (from 5 to 1 million and 800 thousand years ago) and the fifth of planetary diffusion of Homo sapiens (from 15,000 to 500 years ago) (Pievani, 2002: 298–300). See also the various timing tables and related hypotheses, which are not always easy to disentangle (pp. 160, 187).

4. "There has not been, in substance, a synchronized evolution of the main characteristic of the species of hominids (anatomy, technology, social organization, diet, habitat...), but an evolution with heterogeneous rhythms, an evolution on a time lag" (Pievani, 2002: 141).
5. On this semiotico-structuralist point see the consonances with the elaborations of Anderson (1983, 1998), Appadurai (1996), Hall (2006), Clifford (1988, 1997, 2002, 2003).
6. A case of this kind seems to be the volume by Negri and Hardt (2002). For an analytic outlook, from a perspective of international relations and closer to a glocal sensibility, see the volume by Colombo entitled *La disunità del mondo* (2010).
7. On "world-making", see also Goodman (1978).
8. See what has been written on Subject, Discourse ("system of representations"), Identity by Geninasca (1997).
9. See for example Anderson 1983, Robertson 1992, Appadurai 1996, Sedda 2004a, Sloterdijk 2005.
10. Cf. Sahlins (1993, 2000).
11. See Gandhi (1996). For a philosophico-political reflection on exemplarity see Ferrara (2008).
12. See, for example in the European context, the use of the (naked) body by the members of the FEMEN Movement to protest against sex tourism, sexism, discrimination, and dictatorship in Ukraine. The transnational impact and circulation of the images of the women's naked bodies trailed by police forces rapidly situated FEMEN activism beyond the Ukrainian context, putting it directly at the centre of a greater European public sphere.
13. In a previous draft of this chapter, written in Italian, I played on the meaning of the verb "condividere", in English "to share", composed of the Latin prefix *con* – (together) and by the verb *dividere* (to divide). In this paragraph the translators used the verb "to share" in English. Later, we decided to supplement this verb with the compound "*con*-dividing". I thus invite the reader to reflect on the meaning of the Italian word, graphically untranslatable in English.
14. It would be interesting to develop the connection between the idea of *relation*, as a primary idea which generates the parts that enter into relation (see Hjelmslev, 1961), and the idea of *border* (with regard to this we should recall Lotman's (1985) idea that "dialogue precedes and generates language"). On the *poetics of the relation* see Bernabé et al. (1989); Glissant (1996); Chamoiseau (2005).
15. See Sedda (2003).
16. On the fascinating topic of complexity see the essays in Neve et al. (2011). On the other hand, in Pievani (2011) we find a critique to some fissures or uses of the holistic theories of complexity in a "creationist" sense.

References

Anderson, B. (1983) *Imagined Communities*, London: Verso (Italian trans., *Comunità immaginate*, Roma: Manifestolibri, 1996).

Anderson, B. (1998) *The Spectre of Comparisons*, London: Verso.

Appadurai, A. (1996) *Modernity at Large: Cultural Dimensions of Globalization*, Minneapolis and London: University of Minnesota Press (Italian trans., *Modernità in polvere*. Roma: Meltemi, 2001).
Beck, U. (1997) *Was ist Globalisierung? Irrtumer des Globalismus-Antworten auf Globalisierung*, Frankfurt am Main: Suhrkamp Verlag (Italian trans., *Che cos'è la globalizzazione?*, Roma: Carocci, 1999).
Benjamin , W. (1966) *Angelus Novus. Ausgewahlte Schriften 2*, Frankfurt am Main, Suhrkamp (Italian trans., *Angelus Novus*, Turin: Einaudi, 1995).
Bensa, A. (1998) *Nouvelle-Calédonie. Vers l'émancipation*, Paris: Gallimard.
Benveniste, E. (1969) *Le vocabulaire des institutions indoeuropéennes. 1. Economie, parenté, société*, Paris: Les Editions de Minuit (Italian trans., *Il vocabolario delle istituzioni indoeuropee. 1. Economia, parentela, società*, Turin: Einaudi, 1988).
Bernabé, J., P. Chamoiseau, and R. Confiant. (1989) *Éloge de la créolité*, Paris, Gallimard (Italian trans., *Elogio della creolità*, Como–Pavia: Ibis, 1999).
Braudel, F. (1979) *Civilisation materielle, économie et capitalisme, 15–18 siècle*, Paris: A. Colin (Italian trans., *Civiltà materiale, economia, capitalismo*, Turin: Einaudi, 1993).
Chamoiseau, P. (2005) "Universalità e diversalità", "Lo Straniero", anno IX, n. 61, July 2005, Contrasto, pp. 72–77.
Clifford, J. (1988) *The Predicament of Culture: Twentieth-Century Ethnography, Literature and Art*, Cambridge, MA and London: Harvard University Press (Italian trans., *I frutti puri impazziscono*, Turin: Bollati Boringhieri, 1999).
Clifford, J. (1997) *Routes: Travel and Translation in the Late Twentieth Century*, Cambridge, MA and London: Harvard University Press (Italian trans., *Strade. Viaggio e traduzione alla fine del secolo XX*, Turin, Bollati Boringhieri, 1999).
Clifford, J. (2001) "Indigenous Articulations", "The Contemporary Pacific", 13(2), pp. 468–490.
Clifford, J. (2002) "Prendere sul serio le politiche dell'identità", "Aut Aut", n. 312, novembre–dicembre, pp. 97–114.
Clifford, J. (2003) *On the Edges of Anthropology*, Chicago: Prickly Paradigm Press (Italian trans., *Ai margini dell'antropologia. Interviste*, Roma: Meltemi, 2004).
Colombo, A. (2010) *La disunità del mondo. Dopo il secolo globale*, Milan: Feltrinelli.
Diamond, J. (1997) *Guns, Germs and Steel: The Fates of Human Societies*, London and New York: W. W. Norton & Co. (Italian trans., *Armi, acciaio e malattie*, Turin: Einaudi, 2005).
Diamond, J. (2005) *Collapse. How Societies Choose to Fail or Succeed*, New York: Penguin Books (Italian trans., *Collasso*, Turin, Einaudi, 2007).
Eco, U. (2003) *Dire quasi la stessa cosa. Esperienze di traduzione*, Milan: Bompiani.
Fabbri, P. (2000) *Elogio di Babele*, Rome: Meltemi.
Ferrara, A. (2008) *The Force of the Example*, New York: Columbia University Press (Italian trans., *La forza dell'esempio*, Milan: Feltrinelli, 2008).
Friedman, T. L. (2005) *The World is Flat: A Brief History of the Twenty-First Century*, London: Allen Lane.
Geninasca, J. (1997) *La parole littéraire*, Paris: Presses Universitaires de France (Italian trans., *La parola letteraria*, Milan: Bompiani, 2000).
Ghandi, M. K. (1996) *Teoria e pratica della non-violenza*, ed.G. Pontara, Turin: Einaudi.
Glissant, E. (1996) *Introduction à une poétique du divers*, Paris: Gallimard (Italian trans., *Poetica del diverso*, Roma: Meltemi, 1998).

Goodman, N. (1978) *Ways of Worldmaking*, Hassocks: Harvester Press (Italian trans., *Vedere e costruire il mondo*, Rome and Bari: Laterza, 2008).

Greene, B. (2011) *The Hidden Reality: Parallel Universes and the Deep Laws of the Cosmos*, New York: Alfred A. Knopf (Italian trans., 2012, *La realtà nascosta. Universi paralleli e leggi profonde del cosmo*, Turin: Einaudi).

Greimas, A. J. (1970) *Du Sens*, Paris: Éditions du Seuil (Italian trans., *Del senso*, Milan: Bompiani, 1996), 20.

Greimas, A. J. (1983) *Du Sens 2*, Paris: Éditions du Seuil (Italian trans., *Del senso 2*, Milan, Bompiani, 1994).

Hall, S. (2006) *Politiche del quotidiano. Culture, identità e senso* comune, Milan: Il Saggiatore.

Hjelmslev, L. (1961) *Prolegomena to a Theory of Language*, Wisconsin: University of Wisconsin Press (Italian trans., *I fondamenti della teoria del linguaggio*, Turin: Einaudi, 1968).

Lotman, J. M. (1985) *La Semiosfera*, Venice: Marsilio.

Lotman, J. M. (1993) *Kul'tura i vzryv*, Moskva: Gnosis (Italian trans., *La cultura e l'esplosione. Prevedibilità e imprevedibilità*, Milan: Feltrinelli, 1993).

Lotman, J. M (2006) *Tesi per una semiotica delle culture*, ed. F. Sedda, Rome: Meltemi.

Lotman, J. M. and B. A. Uspenskij. (1973) *Tipologia della cultura*, Milan: Bompiani.

Merleau-Ponty, M. (1964) *Le visible et l'invisible*, Paris: Gallimard (Italian trans., *Il visibile e l'invisibile*, Milan: Bompiani, 1999).

Morin, E. (1993) *Terre-patrie*, Paris: Seuil (Italian trans., *Terra-Patria*, Milan: Raffaello Cortina, 1994).

Nancy, J.-L. (1990) *La communauté désoeuvrée*, ed. Christian Bourgois (Italian trans., *La comunità inoperosa*, Napoli: Cronopio, 1995).

Nancy, J.-L. (1996) *Être singulier pluriel*, Paris: Galilée (Italian trans., *Essere singolare plurale*, Turin: Einaudi, 2001).

Negri, T. and M. Hardt. (2002) *Impero. Il nuovo ordine della globalizzazione*, Milan: Rizzoli.

Neve, M., L. Boi, and R. Barbanti. (eds.) (2011) *Paesaggi della complessità. La trama delle cose e gli intrecci tra natura e cultura*, Milan: Mimesis.

Pievani, T. (2002) *Homo Sapiens e altre catastrofi. Per un'archeologia della globalizzazione*, Rome: Meltemi.

Pievani, T. (2011) *La vita inaspettata*, Milan: Raffaello Cortina.

Robertson, R. (1992) *Globalization. Social Theory and Global Culture* (Italian trans., *Globalizzazione. Teoria sociale e cultura globale*, Trieste: Asterios, 1999).

Robertson, R. (1995) *Glocalization: Time-Space and Homogeneity-Heterogeneity*, in M. Featherstone, S. Lash, and R. Robertson (eds.) *Global Modernities*, London: Sage, pp. 25–44.

Robertson, R. and K. White. (2004) *La glocalizzazione rivisitata ed elaborata*, in Sedda 2004a, (ed.), pp. 13–41.

Rosenau, J. (2003) *Distant Proximities. Dynamics beyond Globalization*, Princeton: Princeton University Press.

Rushdie, S. (2002) *Step across this Line. Collected Nonfiction 1992–2002*, New York: Random House (Italian trans., *Superate questa linea. Saggi e articoli 1992–2002*, Milan: Mondadori, 2007).

Sahlins, M. (1993) "'Addio tristi tropi': l'etnografia nel contesto storico del mondo modern", ed. or in 1994, *Assessing Cultural Anthropology*, in R. Borofsky (ed.)

McGraw-Hill (Italian trans., *L'antropologia culturale oggi*, Roma: Meltemi, 2000, pp. 457–475).

Sahlins, M. (2000) "'Sentimental Pessimism' and Ethnographic Experience. Or, Why Culture is not a Disappearing 'Object", in L. Daston (ed.) *Biographies of Scientific Objects*, Chicago and London: University of Chicago Press, pp. 158–202.

Sedda, F. (2003) *Tradurre la tradizione. Sardegna: su ballu, i corpi, la cultura*, Rome: Meltemi.

Sedda, F. (ed.) (2004a) *Glocal. Sul presente a venire*, Rome: Sossella.

Sedda, F. (2004b) "Riflessioni sul glocal a partire dallo studio semiotico della cultura", in Sedda 2004 (ed.), pp. 231–251.

Sedda, F. (2006) *Imperfette traduzioni*, Introduzione a Lotman 2006, pp. 7–68.

Sedda, F. (2012) *Imperfette traduzioni. Semiopolitica delle culture*, Rome: Nuova Cultura.

Sloterdijk, P. (2005) "Die letzte Kugel", in *Im Weltinnenraum des Kapitals*, Frankfurt am Main: Suhrkamp Verlag (Italian trans., *L'ultima sfera. Breve storia filosofica della globalizzazione*, Roma: Carocci, 2005), p. 23.

Tomlinson, J. (1999) *Globalization and Culture*, Chichester: Polity Press (Italian trans., *Sentirsi a casa nel mondo. La cultura come bene globale*, Milan: Feltrinelli, 2001).

Valéry, P. (1945) *Regards sur le monde actuel et autres essais*, Paris: Gallimard (Italian trans., *Sguardi sul mondo attuale*, Milan: Adelphi, 1994).

3

The Glocalizations of Christianity in Europe

A Global-Historical Perspective

Victor Roudometof

To this day, the historical intertwining between religion and globalization remains a relatively understudied area of scholarship (for two notable exceptions, see Beyer, 2006; Warburg, 2006; for a general overview, Roudometof, forthcoming). In contrast to conventional perspectives, adopting a long-term view of globalization necessarily entails decentring the conventional narrative of Western modernization (O'Brien, 2006). Such a global-historical perspective entails the notion that pre-modern globalization was both important and consequential for humanity. It is furthermore important to incorporate into the analysis of the *longue durée* the realization that globalization does not annihilate life worlds and local structures and settings but rather interacts with them, producing new social and cultural configurations. Hence, the process is more accurately referred to as "glocalization". As Robertson (1994) has suggested, glocalization offers a means of comprehending and interpreting cultural variety, hybridity, and fragmentation within the context of the problematic of global–local relations. While Robertson (1991: 282; Robertson and Garrett, 1991: xv) has referred to religion as a "*genre* of expression, communication and legitimation" for collective and individual identities, current perspectives have yet to illuminate the historical specifics of the manner in which these "glocal" identities are articulated within the framework of globalization analysis.

From within these conceptual lenses, then, this chapter is concerned with the development of a global-historical perspective on the problematic of religion. Accordingly, the worldwide spread of universalistic religions involves their simultaneous localization. As religions are reconfigured, new formations emerge in historical time. These new formations are *cultural hybrids* that blend religious universalism with several forms of local (national or ethnic) particularisms. The above are *not* an exclusively contemporary phenomenon. As this chapter shows, the creation of distinct branches of Christianity – such as Orthodox and Catholic Christianity – is a manifestation of this broader process. This chapter's opening section sketches a model of multiple glocalizations of the world's religious traditions. This model is meant to account for the fragmentation of Christianity in Europe – inclusive of the creation of its Eastern and Western branches. Since space considerations exclude a detailed historical narrative (for such a narrative, see Roudometof, 2014), the chapter proceeds with a brief overview of the glocalizations of Chalcedonian Christianity in the two parts of the Mediterranean up to the first fall of Constantinople (1204) to the armies of the Fourth Crusade. In the chapter's third section, I examine in more detail the glocalizations of Eastern Orthodox Christianity in the modern era – and more specifically its nationalization and transnationalization.

A minimal model of multiple glocalizations

Globalization involves *multiple glocalizations of religion* (Beyer, 2007) – that is, it involves the restructuring of universal religiosity alongside local particularity. While this interplay or interpenetration of universalism and particularism constitutes an important facet of globalization per se (see Robertson, 1992), the model sketched in this section is solely concerned with the case of Christianity. Furthermore, as a matter of principle but also historically speaking – and contrary to the impression that might be created by a narrow reading of this chapter – these multiple glocalizations should not been seen as mechanically connected to specific historical eras or periods. Rather, these occur *both* across historical eras and synchronically, subject to the specific cultural and political conditions of a given milieu. Although not claiming to offer an exhaustive account, the four glocalizations that are outlined below present historically concrete examples that involve a fusion between Christianity's universalism and local particularism. These glocalizations are *vernacularization*, *indigenization*, *nationalization*, and *transnationalization*. Each of these represents a distinct historical configuration, and also offers a discrete analytical ordering of the global and the local.

Vernacularization blends Christianity with specific vernacular languages – which are endowed with the privileged ability of offering communication with the sacred. This glocalization is certainly far more common in pre-modern or pre-literate cultures, whereby access to sacred texts was limited and religious efficacy could be tied to specific language. Vernacularization is not identical and should not be confused with *indigenization*, the key difference being that access to a sacred language is completely distinct from membership in a tribe or ethnicity.

Indigenization blends religious universalism with local particularism by adopting religious ritual, expression, and hierarchies into the specifics of a particular ethnicity. Most often, the sense of distinction thus constructed blends religious and ethnic difference. While premodern kingdoms and principalities made regular use of this process in order to bolster their rulers' legitimacy, the ties constructed often endured far beyond specific regimes or states. In such forms of religiosity, group membership is far more closed than in vernacularization; if vernacularization has been associated with empires, indigenization has been associated with ethnic and cultural reproduction and survival. Different religious traditions might possess a greater or lesser affinity with indigenization.

Nationalization is a form of blending universal Christianity and national particularism. Its principal difference from the previous forms is that the nation serves as the foundation for the religious institutions' claim to legitimacy. Nationalization employs religion as a foundation for nation-building or through the intertwining between confessional membership and national identity (Brubaker, 2012). The Church of England is emblematic of such a relationship, but it is not a deviation from broader European trends (see Hastings, 1997; Gorski, 2000). Nationalization is a strategy through which various national churches maintain their central role in society; in spite of secularization, the importance of public or confessional membership remains central to national life. Even within Western Europe, confessionalization involved the establishment of a formal relationship between specific confessions and territorial rulers (MacCulloch, 2009: 639). As a result, people might belong to a national church without necessarily being religious adherents; religions' significance becomes semiotic.

The difference between indigenization and nationalization rests in part on the civic nature of the nation, whereby the people are active citizens conferring legitimacy to political authority, and not mere subjects (Bendix, 1978). Still, the presence of civic bonds alone is insufficient to provide a uniform source of distinction between the two. In numerous occasions, nations coalesce around culturally defined or ethnic membership – examples abound ranging from Poland to Germany (or from Ireland to Greece). In many instances, and specifically in European countries with large Christian majorities, Christianity is a marker signifying national membership, and a symbiotic relationship exists between the faith and the nation (see Kunovich, 2006). If one goes as far as arguing that no substantive difference exists between nations and ethnic groups, then the distinction between indigenization and nationalization is erased. The academic community, though, offers a multitude of perspectives concerning this issue; with primordialist, modernist, and ethno-symbolist perspectives being the most widely accepted interpretations. Of these, practically, only primordialists would argue against the salience of the conceptual distinction between indigenization and nationalization. For modernists, the difference between the two is self-evident; since, for them, nations and nationalism are modern phenomena without deep roots in history. But even the rival viewpoint, that of ethno-symbolism (Smith, 1986, 2001), in spite of its insistence on the pre-modern sources of modern national identity, does acknowledge the existence of a conceptual distinction between *ethnie* (ethnic communities) and modern nations. Consequently, there is sufficient cause to advocate in favour of a conceptual difference between indigenization and nationalization.

Transnationalization represents the flipside of nationalization. That is, the global construction of nation-states and the nationalization of their citizens create a "residual" category of "transnational" people: this category includes all those immigrant groups and expatriate individuals who, while residing within a nation-state, are not viewed as belonging to the nation. To the extent that transnational religion (Levitt, 2007) is a means of describing solutions to newfound situations that people face as a result of migration, it comes as two quite distinct blends of religious universalism and local particularism. First, it is possible for religious universalism to gain the upper hand, whereby religion becomes the central reference for immigrant communities. In such instances, religious transnationalism is often depicted as a religion "going global". In cases in which immigrants share the same vernacular or are members of a church with a centralized administration (such as the Catholic Church), the propensity for such a pattern inevitably increases. Migrants participate in religious multi-ethnic networks that connect them to their co-religionists locally and globally. Their main allegiance is not to their original homeland but to their global religious community; religion in this sense offers a means for "transnational transcendence"

(Csordas, 2009) of identities and boundaries. Second, it is possible for ethnic or national particularism to maintain its centrality for immigrant communities. In such instances, transnational national communities are constructed and religious hierarchies perform dual religious and secular functions that ensure the groups' survival. This classification offers an important means for understanding the different varieties of religious transnationalism. As the discussion in this chapter's third section shows, different branches or religious traditions of Christianity might possess a greater or lesser affinity for one or other type of transnationalism.

It is important to stress that this model of four glocalizations is not the product of speculation or abstract theorizing but instead has been developed in accordance with socio-historical inquiry, and represents an effort to theorize the historical record. While this discussion is mostly concerned with the eastern part of Europe, the model is nevertheless meant to capture historical developments *across* Europe – and possibly even non-European contexts as well. As the next two sections show, the model presents a historical interpretation that covers historical trajectories that are insufficiently incorporated in the conventional narratives of sociology of religion – which, by and large, are characterized by an undue emphasis on Western European developments alone.

The glocalizations of Chalcedonian Christianity

The spread of Christianity across Eurasia resulted first and foremost in its vernacularization and, secondarily, in its indigenization. From the 4th century onwards, Christianity became the Roman Empire's official and dominant religion – famously so under Constantine I the Great (AD 306–337), who also founded Constantinople as the Roman Empire's new seat. When the Council of Chalcedon (AD 451) introduced the formula of Christ having two natures united yet completely distinct, the result was a major split between Chalcedonian and non-Chalcedonian forms of Christianity.[1] Instead of successfully thwarting Christological disputes of the era, the council's decisions were instrumental for self-definition: the Chalcedonian churches started using the term "Orthodox" (literally meaning the correct doctrine) to designate themselves, while their followers believed in a single "Orthodox" (i.e. correct) and "Catholic" (that is, universal) Church (Clendenin, 2002: 34–37; McGuckin, 2008: 18–20).

Initially, this "universal" Chalcedonian Church included Christians both in the western and the eastern parts of the Mediterranean basin, which at that time was still largely united under the auspices of the

Roman Empire. During the reign of Emperor Justinian I (527–565) the imperial armies were able to recapture several of the areas previously lost to barbarian invasions, thereby reconstructing a sense of unity around the Mediterranean. That did not last for long, however: by the 7th century, the Arab invasions and the spread of Islam in the eastern Mediterranean basin and northern Africa placed the Roman Empire on the defensive. The emperors attempted to react to this situation by promoting various theological efforts to bridge the gap between Chalcedonian and non-Chalcedonian versions of Christianity in an effort to reclaim the loyalty of non-Chalcedonian former subjects in Syria, Palestine, and Egypt. These attempts met the strong reaction of the Chalcedonian religious establishment and proved futile. Not only was a large part of the empire forever lost to Islam, but in the subsequent centuries Chalcedonian Christianity itself was further fragmented into the branches or traditions that are conventionally designated Orthodox Christianity and Roman Catholicism.

This fragmentation was slow and gradual, as the vernacularization of Chalcedonian Christianity in the two parts of the Mediterranean contributed to the formation of distinct traditions. Vernacularization involved the rise of different vernacular high-culture languages with their own script (Therborn, 2000: 160). Even before the rise of Christianity, Greek and Latin were high-culture languages in the eastern and western parts of the Mediterranean. After the spread of Christianity, their status as vernacular high-culture script languages further amplified cultural differences that became encoded in religious categories. Thus emerged the "Greek East" and the "Latin West" – the two categories that served as precursors to the branches that later became Orthodox Christianity and Roman Catholicism. In addition to their religious significance, these categories have been also instrumental to the formation of the notions of "East" and "West" within Europe – and the legacy of this historical division remains important to this very day.

The fragmentation of Chalcedonian Christianity into two distinct branches or traditions was a protracted process that lasted roughly from the 8th century until the 15th century. Although a comprehensive comparative-historical analysis cannot be undertaken here, parallel developments – such as, for example, the rise of monasticism and the growing ability of religious hierarchies to withstand political interference – are readily observable in the eastern and western Mediterranean after the turn of the first millennium. This was an era marked by the slow consolidation of ecclesiastical hierarchies, constructions of dogmas and theologies, and the formation of religious orders (Asad, 1993; Morris, 2001; MacCulloch, 2009).

Vernacularization exacerbated the divergences between the "Greek East" and the "Latin West". These divergences include the following: (a) a major difference in the number and status of ecclesiastical hierarchs, with several patriarchs in the East and only the Pope in the West; (b) the impact of Latin and Greek serving as languages of communication, which in due course produced linguistic obstacles in each side's access and knowledge of the other's internal debates; (c) a growing contrast between the two regions' cultural milieu; and (d) a major difference in the role of imperial power in determining the range and potency of ecclesiastical authorities – or what is referred to in the literature as the relationship between *sacerdotium* and *imperium*.

When, in the 4th century, Christianity became the Roman Empire's official religion, complementarity provided the basic principle of governing the relationship between the State and the Christian Church. The ecclesiastical establishment assisted the emperor in the execution of his duties. The high clergy provided spiritual leadership and exercised moral control upon state authority; while the emperor was expected to play a role in protecting, expanding, and serving Christianity. This complementary relationship between the Roman emperor and Christianity's high clergy involved a conception of ecclesiastical governance by the so-called *pentarchy* – the participation of the five ancient patriarchates of Rome, Antioch, Alexandria, Jerusalem, and Constantinople. To be acceptable, ecumenical church councils required the participation of these patriarchs or their representatives.

In due course, theological arguments were constructed and forcefully advocated by both the "Latin" and "Greek" hierarchies as a result of consolidating specific agendas and blueprints that involved the ecclesiastical institutions' own understanding of their purpose and role within the Christian *ecumene*. Since the 9th century, papal claims to primacy were consistently refuted by the Orthodox ecclesiastical establishment. While the Orthodox have been willing to recognize the Pope as *primus inter pares* (first among equals), Orthodox theology rejects papal claims to primacy (*primatus potestatis*) and specifically the Petrine doctrine of papal primacy, that is, the notion that the papacy inherits its superior status from St Peter. For the Orthodox, papal claims to primacy violate the conciliarity of the Christian tradition.[2] This Orthodox perspective echoed the imperial point of view developed by the Eastern Roman elites in Constantinople. In effect, between the 6th and the 11th centuries, Eastern Roman imperial authority contributed extensively to the prestige of the Ecumenical Patriarchate of Constantinople (Meyendorff, 1990: 25), which, while second in rank, was Rome's chief rival. In contrast, the papacy considered its status as deriving from St Peter, the first among the apostles and first bishop of Rome, whereby the Pope, as St Peter's successor, held a position above other bishops, who in turn should yield to his authority.

These historically specific differences contributed to the articulation of differences in ecclesiology that eventually became entrenched. Political developments played a key role in fostering these differences. In the western Mediterranean, the rise of the Carolingian dynasty contributed to the reinterpretation of religious doctrine (in the form of the *Filioque* and the powerful forgery of the *Donation of Constantine*) (Herrin, 1987: 105). The main symbolic marker is Charlemagne's crowing as Holy Roman Emperor by the Pope (800 AD), which was an open act of defiance towards the legitimate Eastern Roman emperor of Constantinople. The crowing symbolized the new trajectory of the papacy, which was increasingly outside the political and military control of the armies of the Eastern Roman Empire, and therefore sought to develop new alliances with the Frankish rulers of the West. In the eastern Mediterranean, the conclusion of the Iconoclast Controversy (726–843 AD) also brought about an incipient sense of religious divergence, of Christian Orthodoxy in the East as distinct from the Christian tradition of the West. This sense was originally codified in the *Synodikon of Orthodoxy* (843), the religious document produced to codify the correct faith at the final conclusion of the Iconoclast Controversy (Louth, 2006).

While vernacularization produced a gradual alienation between "Latin" and "Greek" Christians, the Crusades exacerbated these differences. Western crusaders did not hesitate to employ the rhetoric of heresy to justify their military exploits, whereas the Orthodox side was stunned by the principle of "holy war" evoked by the crusaders. A critical turning point was the 1204 conquest of Constantinople by the soldiers of the Fourth Crusade and the collapse of the Eastern Roman Empire. It is not accidental that, in 2001, Pope John Paul II issued an apology, in which he lamented the fact that "the assailants who set out to secure free access for Christians to the Holy Land, turned against their brothers in the faith. That they were Latin Christians fills Catholics with deep regret" (quoted in Phillips, 2005: xiii). Only after 1204 did Orthodox ecclesiastical authorities begin to operate autonomously and without relying upon political leadership. Between the two falls of Constantinople (1204 and 1453) both doctrinal and liturgical evolution took place, heavily contributing to the crystallization of Orthodox Christianity to the format that is commonly known and practised in the world today. The two abortive acts of union with Rome (1274 and

1438–1439) were, in many respects, instrumental in fostering Orthodox defiance to Catholic objectives of administrative union under the auspices of papal authority.

It was in that era – an era ignored by the conventional narrative of Western modernization – that Catholicism and Orthodoxy emerged as distinct and conflicting traditions. Around this era the notion of "Christendom" was introduced in Western Europe through a 9th-century Anglo-Saxon translation of the *History against the Pagans* by Augustine of Hippo (MacCulloch, 2009: 503). "Christendom" was gradually identified with Latin or Roman Catholic Christianity; and eventually excluded the Eastern variant of Christianity. To the extent later historiography used it as a cornerstone for the meaning of "Europe" (Delanty, 1995), it has provided a justification for excluding the Orthodox part of the continent from Western Europeans' self-image.

In contrast to Roman Catholicism, Orthodox Christianity never adopted a notion of administrative unity as central to its own self-image. Instead, from the 7th century onwards, the Eastern variant of Christianity became woven into the social and cultural fabric of Serbs, Bulgarians, Russians, and Georgians. In most of these instances, though, the establishment of an ecclesiastical relationship vis-à-vis religious hierarchy (e.g. an archbishopric or an autonomous or autocephalous religious organization) implicitly entailed varied degrees of recognition of the authority of the Eastern Roman emperor. For many centuries, Orthodoxy maintained this close association with the Eastern Roman Empire; and its own orientation vis-à-vis the papacy was, in many respects, shaped by the imperial point of view.[3] While, in the western part of the Mediterranean, the use of Latin in church services forestalled indigenization, in the eastern part of the Mediterranean indigenization was promoted as a means of successful Christianization. Hence, as a process, indigenization has a strong elective affinity with Orthodox Christianity. Specific features in the Eastern tradition (such as decentralized administration) made it far more susceptible to indigenization.

As a result, the Eastern variant of Christianity was absorbed into several local ethnic identities. The individual historical trajectories of medieval Georgia, Bulgaria, Russia, and Serbia offer prominent examples of this trend (for overviews, see van den Bercken, 1999; Gonis, 2001; Gvosdev, 2001) – however, space restrictions prevent their detailed examination here (see Roudometof, 2014). Perhaps the most widely known example involves the construction of the Cyrillic alphabet and the use of Old Slavonic in liturgy (with Old Slavonic providing the original point of reference for modern Slavic languages). But the indigenization of Orthodoxy was not predicated solely on the creation of a distinct liturgical language. It was further strengthened by the initial processes of granting autonomy or autocephaly to various archbishoprics, related to or offered in direct negotiation with Bulgarian, Serb, or Russian rulers. The foundation of these seats offered local rulers a sacred element to their authority and strengthened acceptance and legitimacy of their rule. Both sacred authority and public authority were concurrently employed as elements that would foster a sense of identity and cohesion. Therein lay the origins of the strong association between the faith and specific cultural identities of various Orthodox communities and nations throughout Eastern and South-Eastern Europe.

The glocalizations of Christianity in Eastern Europe: The modern era

In this section, I turn to the glocalizations of Eastern Orthodox Christianity in the early modern and modern periods. In large part, this is a reflection of the fact that, post-1500, Western European religious history is the subject of numerous studies, and the confessionalization of religion in the aftermath of Western Europe's religious wars is all too well known, as is the association between specific churches and modern nations. The nationalization of Christianity in Western Europe is, after all, an important facet of conventional historical narratives of secularization (see Beyer, 2012, for a recent reappraisal). The story of Europe's Eastern half is far less popular – but it also demonstrates the nationalization and transnationalization of Christianity.

Until the 18th century, the majority of Orthodox Christians lived in the Ottoman and Russian Empires. Most of them were under the pastoral care of two institutions: the Russian Orthodox Church, which had its primate elevated in 1589 to the status of a patriarch, and the Ecumenical Patriarchate of Constantinople. However, in the modern era of nations and nationalism, these two institutions evolved very differently. In the Russian case, the patriarchate was abolished in 1721 and was not revived until 1917, only to survive successive rounds of Soviet persecution at great cost. In the Ottoman case, the authority of the Ecumenical Patriarchate was fragmented as a result of the rise of local nationalist movements. Throughout the 19th century, when Greece, Serbia, Romania, and Bulgaria were territorially disaggregated from the Ottoman Empire and became either independent (e.g. Kingdom of Greece, 1833) or autonomous states (e.g. pre-1878

Serbia, pre-1908 Bulgaria), they developed their own secular political leadership, which in turn led to a modern synthesis between Church and nation (for details see Roudometof, 2001, 2014). This synthesis was predicated upon nationalism's success as the principal legitimizing force in the modern world. It connected national churches in Romania, Serbia, Bulgaria, and Greece with their respective nation-states and offered a model for cross-societal emulation (for an overview of individual cases see Kitromilides, 2006). Through the modern synthesis a church–nation link was constructed, linking the Orthodox confession with each nation. Administrative independence in the form of national autocephaly became a means of showcasing national independence.

In order to construct such a link it was imperative for religious markers and institutions to *relate* to the newly crafted "national" political identities and to adapt themselves to the emerging realities of the era of the nation-state. This altered the structural foundations and cultural significance of Orthodox Christianity. Orthodox institutions became emblematic not only of universal Christianity but also of national particularism. To belong to the nation one also has to belong to the national church. In 19th-century Ottoman-held Macedonia, Serbs, Greeks, and Bulgarians used paramilitary groups to coerce the local population to declare as their confession the respective Serb, Bulgarian, or Greek versions of Orthodoxy (for a brief overview see Roudometof, 2002: 84–89). That might be the most extreme application of this mentality. Its most spectacular application concerned the 1923 Lausanne Treaty, whereby the Orthodox Christian and Muslim populations of Greece and Turkey were compulsorily sent to the two countries where they supposedly belonged.

This tension between Christian universalism and ethnic nationalism was felt deeply within ecclesiastical institutions, in particular over the issue of national autocephaly. In an era of nations and nationalisms, the ancient principle of territoriality was resurrected to obtain the autocephaly of national churches. In terms of ecclesiastical governance, the establishment of jurisdictional boundaries in Orthodox dioceses was initially based on a correspondence with the Roman Empire's municipal system – as stated in Canon 17 of the Council of Chalcedon and Canon 38 of the Council in Trullo. In the modern era, this correlation of the territorial and the nationality principle essentially implied that an autocephalous church should be established within a nation-state. This principle was explicitly invoked by Ecumenical Patriarch Joachim III in his 1879 letter concerning the recognition of the Serb Orthodox Church (cited in Bogolepov, 2001: 11–15). On this basis, granting autocephaly is conditioned upon a church's location within a sovereign state. Although such independence is clearly related to national self-assertion, jurisdiction is grounded on the territoriality principle. For example, the Church of Serbia's jurisdiction was confined to the domain of the Serb state – and not to the other communities of Serbs lying outside the state's boundaries.

In canon law, however, ethnic principles have also been invoked when dealing with faraway places, nomadic tribes, pagans, non-Christian "barbarians", and so on. A major historical example is the establishment of the original Kiev metropolitan seat, whereby its holder was metropolitan of Kiev and All of Rus' (that is, the leader of a people and not of a territorially construed entity). In the modern era, the nationality principle as a foundation for autocephaly became contested. Orthodoxy's ambivalence towards ethnic nationalism is well known. As early as 1872, the Ecumenical Patriarchate convened a synod that condemned the doctrine of *ethnofyletismos* – a term that practically means what is typically referred to as "ethnic nationalism" today. The synod was convened in order to address the Ottoman decree (*firman*) that established the Bulgarian Exarchate (1870). The decree did not set clearly defined territorial boundaries. Consequently, competing claims by rival jurisdictions could be put forward with regard to the same locale. The 1872 synod led to the official excommunication of the Bulgarian Exarchate and its followers, considered heretics who rejected religious unity in favour of ethno-national bonds. The subsequent schism (which lasted from 1872 until 1945) represented the recognition of a major shift in the nature of church affiliation, whereby the nationality principle was introduced openly as the foundation for constructing separate national churches even within the boundaries of a single state.[4]

To move from the recent past to the present, consider the following exchange Ghodsee (2009: 227) had with Krassimir, a Bulgarian taxi driver, in 2007:

Question: Are you a Christian?
Answer: Yes, of course.
Q: Do you believe in God?
A: No.
Q: How are you a Christian if you do not believe in God?
A: I am [Orthodox] Christian because I am Bulgarian. Boris baptized the Bulgarians to make a Bulgarian Kingdom. [So] Bulgarians are [Orthodox] Christians.

In the above example, the use of Orthodox Christianity as a cultural marker that signifies inclusion in the nation is abundantly clear and self-reflexively used by the informant. Echoes of this discursive understanding of religion abound throughout contemporary Eastern European nations. From the Moscow Patriarchate's (2000) *Bases of the Social Concept of the Russian Orthodox Church* to numerous pronouncements of religious leaders in public discourse, this understanding forms the backbone of the contemporary mode of existence for the majority of Orthodox Christians in Eastern and South-Eastern Europe. In large part, this relationship has grown out of Orthodox Christianity's propensity to assume a "taken-for-granted unity between religion and community" (Berger, 2005: 441). The Church, as Orthodox theologians tirelessly repeat, is not simply the religious hierarchy or the formal institution but the entire body of those who are publicly affiliated with the faith. The importance of the faith lies at the level of public culture and community, and in contemporary nations this culture is a national culture. Through its nationalization Orthodox Christianity has further moulded itself into the fabric of the modern Eastern and South-Eastern European nations, and nearly all of its adherents today would add an ethnic or a national modifier ("Greek", "Bulgarian", "Russian", and so on) to their identification as Orthodox Christians.

Although its origins can be traced to the 19th century, this process has continued throughout the course of the 20th century with new states – sometimes communist ones – fostering ecclesiastical independence as a means of bolstering national aspirations and hence gaining legitimacy among the population. The Macedonian case, in which the local communists sponsored the uncanonical independence of the local church from the Serbian Orthodox Church, is a good case in point (for an overview, see Cepreganov and Shashko, 2010). In Estonia, Moldova, and Ukraine, nationalist movements also used ecclesiastical autocephaly for the same purposes, but their objectives were frustrated due to the incorporation of these countries into the USSR. As a result, these issues resurfaced after the collapse of communism (Sysyn, 2003: 88–119; Turcescu and Stan, 2003:443–465; Payne, 2007: 831–852).

These issues are not always geographically contained to existing nation-states, but also extend into Orthodox transnational immigrant communities. From the 19th century onwards, hundreds of thousands of Orthodox Christians migrated out of the traditional Eastern European heartlands to new destinations, most notably overseas (to Australia, Canada, and, most importantly, the United States). During the course of the 20th century another, far more silent and less well-documented, migration wave directed hundreds of thousands, if not millions, of Orthodox immigrants into Western Europe (see Mayer and Hammerli, 2014). In most cases, the result was the creation of parishes and communities connecting the immigrants with their original homeland and their mother churches.

The church–nation link between Orthodoxy and national identity was thus not confined within the "new" (e.g. post-19th-century) Orthodox nation-states of South-Eastern and Eastern Europe, but was exported – via the ecclesiastical institutions' own transnationalization – both into the Orthodox populations of the Ottoman Empire as well as among immigrant transatlantic or Western European communities (for examples, see Danforth, 2000; Roudometof, 2000; Heckel, 2006). The fragmentation into a multitude of ethnic groups and the institution of separate ecclesiastical units for each of these has further added to the difficulties of studying such a diverse and heterogeneous population – as many of these groups are too small to attract the attention of social scientists, and the existence of complicated and often overlapping ecclesiastical arrangements does not make things easier. Moreover, the 1917 Bolshevik Revolution and the post-1945 imposition of communist rule in Eastern Europe further caused many of these communities to break their traditional ties with their motherland churches. This was famously done in the case of Russian Orthodox communities outside the USSR's borders. However, in the post-World War II period the Ukrainian and the Estonian churches also maintained their own separate refugee ecclesiastical organizations; while after the imposition of communist rule in many Eastern European countries, the US-based communities sought to break off their ties with their mother churches – which were at the time under the effective control of these countries' communist regimes. Some of them sought the support of the Ecumenical Patriarchate in order to maintain their canonical status. Following the collapse of communism in Eastern Europe, many expatriate churches were reunified with their mother churches. Other churches, though, having gained a sense of identity remained autocephalous – such as, for the example, the Orthodox Church in America, which, until 1970 was a *metropolia* of the Russian Orthodox Church.

Certainly, the predominant pattern of Orthodox transnationalism has been that of various Orthodox national groups which employ this religious tradition as a means of maintaining and reproducing their ethnic or national identities in a new cultural milieu. Moreover, this process is far from complete – as the already mentioned cases of Ukraine, Moldova, and Estonia demonstrate. No Orthodox diaspora per se exists; Orthodox theology supports the preservation of religious ties through the institution of the local (i.e. national) church and not through a single administrative jurisdiction that could unite peoples of diverse origins under a single ecclesiastical hierarchy (Hammerli, 2010).

Conclusions

In this chapter, I argued in favour of a model of *multiple glocalizations* of Christianity in Europe and suggested that this model offers a conceptual map that accounts for religious change and fragmentation both in Western and Eastern Europe. Unlike the conventional narrative of modernization and secularization with its undue reliance upon the modern era and Western European historical developments, the proposed model can be used to interrogate historical developments from the 4th to the 21st centuries. Furthermore, by focusing on the fusions between Christianity and local identities, this model shows the relevance and potency of glocalization as a heuristic capable of explaining historical events *throughout* Europe. In the narrative sketched in this chapter, four glocalizations were identified: vernacularization, indigenization, nationalization, and transnationalization. In the course of the discussion, this chapter has offered particular historical illustrations of these glocalizations, thereby grounding the proposed interpretation in the historical record itself.

A central claim advanced in this chapter is that Roman Catholicism and Orthodox Christianity represent religious traditions that emerged in the context of Chalcedonian Christianity's long-term vernacularization. In this sense, these traditions are themselves the products of historically formed combinations of universalism and particularism. Moreover, this chapter has argued that, unlike Roman Catholicism, Orthodox Christianity has displayed an elective affinity towards indigenization, whereby the contours of universal Christianity were fused with local, regional, or ethnic identities – the cases of Georgia, Russia, Serbia, and Bulgaria were briefly mentioned as suitable examples. Space considerations, however, did not allow for a more detailed historical exploration of these individual cases.

In the early modern and modern eras, Christianity has been subject to nationalization and transnationalization. Since these trends are quite well established in reference to the historical developments in Western Europe, in the third section attention was focused on the historical developments in the eastern part of Europe. Eastern Orthodox Christianity, the region's dominant faith, was consolidated in the era between the first (1204) and second (1453) falls of Constantinople. Initially, its institutions were deeply intertwined with the Russian and Ottoman Empires, but, over time, these were subjected to nationalization. This nationalization of Orthodoxy led to its redeployment as a facet of local national identities. This historical process was initiated in 19th-century South-Eastern Europe and was more recently applied to the post-1989 post-Soviet constellation. Several contemporary ecclesiastical disputes (in Estonia, Ukraine, and Moldova) reflect this contemporary application of a modern synthesis between Orthodoxy and nationality.

This nationalization is accompanied by transnationalization; in fact, the two are intimately related. Through the construction of nation-states and international migration, new categories of transnational peoples are continuously created. In the case of Orthodoxy, the nationalization operated not only in the countries of South-Eastern and Eastern Europe, but also in the numerous transnational communities of Orthodox immigrants in their transatlantic destinations (Australia, Canada, and the United States). In most of these cases, the immigrants' transnationalism does not privilege religious universalism, but, rather, it uses religion as a symbolic means to maintain and reconstruct national relations with the country of origin. Overall, Orthodoxy's transnationalism belongs to the second of the two variants of religious transnationalism outlined in this chapter's first section – and stands in sharp contrast to the first variant of religious transnationalism, in which religious universalism becomes a central reference point for religious communities dispersed across borders.

While the discussion in this chapter has not address in detail the situation in Western Europe, the knowledgeable reader can easily discern that vernacularization, nationalization, and transnationalization of religion are equally operative concepts for analysing developments in Western Europe. There is a rich body of literature that documents these trends in Western Europe, and, hence, this chapter has stressed the events in the other half of the continent. As a final remark, it is important to note the scope restrictions of the model of multiple glocalizations set forth in this chapter. In this chapter and for current purposes, this model refers only to Christianity or other religions or religious traditions that are explicitly universalistic – that is, these are open to all people irrespective of ethnic or gender or caste distinctions. The extent to which religious traditions or faiths that are explicitly particularistic (such as Judaism, for example) can be interpreted using this model remains a topic for further discussion.

Notes

1. Several churches that did not accept the council's formula broke away to form the non-Chalcedonian churches – including the Coptic, Armenian, Assyrian, and Ethiopian churches. Some of them did not participate in that council or even in earlier councils. In Ethiopia, Armenia, and Egypt, these non-Chalcedonian churches were intertwined with the preservation and reproduction of local identities. Their own glocalisms, though, fall outside the scope of this discussion. See MacCulloch (2009) for overviews.
2. For theological discussions, see Pelikan (1977: 156, 163–170) and Papadakis (2003: 232–233; for the Orthodox interpretation, see 236–255). Papal supremacy was deeply implicated in two theological issues of contention: the question over the proper minister for the sacrament of confirmation (that is, whether this could be done by a priest, as in the East, or only by a bishop, as in the West) and the question of the compulsory celibacy of the clergy (Pelikan, 1977: 174). At stake was the Pope's right to unilaterally issue binding decisions on these matters, which was contested because, in the Orthodox theological view, such matters could only be decided by a synod.
3. Eastern European rulers in general were hesitant to claim the status of the Roman title of *basileus*. Shepard (2006: 10–11) notes that a "standing caveat to the aspirations of the *Rus* and other rulers was the [ecumenical patriarchate's]...commitment to the idea that Christendom's unity was underpinned by the presence of a 'Roman' empire in Constantinople".
4. Traditionally, the 1872 decision is viewed as part of the Greek–Bulgarian nationalist conflict over Ottoman-held Macedonia (for the 1872 text and further discussion, see Meyendorff et al., 1993). Bulgarian nationalists viewed the decision as part of patriarchal support for Greece's claims, whereas Greek nationalists viewed the establishment of the Bulgarian Exarchate as a proxy for justifying the future annexation of pro-Exarchate regions into the Bulgarian state.

References

Asad, T. (1993) *Genealogies of Religion: Discipline and Reasons of Power in Christianity and Islam*, Baltimore, MD: Johns Hopkins University Press.

Bendix, R. (1978) *Kings or People? Power and the Mandate to Rule*, Berkeley: University of California Press.

Berger, P. (2005) "Orthodoxy and Global Pluralism", *Demokratizatsiya: The Journal of Post-Soviet Democratization*, 13 (3): 437–448.

Beyer, P. (2006) *Religions in Global Society*, London: Sage.

Beyer, P. (2007) "Globalization and Glocalisation", in J. A. Beckford and N. J. Demerath, III (eds.) *The Sage Handbook of the Sociology of Religion*, London: Sage, pp. 98–117.

Beyer, P. (2012) "Socially Engaged Religion in a Post-Westphalian Global Context: Remodeling the Secular/Religious Distinction", *Sociology of Religion*, 74 (3): 297–313.

Bogolepov, A. (2001) *Toward an American Orthodox Church: The Establishment of an Autocephalous Orthodox Church*, Crestwood, NY: St. Vladimir's Seminary Press.

Brubaker, R. (2012) "Religion and Nationalism: Four Approaches", *Nations and Nationalism*, 18 (1): 2–20.

Cepreganov, T. and P. H. Shashko. (2010) "The Macedonian Orthodox Church", in L. Leustean (ed.) *Eastern Christianity and the Cold War, 1945–91*, London: Routledge, pp. 173–188.

Clendenin, D. B. (2002) *Eastern Orthodox Christianity: A Western Perspective*, Grand Rapids, MI: Baker Books.

Csordas, T. J. (2009) *Transnational Transcendence: Essays on Religion and Globalization*, Berkeley: University of California Press.

Danforth, L. (2000) "Ecclesiastical Nationalism and the Macedonian Question in the Australian Diaspora", in V. Roudometof (ed.) *The Macedonian Question: Culture, Historiography, Politics*, Boulder, CO: East European Monographs, pp. 25–54.

Delanty, G. (1995) *Inventing Europe: Idea, Identity, Reality*, London: Palgrave Macmillan.

Ghodsee, K. (2009) "Symphonic Secularism: Eastern Orthodoxy, Ethnic Identity and Religious Freedoms in Contemporary Bulgaria", *Anthropology of East Europe Review*, 27 (2): 227–252.

Gonis, D. B. (2001) *History of the Orthodox Churches of Bulgaria and Serbia*, Athens: Armos. (In Greek)

Gorski, P. S. (2000) "The Mosaic Moment: An Early Modernist Critique of Modernist Theories of Nationalism", *American Journal of Sociology*, 5 (105): 1428–1468.

Gvosdev, N. (2001) *An Examination of Church–State Relations in the Byzantine and Russian Empires with an Emphasis on Ideology and Models of Interaction*, Lewiston, NY: Edwin Mellen.

Hammerli, M. (2010) "Orthodox Diaspora? A Sociological and Theological Problematization of a Stock Phrase", *International Journal for the Study of the Christian Church*, 10 (2–3): 97–115.

Hastings, A. (1997) *The Construction of Nationhood: Ethnicity, Religion and Nationalism*, Cambridge: Cambridge University Press.

Heckel, S. (2006) "Diaspora Problems of the Russian Emigration", in M. Angold (ed.) *The Cambridge History of Christianity, Vol. 5: Eastern Christianity*, Cambridge: Cambridge University Press, pp. 539–557.

Herrin, J. (1987) *The Formation of Christendom*, Oxford: Basil Blackwell.

Kitromilides, P. M. (2006) "The Legacy of the French Revolution: Orthodoxy and Nationalism", in Michael Angold (ed.) *The Cambridge History of Christianit*, Vol. 5: *Eastern Christianity*, Cambridge: Cambridge University Press, pp. 229–249.

Kunovich, R. M. (2006) "An Exploration of the Salience of Christianity for National Identity in Europe", *Sociological Perspectives*, 49 (4): 435–460.

Levitt, P. (2007) *God Needs No Passport: How Immigrants are Changing the American Religious Landscape*, New York: Free Press.

Louth, A. (2006) "Introduction", in A. Louth and A. Casiday (eds.) *Byzantine Orthodoxies*, Aldershot: Ashgate/Valorium, pp. 1–12.

MacCulloch, D. (2009) *A History of Christianity: The First Three Thousand Years*, London: Penguin.

Mayer, J. F. and M. Hammerli. (eds.) (2014) *Orthodox Identities in Western Europe: Migration, Settlement and Innovation*. Aldershot: Ashgate.

McGuckin, J. A. (2008) *The Orthodox Church: An Introduction to Its History, Doctrine and Spiritual Culture*, London: Basil Blackwell.

Meyendorff, J. (1990) *The Byzantine Legacy in the Orthodox Church*, Athens: Armos. (In Greek)

Meyendorff, J. G., G. D. Kapsanes, G. Metallinos, P. Zerbos, S. Karanikolas, I. Agourides, D. V. Bulović, E. Gones, and E. Phratseas. (1993) *The Balkans and Orthodoxy*, Athens: Minima. (In Greek)

Morris, C. (2001) *The Papal Monarchy: The Western Church from 1050 to 1250*, Oxford: Clarendon Press.

Moscow Patriarchate. (2000) *Bases of the Social Concept of the Russian Orthodox Church*, Moscow: Russian Orthodox Church, http://orthodoxeurope.org/print/3/14.aspx, accessed 28 June 2011.

O'Brien, P. K. (2006) "Historiographical Traditions and Modern Imperatives for the Restoration of Global History", *Journal of Global History*, 1: 3–40.

Papadakis, A. (with John Meyendorff) (2003) *The Christian East and the Rise of the Papacy: The Church 1071–1453 A.D*, Athens: Educational Foundation of the National Bank of Greece. (In Greek)

Payne, D. P. (2007) "Nationalism and the Local Church: The Source of Ecclesiastical Conflict in the Orthodox Commonwealth", *Nationalities Papers*, 35 (5): 831–852.

Pelikan, J. (1977) *The Spirit of Eastern Christendom (600–1700)*, Chicago: University of Chicago Press.

Phillips, J. (2005) *The Fourth Crusade and the Sack of Constantinople*, London: Pimlico.

Robertson, R. (1991) "Globalization, Modernization, and Postmodernization: The Ambiguous Position of Religion", in R. Robertson and W. Garrett (eds.) *Religion and Global Order*. New York: Paragon House, pp. 281–291.

Robertson, R. (1992) *Globalization*, London: Sage.

Robertson, R. (1994) "Globalisation or Glocalisation?", *The Journal of International Communication*, 1 (1): 33–52.

Robertson, R. and W. Garrett. (1991) "Religion and Globalization. An Introduction", in R. Robertson and W. Garrett (eds.) *Religion and Global Order*, New York: Paragon House, pp. ix–xxiii.

Roudometof, V. (2000) "Transnationalism and Globalization: The Greek-Orthodox Diaspora between Orthodox Universalism and Transnational Nationalism", *Diaspora*, 9 (3): 361–398.

Roudometof, V. (2001) *Nationalism, Globalization and Orthodoxy: The Social Origins of Ethnic Conflict in the Balkans*, Westport, CT: Greenwood.

Roudometof, V. (2002) *Collective Memory, National Identity and Ethnic Conflict: Greece, Bulgaria and the Macedonian Question*, Westport, CT: Praeger.

Roudometof, V. (2014) *Globalization and Orthodox Christianity: The Transformations of a Religious Tradition*, London: Routledge.

Roudometof, V. (forthcoming) "Religion and Globalization", in Manfred B. Steger, Paul Battersby, and Joseph Siracusa (eds.) *The Sage Handbook of Globalization*, London: Sage.

Shepard, J. (2006) "The Byzantine Commonwealth, 1000–1500", in M. Angold (ed.) *The Cambridge History of Christianity, Vol 5: Eastern Christianity*, Cambridge: Cambridge University Press, pp. 3–52.

Smith, A. D. (1986) *The Ethnic Origins of Nations*, Oxford: Basil Blackwell.

Smith, A. D. (2001) *Nationalism: Theory, Ideology, History,* Malden, MA: Polity Press.

Sysyn, F. E. (2003) "The Third Rebirth of the Ukrainian Autocephalous Orthodox Church and the Religious Situation in Ukraine, 1989–1991", in S. Plokhy and F. E. Sysyn (eds.) *Religion and Nation in Modern Ukraine,* Alberta: Canadian Institute of Ukrainian Studies, pp. 88–119.

Therborn, G. (2000) "Globalizations: Dimensions, Historical Waves, Regional Effects, Normative Governance", *International Sociology,* 15 (2): 151–179.

Turcescu, L. and L. Stan. (2003) "Church–State Conflict in Moldova: The Bessarabian Metropolitanate", *Communist and Post-Communist Studies,* 36: 443–465.

Van den Bercken, W. (1999) *Holy Russia and Christian Europe. East and West in the Religious Ideology of Russia,* London: SCM Press.

Warburg, M. (2006) *Citizens of the World: A History and Sociology of the Baha'i from a Globalization Perspective,* Leiden: Brill.

4

European Television Programming

Exemplifying and Theorizing Glocalization in the Media

Andrea Esser

When, in the 1980s and early 1990s, private commercial television was introduced in the majority of European countries, old fears about the hegemony of American popular culture resurfaced. However, concerns that the attendant influx of American programmes would weaken national cultures and diminish Europe's cultural diversity soon eased. Domestic programmes mostly seemed to draw higher audience figures, and from the mid-1990s national production sectors and output were growing. In academia, this led to the quickly cemented and widespread belief that audiences per se prefer local to imported programmes – the appeal of the latter diminished by a "cultural discount" (Hoskins and Mirus, 1988) – and most media scholars came to agree that national television markets would remain strong, followed in importance by geo-linguistic or geo-cultural markets offering close "cultural proximity" (Straubhaar, 1991, 2007; Sinclair et al., 1996; Keane et al., 2007). Television's internationalization, they opined, was confined by entrenched cultural difference and resilience.

Drawing on Roland Robertson's glocalization theory (1991, 1994, 2014), I want to argue that this assessment does not recognize the de facto complexity of the development of television and culture more generally. Grounded in a theoretical fallacy – a binary understanding of the local and the global – scholars' affirmation of the local resulted in the repudiation of television's internationalization in the form of first glocal television channels and then glocal programmes, so-called TV formats. TV formats, the focus of this chapter, are programmes sold internationally for local adaptation. Prominent examples include, *Big Brother, Who Wants to Be a Millionaire?, Strictly Come Dancing,* and *The Voice*. The past

15 years have seen an exponential growth in the trade of such formats, the majority of which presently originate in Europe.

TV formats exemplify the concept of glocalization, seminally introduced by Robertson in the early 1990s, but unfortunately not always correctly understood and applied. Misleadingly, we can find the concept wrongly confined to the notions of hybridity and heterogeneity (for example, Ritzer, 2004; Straubhaar and Duarte, 2005; Straubhaar, 2007), or wrongly interpreted as applying to separate entities. As Ritzer notes: "We can have greater homogenization of some aspects of our lives (...) along with the greater heterogenization of other aspects" (2000: 177). This lapse in understanding the "duality of glocality" (Giulianotti and Robertson, 2007: 182) also resulted in a distorted understanding of what is happening in television.

To offer a more nuanced account, which adequately considers the fact that formats (as well as transnational channels) in their localized form have a major stake in advancing television's internationalization, the first part of this chapter provides a thick description of the format phenomenon and the increasingly multi-directional and complex trade flows emanating from it. To illuminate formats' glocalness, this more descriptive part also looks at some of the aspects involved in localization. The empirical format study makes concrete Robertson's theorized simultaneity of universal and unique impulses within globalizing processes, and shows that homogenization and heterogenization are not exclusionary but coincide.

The second half of the chapter explores a number of conceptual deficiencies. The empirical frame of the TV format study is used here as an exemplary aid to critically reflect on some of the findings, which do not fit prior theorization in media scholarship. First, cultural reductionism, essentialism, and the increasingly untenable cultural–economic dichotomy are addressed. From there the "local" is explored. Most commonly used as a synonym for the national in research concerned with the internationalization of television, the concept of the "local", like the premise of the "preference for the local" (for example, Straubhaar, 1991; Hallenberger, 2002) thus far has evaded closer scrutiny. Finally, attention will be given to the essentialist and ideologically charged notions of "delocalization" and "deculturalization" and the related resistance amongst those predominately concerned with culture towards conceptualizations of "universals" and "cosmopolitanism". As with the chapter's first half, I hope that these format study-derived reflections contribute to a more generally valid understanding of the inseparable and mostly non-conflictual local–global and cultural–economic links.

Introducing television formats

It was not long after television was established that a number of successful TV shows came to be copied across national borders and even continents (Chalaby, 2012). But for decades, "borrowing" programme ideas remained ad hoc and the directions of flow were limited. Above all, it was finished, "canned" programmes that were being traded. In the last 15 years, however, a second trade tier has emerged. The liberalization and commercialization of television globally, leading towards greater standardization, as well as technological developments facilitating global observation and communication, have established and systematized the format trade.

To clarify, what is traded is not just an idea for a programme such as *Big Brother* but the elaboration of the idea, sold in the form of a "production bible", a booklet that comprises any information of value to future production teams. This can include technical requirements, a shooting schedule, a crew list, a budget sample, audience ratings from the original and other adaptations, marketing tips, software for the graphics, and scripts where relevant. Often the bible is accompanied by a so-called "flying producer". This glocalization agent's task is twofold: to support local production teams through knowledge transfer and to ensure brand protection.

The business of selling formats began to form in the early 1990s, when private commercial television was growing across Europe and demand for content was rapidly rising. American talk shows and game shows, such as *The Price is Right* or *Wheel of Fortune*, proved popular with viewers and allowed broadcasters to schedule programmes that were cheap to produce, suited to serialization, and were perceived as local. But it was not until the transnational success of the European "super-formats", *Who Wants to Be a Millionaire?* (1998), *Big Brother* (1999), and *Survivor* (2000), that the business accelerated (Chalaby, 2011).

The last decade has witnessed the popularity of, especially, factual entertainment formats: makeover shows (e.g. *10 Years Younger, The Swan*), dating shows (*The Bachelor, The Dating Game*), childcare (*Supernanny, The Baby Borrowers*), renovating and cleaning (*Changing Rooms, How Clean Is Your House?*), cookery shows (*Come Dine With Me, The Great British Bake-Off*), and potentially life-changing social experiments (*Wife Swap, Brat Camp, Blood, Sweat and T-Shirts*). Talent show formats (*Idol, Got Talent, The Voice*) have been flooding television screens across Europe and globally, and game show formats, too, are still popular (*Million Pound Drop, Fort Boyard*).

Today, internationally formatted programmes constitute a substantial share of the overall programme offerings of many TV channels; and they are not just cheap schedule fillers but popular primetime fare used by major terrestrial channels (Esser, 2013a; Jensen, 2013). In European countries, which from a global perspective are particularly active format exporters and importers, this is highly notable. Table 4.1 lists formats that were amongst the most watched programmes in several European

Table 4.1 Formats in multiple European top 10/20 TV programme lists, 2004–2012

International format	European countries where the format was in the top 10/20 programme lists (based on audience ratings) in at least three countries
Big Brother	Bulgaria, Croatia, Portugal, Serbia, Spain
Dancing with the Stars/Strictly Come Dancing	Austria, Belgium (north), Croatia, Czech Republic, Denmark, Estonia, Finland, Italy, Latvia, Norway, Sweden, UK
Deal or No Deal	Czech Republic, Italy, Netherlands, Slovenia
Farmer Wants a Wife	Belgium (north and south), Croatia, Estonia, France, Germany, Hungary, Netherlands
Got Talent	Belgium (north and south), Bulgaria, Cyprus, Italy, Netherlands, Romania, Slovakia, Switzerland (German speaking), UK
Idols	Belgium, Bulgaria, Estonia, Germany, Hungary, Norway, Slovakia, Sweden, Switzerland
The Bachelor	Czech Republic, France, Hungary
The Farm	Norway, Slovakia, Slovenia
The Voice	Belgium (north and south), Czech Republic, Denmark, France, Hungary, Ireland, Netherlands, Slovakia, Spain, UK
The X Factor	Denmark, Hungary, Slovenia, UK
Who Wants to Be a Millionaire?	Austria, Croatia, Estonia, France, Germany, Hungary, Italy, Netherlands, Slovakia, Slovenia, Sweden, UK
Wife Swap	Belgium (north), Czech Republic, France, Slovakia

Note: This list is not complete as this kind of information is not available in the same form for all countries. The list would also yield a few additions both in terms of the number of formats and countries if analysis of the remaining interim years were added.
Source: Collated by the author based on countries' top 10/20 programme lists in IP Network, Television (2005, 2008, 2013).

countries in the past ten years, making it into various Top 10/20 TV programme lists.

Table 4.1 only considers Europe. But the most popular formats come to span the globe. *Who Wants to Be a Millionaire?*, the most successful format to date, has spawned more than 80 local adaptations around the world, achieving high audience ratings globally. In the USA it became the first highly successful game show on primetime television since the 1960s, in India, it "emptied the nation's streets" when aired, and in the Middle East, too, it was one of the most popular programmes (Bielby and Harrington, 2008: 112).

Global diffusion and multi-directional flows

Whereas clear and limited patterns of TV programme flows existed in the past, the format trade is becoming increasingly global, both in terms of diffusion and directionality. *America's Next Top Model* (UPN/The CW, 2003–), for instance, covers all continents. Six years after its launch, the reality TV show aired in over 100 countries in its original version and there were 25 licensed local (national and regional) productions (Lettman, 2009). Ten years later and the number of adaptations has almost doubled (Table 4.2):

Table 4.2 Local adaptations of *America's Next Top Model*

Africa	Africa, West Africa
Asia	Asia, China, South Korea, Thailand, Vietnam
Australia	Australia, New Zealand
Europe	Albania, Austria, Belgium, Benelux, Bosnia and Herzegovina, Croatia, Denmark, Estonia, Finland, France, Germany, Georgia, Greece, Hungary, Ireland, Italy, Netherlands, Norway, Poland, Romania, Russia, Scandinavia, Serbia, Slovakia, Slovenia, Spain, Sweden, Turkey, United Kingdom
Latin America	Brazil, Central America, Colombia, Mexico, Peru
North America	USA (original), Canada

Source: Lettman/CBS Television Distribution 2009; updated with various online industry sources.

Yo soy Betty, la Fea (*Ugly Betty*), a Colombian-scripted fiction format, has been broadcast in its original version in many countries and has been locally adapted in 19. The telenovela, too, has achieved outstanding ratings on all continents (Table 4.3).

Table 4.3 Local adaptations of *Yo Soy Betty, La Fea*

Asia	China, India, Israel, Vietnam, Philippines
Europe	Belgium, Croatia, Czech Republic, Germany, Greece, Netherlands, Poland, Russia, Spain, Turkey
Latin America	Colombia (original), Mexico, Brazil
North America	USA
Optioned for	Italy, France, Dubai

Source: Waked/RCN (2009); Lippert (2011).

An interesting aspect of *Betty, La Fea* is that not just the original version but some adaptations, too, are being sold internationally, diffusing the format even more widely. For example, the German adaptation, *Verliebt in Berlin*, was broadcast in Hungary (*Lisa csak egy van*) and in a dubbed French version (*Le destin de Lisa*) in France, Belgium, Switzerland, and Canada. Russia's adaptation, *Ne Rodis Krasivoy*, was shown in most nations formerly part of the USSR, and the US version, *Ugly Betty*, was also shown in numerous countries, including Australia, Britain, Germany, Italy, Japan, Spain, and Sweden amongst others (IMDb). Traditional trade ties are still visible here and language, not surprisingly, continues to play an important role. However, the picture is becoming increasingly global and multifaceted. Formatting allows television programmes to be diffused more widely and makes trade patterns more intricate and multi-directional.

Most of the early format sales originated in either the USA, Australia, or Britain (Chalaby, 2012). But since the 1990s, when format sale turned into a recognized business practice, European companies have been at the forefront. Dutch company Endemol were the first to embark on the format business, successfully selling entertainment shows including *Deal or No Deal*, *The Mini Playback Show*, *All You Need is Love*, *Love Letters*, *Soundmix Show*, and *Now or Never* (Esser, 2001). Other early attempts to develop and sell formats came out of Scandinavia, including *Survivor*, *The Big Class Reunion*, *The Bar*, and *The Farm*, and from the British indie sector, meaning those production companies, for instance RDF Media (*Wife Swap*, *Faking It*), not aligned to broadcasters.

The well-established indie sector, combined with a favourable policy change in the country, led to the blossoming of British format development (Chalaby, 2010), turning the UK into the world's most successful format exporter, with the Netherlands and the USA in second place (Jäger and Behrens, 2009). But producers from all over the world are now jumping on the bandwagon: French and German companies have had a few noteworthy successes, including comedy formats *Camera Café* (sold to over 55 countries) and *Schillerstrasse* (sold to over twenty territories on four different continents); and Japan and Israel came into the format market's limelight in the late 2000s.

To sum up, formats, as shown, have made television content more international both in terms of scale and by further opening up export markets. TV executives globally are not just looking towards the USA, traditional trade partners, and culturally proximate countries, but are scanning the globe for programme ideas. Moreover, US executives no longer view themselves exclusively as television exporters but are open to the import of formats and the know-how that comes with this (Esser, 2010). More than ever before in the history of television content is shared across borders, is originating from a multiplicity of countries, and is spreading across several continents. As a consequence, TV markets globally are further homogenized. However, this is a dual trajectory as the nature of formats also causes heterogenization.

The glocalization process: adapting TV formats

As fascinating as the scale, directionality, and global diffusion of formats is their intricate local–global texture. Broadcasters' selection of international formats depends on their success in the world's format showcase markets (the USA, the UK, and the Netherlands, plus some regional showcase markets and the "hot" format market of the day), formats' sales track records, and audience ratings in other countries (Scott, 2002: 6). Once the format is bought local producers are asked to adapt it.

The degree of adaptation differs considerably between formats. In the case of *Who Wants to Be a Millionaire?*, the original licensor, Celador, was reported to dictate the ground rules right down to the colours of the set. Other than "the language and the face presenting it there is little difference from one country to the next" (Walker, 2002: 14). Fremantle's *Got Talent* and *The X Factor*, too, are easy to identify, though it has to be noted that the production value differs significantly between adaptations and has a visible impact on the overall look and feel.

In principle, changes to game and talent shows pertaining to formal features (e.g. prizes, title, studio set) are easy and quick to make. But the economic calculus of licensors, who aim for their formats to become internationally recognizable brands, means there is a strong incentive not to allow for too much flexibility (Hallenberger, 2002; Müller, 2002). Exempting the necessary concessions relative to the individual market situation, in practice the degree of flexibility depends on the desirability of a format and the resulting negotiating power of the licensor (Cirone, 2008; Peek, 2008; Rettler, 2008).

Even in the case of fiction, guided by agreement that scripted formats require more adaptation if they are to be successful than unscripted game or reality TV shows, we can find attempts to safeguard the brand through tight overview. For instance, Dick Wolf, creator of *Law & Order*, reportedly insisted on elaborate control of the French adaptation, *Paris enquêtes criminelles*. The bible for this show is said to be 1,000 pages long and Maxime Lombardini, who produced the French adaptation, commented: "Absolutely nothing has been left to interpretation" (in Barnes, 2007).

But inevitably there are notable and at times considerable variations to be found between adaptations. Unfortunately, it is not possible within the scope of this chapter to give examples. The interested reader could look at Skovmand's (1992), Mikos' (1995), or Hetsroni's (2004) cross-cultural analyses of game shows, Larkey's (2009) comparative analysis of *The Office*, or Mikos and Perrotta's (2012) analysis of various *Betty, La Fea* adaptations. Much of format scholarship is dedicated to highlighting difference through local particularities, or to showing how a particular format affords local imaginations and means of identification.

Ways in which the local is reflected include language and dialect, familiar places and faces, characters, humour, and reference to past and current social, political, and cultural events and themes (Waisbord, 2004; Adriaens and Biltereyst, 2012; de Bruin, 2012). In addition, it has been noted (Mikos, 1995; Mikos and Perrotta, 2012) that each country has developed aesthetic and other standards that structure a programme's production and course of action. Whilst differences are clearly visible, it is important to acknowledge that the factors spawning variations in format adaptation are too manifold and diffuse to be nonchalantly assigned to cultural and especially national cultural differences, as happens all too frequently in both academic and industry discourse. A number of reasons seem to cause this cultural reductionism and essentialism, leading us to the second part of this chapter.

Deconstructing 'television culture'

Eggo Müller (2002: 467–468) has rightly pointed out that, although it is easy to describe variations between adaptations, a culture-based comparative analysis of formats is problematic. With economic and structural forces influencing production in major ways it is near impossible, he argues, to ascribe difference to national cultural particularities. My interviews confirmed that vastly differing production budgets, for one, are crucial in effecting difference. For instance, the executive producer of *Britain's Next Top Model*, produced for and broadcast on niche channel Living, mentioned that the team had to be "creative" to make up for the lack in budget, which is substantially smaller than that of the original, *America's Next Top Model* (Morgan, 2008). One consequence is that the British models go on fewer international shoots, making the show less glamorous.

In the German adaptation financial implications, too, resulted in changes to the format, but in different ways and for different reasons. In Germany, the format is produced for a primetime slot of a major terrestrial channel (Pro7). Unlike in the case of Living, a production of high value was both feasible and mandatory. Moreover, when the show proved hugely successful with audiences and, consequently, sponsors, some episodes were extended from 60 to 100 minutes. The longer the episode the cheaper the production costs per minutes, the producer, Holger Rettler (2008), explained. The prolongation made economic sense.

There is no scope for further examples, but interviews with producers clearly show that format variations are grounded in a complex matrix of cultural, economic, structural, media-systemic, scheduling-related, and even circumstantial factors (Lippert, 2011; Jensen, 2012; Esser, 2013b; Carini, 2013). Müller convincingly concludes,

> we can [therefore] only describe the local adaptation of a format as the result of a respective national or regional television culture if we understand the latter as a complex network of economic, institutional, and cultural practices, for which international relations, experiences and orientations play a significant role.
>
> (2002: 469; my translation)

The last line of Müller's quote, too, is significant. Not just because of the de facto influence that international business relations and knowledge transfer have, but also from a conceptual point of view. Robertson has long argued that the local can only be defined in relation to the global. Regarding television he notes:

> An "international" TV enterprise like CNN produces and reproduces a particular pattern of relations between localities, a pattern which depends on a kind of recipe of locality. This standardisation renders meaningful the very *idea* of locality, but at the same time diminishes the notion that localities are "things in themselves".
>
> (Robertson, 1994: 38)

Robertson here rightly challenges the idea that the local is an indigenous source of cultural identity. Like Massey (1994), he argues that a sense of the local and of place can only be constructed and understood if it includes a consciousness of its links with the wider world. Moreover, important in this, Robertson maintains, is that we think "from the whole to the part". Or differently expressed, "one cannot 'imagine' a locality or a place in the absence of imagining a context in which the locality or the place is situated" (2011: 9) – a compelling critique of Anderson's (1983) "outward-looking" imaginings.

A second important point contained in the quote is the contestation of the widespread assumption that globalization is driven by commerce and halted by culture, forcing transnational corporations to cater to "local sensibilities" (see, for example, Ferguson, 1992; Mikos, 1995; Robins, 1997; Moran, 1998; Waisbord, 2004; Sinclair and Wilken, 2009). Robertson describes the economic and the cultural realms as inseparably linked because of the vested interest that capitalism has in advocating difference. Thus, rather than a relationship of tension he suggests that the economic becomes co-invested in constructing cultural difference (1994, 2014). Or, as Lash and Lury say, the cultural becomes an integral part of the economic. In *Global Culture Industry: The Mediation of Things* (2007), they make the compelling case that the 21st century is marked by the collapse of the base and the superstructure; where things become media and media become things.

Querying the national as the local

Moving away from cultural reductionism and the untenable cultural–economic dichotomy but remaining with the problem of cultural essentialism, I now want to turn to the common equation of the national with the local, in research concerned with the internationalization of television. In many ways it is not unintelligible that media scholars as well as the majority of TV executives still think predominately in national terms. As a result of the extensive and abiding ideological work undertaken to create national cultures and identities, television historically is nationally determined, and broadcasting policy is discussed and implemented at the national level. (Although in several European countries, including Belgium, Germany, Spain, and Switzerland, the subnational level is also important or even more important, and, within the EU, television policy today originates in Brussels to a fair extent.) Because of the national set-up and erstwhile tightly controlled broadcast signals, programme rights, too, historically are sold on a national basis. (Again, though, this happens increasingly on the basis of language territories and, especially in the case of formats, multi-territory and global deals.) Finally, as a corollary of much national determination, some distinct national viewing habits have developed over time, for instance, regarding peak viewing times.

If we disregard the above listed exceptions and many more I could list, it is hence not illogical to assume a format is adapted with a national audience in mind (see, for example, Waisbord, 2004; Larkey, 2009; Sharp, 2012; Mirrlees, 2013). However, the "local" adaptation is not always nor necessarily nationally inflected, as three of my interviewees, Michael Esser (2008), head writer of the German adaptation of *Betty, la Fea*, and Holger Rettler (2008) and Sophie Morgan (2008), producers of *Next Top Model* in Germany and Britain, respectively, explained. Esser and Morgan in particular stressed that producers do not think about national identity and how to express it. Esser noted that production teams think of what has worked, or not worked, in the past. Morgan, when asked about the many ostentatious symbols of London in *Britain's Next Top Model*, responded that the idea was to stress London's role as a fashion capital. Both refuted my suggestion that intentions of employing visual tools of "banal nationalism" (Billig, 1995) may have played a role in creating a local–national feel.

One could argue, of course, that what has worked/not worked alludes to the national market. But Rettler also pointed out that a programme is adapted in light of the channel it is produced for rather than the nation. *Germany's Next Top Model (GNTM)*, he explained, would have looked very different on German channel RTL than it did on Pro7, for which it is produced. Pro7's overall programme strategy presents itself as American, international, young. It is hence fitting, Rettler said, that in *GNTM*, the aspiring models travel a lot, much more than in other adaptations. Moreover, a substantial part of the German version is filmed in LA, where the German presenter, Heidi Klum, lives. The reason for the LA location is practical, Rettler admitted, but it suited Pro7's identity. His point about the impact channel identity has on "local" adaptations was corroborated by other industry sources (Feistauer, 2008; Peek, 2008; Traverso, 2008), and should make us question the accuracy and theoretical value of labelling any production, including the original version of a format, as "national".

In addition to suggesting a lesser role for the national at production level (at least in larger television markets), the example of *Next Top Model* exposes the fragmented and fluid composition of supposedly national TV audiences. Moreover, it challenges the thesis of the "preference for the local". In the UK, both the domestic and the original version are shown in the same primetime slot on Living. In light of the unquestioned and underexplored notion of the "preference for the local", we would expect the adaptation to attract the larger audience. This is not the case. In 2008, the average audience size of *America's Next Top Model (ANTM)* on Living was 553,000 adults, whereas *Britain's Next Top Model (BNTM)* only attracted 412,000 viewers (Rufaie, 2008). In other words, a greater number of viewers in the UK found the more costly, glamorous American version more appealing than the domestic production. To elucidate matters further, Living's research showed that, whilst both versions attracted young professional women, on average only about a third of *ANTM*'s audience watched *BNTM*. Living's audience researchers concluded from this that the format had three main UK audiences: women who prefer the high production value of the US version, women who prefer a local feel and the opportunities offered for identification, and women who like the *NTM* format as such and watch several versions (Rufaie, 2008).

Intra-national or intra-cultural differences are largely neglected in television scholarship. They have been highlighted in only a small number of, mostly media diaspora, studies. Aksoy and Robins (2000) seminally revealed the diverse and varied media consumption amongst Turkish migrants in Germany. The generational differences they found, amongst others, were also noted by Straubhaar (2007), who interviewed Latin American immigrants in the USA, and by Frau-Meigs (2006) in her exploration of *Big Brother* audiences across Europe. In Frau-Meigs' view, generational differences were conspicuous and hinted at an emerging transnational television culture.

Straubhaar (2007), who argues for the continued dominance of the national television framework and the importance of cultural proximity, interestingly also mentions how the Brazilian poor and working class turn away from national channel TV Globo because they prefer Mexican to Brazilian telenovelas. The Brazilian elite, on the other hand, turn to international pay-TV channels (Straubhaar, 2007: 247), just like the affluent television viewers in African countries (Ndlela, 2012). As Tomlinson astutely remarked, "[c]ulture is entirely – even definitively – the work of human beings" and thus cannot, like flora and fauna, "naturally belong" to a geographical area (1991: 23).

Of course, the impossibility of a single, monolithic national culture does not mean that national imaginations or identities do not exist. The experience of belonging that people have is real, and at least at times is clearly and strongly national (Tomlinson, 1991; Robertson, 2011). Also, there is a "lived reality" of national identity through daily imaginations and representations (Tomlinson, 1991; Billig, 1995). However, there are also many other identities, including those of other large communities (Beck, 2006; Aksoy and Robins, 2008; Robertson, 2011, 2014). Ranking identities "from local to global" is empirically indefensible. More realistic and convincing is that we "foreground" one or the other of our multiple identities at each particular moment in time, no matter how short (Omoniyi, 2006).

Reflections on conceptualizations of "delocalization" and its alternatives

The preceding discussions suggest that, as researchers, we must try harder to resist the hegemonic myth of national cultures. The case for a conceptual shift from space to time has been convincingly made (Tomlinson, 1991; Robertson, 2011, 2014) and few, I believe, would disagree in theory. But the attraction of the idea of a monolithic, pure and stable space–culture relationship seems to remain, no matter how conflicted and untenable. It is reflected in the preoccupation of cultural policy-makers and academics with cultural sovereignty, or the everyday talk and branding of, for example, television programmes and national cuisines. It is also implied in the concept of "deterritorialization". The idea, of course, is to theorize "*the loss* of the 'natural' relation of culture to geographical and social territories" (Canclini, 1995: 229; my italics). But it also confirms the belief in a once much stronger and presumably stable space–culture relationship.

In the case of television research we find the related concepts of "delocalization" (Straubhaar, 2007) and "deculturalization" (Bielby and Harrington, 2008) used to describe strategies designed to give television programmes greater international appeal. According to Waisbord, who draws on Ritzer (2000) and looks at TV formats specifically, "[f]ormats purposefully eviscerate the national.... Because formats explicitly empty out signs of the national, they can become nationalized – that is customized to domestic cultures" (Waisbord, 2004: 368). To me these conceptualizations are misleading. As Mjos' (2010) study of Discovery's documentary programming has shown, certain topics or genres lend themselves to international distribution whilst others do not. This, I agree, can have profound and negative consequences for media production and provision overall and it is hence vital that we turn our attention to what is no longer being produced.

However, attempting to find and to produce something that appeals to audiences across borders is not the same as "eviscerating" or "emptying out" culture. We have to ask ourselves: Is the negative judgement implied in "*de*territorialization", "*de*localization", and "*de*culturalization" as ideologically charged as that in such criticized concepts as "cosmopolitanism" and "universalism"? Hepp, for example, has rightly noted that today's key global media cities are "microcosms of globalization", absorbing a large variety of cultural contexts and in turn stimulating creativity and nurturing hybridization (2005: 142ff.). This could be one reason for the international appeal of the cultural products created there. But is deterritorialization the right word to use then? Should not a more positive conceptualization, the possibility that these cultural workers have a "cosmopolitan identity" in their identity repertoire, at least be considered?

The same question applies to "universals". Although sociologists, neurologists, psychoanalysts, management and organization theorists, linguistic and literary structuralists all take universals for granted, amongst those preoccupied with culture, universals are met with scepticism and renunciation. In Britain, the birthplace of cultural studies, resistance to the idea of universally shared features seems especially strong, but unease is notable globally. In the work of media scholars the concept is mostly avoided. For instance, US-based film and television scholar Selznick, in her book, *Global Television: Co-Producing Culture* (2008), mentions "universal appeal" and "universal themes" only a mere handful of times, in passing and mostly in quotation marks. Australian cultural theorist Barker in his book, *Global Television: An Introduction*, speaks of the "*apparently* global themes" of serials (1997: 93; my italics).

Others, concerned with understanding the widespread appeal of particular television programmes and genres, have offered less threatening explanatory models. Singhal and Udornpim (1997) speak of "cultural shareability". Olson (1999) explains the success of American programmes as a result of, amongst other things, the country's melting pot history and a resulting storytelling that favours "narrative transparency". That is, narratives whose polysemy encourages viewers from diverse cultural backgrounds to read them as though they are indigenous. Straubhaar (2007), in an attempt to explain the unexpected cross-border success of some TV programmes, expanded on his notion of "cultural proximity" to include "proximities" relating to genre, values, and themes to which different cultures can relate.

The notable caution or even resistance that scholars concerned with culture and the media show towards the possibility of universal traits has to be understood in the context of the charge that there is always some 'project of domination' underlying claims of universality and of the gridlocked nature versus nurture debate (Tomlinson, 1991, 1999). For proponents of the latter, culture itself is centred on difference and any kind of universalism is hence to be rejected. It threatens the "natural" plurality of different ways of life. However, as Tomlinson – who himself has claimed that universalism ignores the problem of interpretation (1991: 54) – has also convincingly argued that "culture is associated with difference only contingently and not necessarily" (Tomlinson, 1999: 68). Culture and difference relate through the work of history, where varying local circumstances, combined with the gradual emergence of particular practices, result in a rich array of cultural difference. This means,

> difference does not arise as the telos of cultural practices, but simply as its consequence. Cultural work may produce difference but this is not the same as saying that culture is founded in difference. (...) So if culture is not wedded essentially to difference, it also follows that it is not antithetical to universals as such.
>
> (Tomlinson, 1999: 68–69)

In my format research, I found no evidence for the "evisceration" of (de facto inexistent) national cultures nor for the "nationalization" of adaptations. What I came across instead, again and again, was TV executives looking for "universals". Michael Esser tellingly noted: "the challenge in adapting a format is not to localise it but to identify what's universal about it. Only the latter will guarantee access to your own audience" (in Lippert, 2011: 253). The unexpected international success of *Betty, La Fea,* which he adapted for the German-language channel Sat.1, where the format also proved hugely successful, could be seen as an indicator that he is right.

Conclusion

In this chapter, television formats were used to demonstrate the duality of glocality, the interdependence of the local and the global, and the co-presence of homogenizing and heterogenizing impulses. Formats demonstrate convergence of the form of particularities, including whole genres that become popular globally, formatted content brands, production techniques, and successful marketing and cross-media strategies.

As this globally shared knowledge is being appropriated, local specificities are both established and reasserted. Globalization is revealed as a "self-limiting – indeed, self-defeating process" (Robertson, 2014: 32). This is not to say there are no negative aspects to globalization, only that we need to look more carefully than both cultural imperialism theorists and those highlighting "local resistance" and localization have us believe.

A second common dichotomization that was questioned was that of the cultural-economic. I argued that the widely held assumption that internationalization is driven by commerce and halted by culture is too simplistic. Not only are cultures not essentialist and unable to act, but in today's world particularly it also seems much more appropriate to view the two conceptual realms – components of what was always a crude taxonomy – as inseparably linked: the cultural has become an integral part of the economic and economic forces contribute to creating cultural difference in major ways. As Robertson contends, "'being different' is one of the major motifs of our time" – glocalization, rather than standardization, is becoming the norm (2014: 30). Adaptation to the local should not be understood in an essentialist sense though. A locality or place is constructed by context, constructs new contexts, and, as such, is inherently unstable and always changing.

Based on these insights, the geographical territory–culture relationship, and especially the idea that it is a national TV audience which constitutes the local, were also challenged. I addressed the significance of channel identity and subnational target audiences, and the diversity and complexity of television consumption, including notable generational differences, transnational and cross-border audiences, and different audiences and viewer motives for one and the same format. Acknowledging this complexity is not to deny the continuing influence of banal nationalism or established national television structures. But it does mean we have to beware of cultural essentialism and the naturalized, hegemonic notion of national cultures. The propositions to counter these pitfalls with methodological glocalism (Robertson, 2014), cosmopolitanism (Beck, 2006), or a perspective of transculturality (Hepp, 2009) are steps in the right direction and should be given more attention.

Acknowledgements

I would like to express my deep gratitude to all the television industry professionals I interviewed and spoke to for their time and insightful contributions, to Roland Robertson for his always enlightening comments and reading recommendations, and to Pia Majbritt Jensen, Jakob Isak Nielsen, Iris Rittenhofer, and Anne Marit Waade, for their valuable feedback on an early draft of this chapter.

Interviews and other direct communication with TV executives

(Company names and job titles at time of interview)

Bachmaier, J. (2012) EVP for EMEA, BBC Worldwide, workshop, 11 May 2012, London: University of Roehampton.

Baur, J. (2008) Head of Development, Grundy UFA TV Produktions GmbH, interview, 07 October 2008, Berlin.

Beale, M. (2012) Director of International Formats, ITV Studios, workshop, 11 May 2012, London: University of Roehampton.

Cirone, N. (2008) Television Consultant, telephone interview, 15 December 2008.

Esser, M. (2008) Head-writer of *Verliebt in Berlin*, Dramaworks GmbH, interview, 09 October 2008, Berlin.

Feistauer, K. (2008) Director Programme Controller, Discovery Communications, interview, 03 November 2008, London.

Lettman, R. (2009) Sales executive, CBS Studios International, email communication, 28 October 2009.

McGonigal, M. (2012) Managing Director, CrowTV, workshop, 11 May 2012, London: University of Roehampton.

Morgan, S. (2008) Commissioning Editor, Living, interview, 27 November 2008, London.

Peek, J. (2008) Director, Tape Consultancy, interview, 15 December 2008, London.

Pflueger, K. (2012) Program Director, RTL Hrvatska, workshop, 11 May 2012, London: University of Roehampton.

Remirez, A. (2008) Head of Fiction, Sat.1, interview, 07 October 2008, Berlin.

Rettler, H. (2008) CEO, Tresor TV, interview, 29 May 2008, Cologne.

Rufaie, A. (2008) Director of Audience Research, Living, email correspondence, 28 November 2008.

Traverso, A. (2008) SVP Commercial Development, Hit Entertainment, interview, 03 November 2008, London.

Waked, L. M. (2009) Sales Executive, RCN Television, email communication, 26 October 2009.

Wallace, V. (2009) SVP Global Acquisition and Development, Fremantle Media, interview, 22 June 2009, London.

References

Adriaens, F. and Biltereyst, D. (2012) "Glocalized Telenovelas and National Identities: A 'Textual Cum Production' Analysis of the 'Telenovela' Sara, the Flemish Adaptation of Yo soy Betty, la Fea", *Television & New Media*, 13 (6): 551–567.

Aksoy, A. and K. Robins. (2000) "Thinking across Spaces: Transnational Television from Turkey", *European Journal of Cultural Studies*, 3 (3): 343–365.

Aksoy, A. and K. Robins. (2008) "Banal Transnationalism: The Difference that Television Makes", Working Paper, WPTC-02-08, accessed 2 July 2010, http://www.transcomm.ox.ac.uk/working%20papers/WPTC-02-08%20Robins.pdf.

Anderson, B. (1983) *Imagined Communities: Reflections on the Origin and Spread of Nationalism*, London: Verso.

Barker, C. (1997) *Global Television: An Introduction*, Oxford: Blackwell.

Barnes, B. (2007) "A New Accent for 'Law & Order' ", *Wall Street Journal Europe*, 1 March 2007, accessed 14 July 2008, http://www.lawandorder-fr.com/articles/?article=638.

Beck, U. (2006) *Cosmopolitan Vision*, Cambridge: Polity.

Bielby, D. and C. L. Harrington. (2008) *Global TV: Exporting Television and Culture in the World Market*, New York: New York University Press.

Billig, M. (1995) *Banal Nationalism*, London: Sage.

Bruin, de J. (2012) "NZ Idol: Nation Building through Format Adaptation", in T. Oren and S. Shahaf (eds.) *Global Television Formats*, London: Routledge, pp. 223–241.

Canclini, N. G. (1995) *Hybrid Cultures: Strategies for Entering and Leaving Modernity*, Minneapolis: University of Minnesota Press.

Carini, S. (2013) "Recreating Betty's World in Spain", in J. McCabe and K. Akass (eds.) *From Telenovela to International Brand. TV's Betty Goes Global*, London: I.B. Tauris, pp. 114–125.

Chalaby, J. (2010) "The Rise of Britain's Super-Indies: Policy-Making in the Age of the Global Media Market", *The International Communication Gazette*, 72 (8): 675–693.

Chalaby, J. (2011) "The Making of an Entertainment Revolution: How the TV Format Trade became a Global Industry", *European Journal of Communication*, 26 (4): 293–309.

Chalaby, J. (2012) "At the Origin of a Global Industry: The TV Format Trade as an Anglo-American Invention", *Media, Culture and Society*, 34 (1): 36–52.

Esser, A. (2001) *The Transnationalisation of Television in Europe 1985–1997*, unpublished PhD thesis, London: South Bank University.

Esser, A. (2010) "Television Formats: Primetime Staple, Global Market", *Popular Communication*, 8 (4): 273–292.

Esser, A. (2013a) "Television Formats and Commercialisation", in K. Donders, C. Pauwels, and J. Loisen (eds.) *Private Television in Europe: Content, Markets and Policy*, Basingstoke: Palgrave Macmillan, pp. 151–168.

Esser, A. (2013b) "Interviews with TV Executives Involved in the German Adaptation, Verliebt in Berlin", in J. McCabe and K. Akass (eds.) *TV's Betty Goes Global. From Telenovela to International Brand*, London: I. B. Tauris, pp. 72–82.

Ferguson, M. (1992) "The Mythology about Globalization", *European Journal of Communication*, 7 (1): 69–93.

Frau-Meigs, D. (2006) "Big Brother and Reality TV in Europe. Towards a Theory of Situated Acculturation by the Media", *European Journal of Communication*, 21 (1): 33–56.

Giulianotti, R. and R. Robertson. (2007) "Recovering the Social: Globalization, Football and Transnationalism", *Global Networks: A Journal of Transnational Affairs*, 7 (2): 166–186.

Hallenberger, G. (2002) 'Fernsehformate und internationaler Formathandel', in Hans-Bredow-Institut (ed.) *Internationales Handbuch Medien 2002/2003*, Hamburg: Nomos Verlagsgesellschaft, pp. 130–137.

Hepp, A. (2005) "Medienkultur", in A. Hepp, F. Krotz and C. Winter (eds.) *Globalisierung der Medienkommunikation. Eine Einführung*. Wiesbaden: VS Verlag, pp. 137–162.

Hepp, A. (2009) "Transculturality as a Perspective: Researching Media Cultures Comparatively", *Forum Qualitative Sozialforschung*, 10 (1), Art. 26, http://nbn-resolving.de/urn:nbn:de:0114-fqs0901267, accessed 22 March 2014.

Hetsroni, A. (2004) "The Millionaire Project: A Cross-Cultural Analysis of Quiz Shows from the United States, Russia, Poland, Norway, Finland, Israel, and Saudi Arabia", *Mass Communication & Society*, 7 (2): 133–156.

Hoskins, C. and R. Mirus. (1988) "Reasons for the U.S. Dominance of the International Trade in Television Programs", *Media, Culture & Society*, 10: 499–515.

IP Network, Television (2005) *International Key Facts*, Luxembourg: IP/RTL Group.

IP Network, Television (2008) *International Key Facts*, Luxembourg: IP/RTL Group.

IP Network, Television (2012) *International Key Facts*, Luxembourg: IP/RTL Group.

Jäger, E. and S. Behrens. (2009) *The FRAPA Report 2009. TV Formats to the World*, Cologne/Hürth: FRAPA.

Jensen, P. M. (2007) "Danish and Australian Television: The Impact of Format Adaptation", *Media International Australia*, 124: 119–133.Jensen, P. M. (2012) "How Media System Rather than Culture Determines National Variation: Danish Idols and Australian Idol Compared", in K. Zwaan and J. de Bruin (eds.) *Adapting Idols*. Farnham: Ashgate, pp. 27–40.

Jensen, P. M. (2013) "The Use of Format Adaptation in Danish Public Service Programming", *Critical Studies in Television*, 8 (2): 85–103.

Keane, M., A. Fung, and A. Moran. (2007) *New Television, Globalisation, and the East Asian Cultural Imagination*. Hong Kong: Hong Kong University Press.

Lagarto, T. "Ugly is the New Beautiful. An International Bettybase", fan website, last accessed 2 March 2014, http://www.jerriblank.com/betty/about.html.

Larkey, E. (2009) "Transcultural Localization Strategies of Global TV Formats: *The Office* and *Stromberg*", in A. Moran (ed.) *TV Formats Worldwide*, Bristol: Intellect, pp. 187–201.

Lash, S. and C. Lury. (2007) *Global Culture Industry: The Mediation of Things*, Cambridge: Polity.

Lippert, B. (2011) *Telenovela Formats. Localized Versions of a Universal Love*, Göttingen: Sierke Verlag.

Massey, D. (1994) *Space, Place and Gender*, Cambridge: Polity.

Mikos, L. (1995) "Internationale Fernsehformate und nationale Seh-ge-wohnheiten", in L Erbring (ed.) *Kommunikationsraum Europa*, Konstanz: Verlag Ölschläger, pp. 169–180.

Mikos, L. and Perrotta, M. (2012) "Travelling Style: Aesthetic Differences and Similarities in National Adaptations of Yo Soy Betty, La Fea", *International Journal of Cultural Studies*, 15 (1): 81–97.

Mirrlees, T. (2013) *Global Entertainment Media. Between Cultural Imperialism and Cultural Globalization*, New York: Routledge.

Mjos, O. (2010) *Media Globalization and the Discovery Channel Networks*, London: Routledge.

Moran, A. (1998) *Copycat TV: Globalization, Program Formats and Cultural Identity*, Luton: Luton Press.

Müller, E. (2002) 'Unterhaltungsshows transkulturell: Fernsehformate zwischen Akkomodation und Assimilation', in A. Hepp and M. Löffelholz (eds.) *Transkulturelle Kommunikation*, Konstanz: UVK, pp. 456–473.

Ndlela, M. N. (2012) "Global Television Formats in Africa: Localizing *Idol*", in T. Oren and S. Shahaf (eds.) *Global Television Formats*, London: Routledge, pp. 242–259.

Olson, S. R. (1999) *Hollywood Planet: Global Media and the Competitive Advantage of Narrative Transparency*, London: Routledge.

Omoniyi, T. (2006) "Hierarchy of Identities", in T. Omoniyi and G. White (eds.) *The Sociolinguistics of Identity*, London: Bloomsbury, pp. 11–33.

Ritzer, G. (2000) *The McDonaldization of Society*. Thousand Oaks, CA: Pine Forge Press.

Ritzer, G. (2004) *The Globalization of Nothing*, Thousand Oaks, CA: Pine Forge Press.

Robertson, R. (1991) "Social Theory, Cultural Relativity and the Problem of Globality", in A. D. King (ed.) *Culture, Globalization and the World-System*, Basingstoke: Macmillan, pp. 69–90.

Robertson, R. (1994) "Globalization or Glocalization?", *Journal of International Communication*, 1 (1): 33–52.

Robertson, R. (2011) "Global Connectivity and Global Consciousness", *American Behavioural Scientist*, 55 (10): 1336–1345.

Robertson, R. (2014) "Situating Glocalization: A Relatively Autobiographical Intervention', in G. Drori, M. A. Höllerer, and P. Walgenbach (eds.) *Global Themes and Local Variations in Organization and Management*, London: Routledge, pp. 25–36.

Robins, K. (1997) "What in the World's Going On?", in P. Dugay (ed.) *Production of Culture. Cultures of Production*, London: Sage.

Scott, K. (2002) "Format Buyers' Voxpop", *Television Business International*, Guide to Formats, April/May 2002, pp. 4–12.

Selznick, B. (2008) *Global Television: Co-Producing Culture*, Philadelphia: Temple University Press.

Sharp, S. (2012) "Global Franchising, Gender and Genre: The Case of Domestic Reality Television", in T. Oren and S. Shahaf (eds.) *Global Television Formats*, London: Routledge, pp. 346–365.

Sinclair, J. and R. Wilken. (2009) "Strategic Regionalization in Marketing Campaigns: Beyond the Standardization/Glocalization Debate", *Continuum: Journal of Media & Cultural Studies*, 23 (2): 147–157.

Sinclair, J., E. Jacka, and S. Cunningham (1996) "Peripheral Vision", in J. Sinclair, E. Jacka, and S. Cunningham (eds.) *New Patterns in Global Television*, Oxford: Oxford University Press, pp. 1–32.

Singhal, A. and K. Udornpim. (1997) "Cultural Shareability, Archetypes and Television Soaps.'Oshindrome' in Thailand", *Gazette*, 59 (3): 171–188.

Skovmand, M. (1992) "Barbarous TV International: Syndicated Wheels of Fortune', in M. Skovmand and K. C. Schrøder (eds.) *Media Cultures. Reappraising Transnational Media*, London: Routledge, pp. 84–103.

Straubhaar, J. (1991) "Beyond Media Imperialism: Asymmetrical Interdependence and Cultural Proximity", *Critical Studies in Mass Communication*, 8: 1–11.

Straubhaar, J. (2007) *World Television. From Global to Local*, London: Sage.
Straubhaar, J. and Duarte, L. G. (2005) "Adapting US Transnational Television Channels to a Complex World: From Cultural Imperialism to Localization to Hybridization," in J. K. Chalaby (ed.) *Transnational Television Worldwide*. London: I. B. Tauris, pp. 216–253.
Tomlinson, J. (1991) *Cultural Imperialism. A Critical Introduction*, London: Pinter Publishers.
Tomlinson, J. (1999) *Globalization and Culture*, Chicago: University of Chicago Press.
Waisbord, S. (2004) "McTV. Understanding the Global Popularity of Television Formats", *Television & New Media*, 5 (4): 359–383.
Walker, A. (2002) "Theories of Evolution", *Television Business International*, Guide to Formats, April/May 2002, p. 14.

5
Glocalization Effects of Immigrants' Activities on the Host Society

An Exploration of a Neglected Theme

Ewa Morawska

International migration seems an ideal field to explore the workings of glocalization understood as the process of simultaneous homogenization and heterogenization of economic, sociocultural, and political forms (Robertson, 1994; Robertson and White, 2005), yet curiously this connection has attracted minimal attention from scholars and, such that there is, is almost exclusively from those not directly affiliated with (im)migration studies (Giulianotti and Robertson, 2004, 2007; for a rare exception, see Fitzgerald, 2004, on the transformative penetration of Mexican hometown politics onto the agenda of a local branch of the American labour union). In considerable part this neglect reflects, I believe, a "nichification" of (im)migration studies within its own field-specific agendas, meetings, journals, and research networks – evidence of the very success of this specialization but at the cost of a parochialism of interests and pursuits.[1] If at all echoed in these studies, the concerns of mainstream disciplines represented by (im)migration specialists are those of anthropology as a new and vocal presence in the field since the 1990s. Probably most commonly invoked has been Arjun Appadurai's (1996) concept of "multi-scalar scapes", used to denote the simultaneity of the multi-level, in this case, global and local dimensions of human actors' experience in the contemporary world. Although the premise of the simultaneity of the global and the local is shared by the notion of multi-scalar scapes and that of glocalization, no effort has yet been made to try to clarify theoretically or illustrate empirically the relationship of these two ideas (an interdisciplinary volume, *Deciphering the Global: Its Scales, Spaces, and Subjects* (2007), edited by the sociologist Saskia Sassen, which includes several essays by anthropologists who frame their discussions in terms of multi-scalar scapes, does not contain a single mention of glocalization).

The purpose of this discussion is threefold: to elucidate the relation between the notions of glocalization and globalization's multi-scalar scapes; to elaborate the glocalization–(im)migration link, the conceptualization of which, by Giulianotti and Robertson (2007), I do not find entirely satisfactory; and to bring the overspecialized study of (im)migration closer to the ongoing debate in the mainstream social sciences about the global, glocal, and local developments in the contemporary world.

This chapter consists of three sections. In the first part I propose a way to position vis-à-vis each other, the notions of glocalization and multi-scalar spaces of globalization, and I suggest some modifications of the conceptualization of glocalization in relation to (im)migration as formulated by Giulianotti and Robertson. In the remaining two sections I illustrate my propositions with empirical cases. Although by definition of their subject matter studies of international migration have transgressed national boundaries, these cosmopolitan foundations have not saved the practitioners of this field from a narrow, one-sided perspective in their works. The almost exclusive focus of theory and research regarding the effects of the encounters between immigrants and the receiver countries they settle in has been on the modes of adaptation of those newcomers into the host societies and the patterns of accompanying transformation of their home-country identifications, cultural practices, and social and civic commitments. I focus here on a thus far neglected reverse outcome of these encounters, namely, the glocalizing impact of immigrants' activities on the host society.

The empirical part of the chapter includes two sets of analyses: I first comparatively consider the effects on the receiver, American society of the turn of the last century versus contemporary immigrants, and, next, I examine this impact of differently positioned groups among the latter. The information about these groups and their influence on the receiver-country people and institutions comes from my longitudinal historical-sociological study of past and present immigration and ethnicity in the United States.[2]

Exploring glocalization

The basic affinity between the concepts of globalization's multi-scalar scapes and glocalization is the earlier-noted recognition by scholars who use these ideas of the simultaneity of the global and the local dimensions of sociocultural developments in the contemporary world. It is implied in the very term "glocalization" coined by the sociologists, whereas anthropologists, whose professional concerns traditionally focus on ground-level sociocultural phenomena, define globalization as naturally multi-scalar in character so that its processes evolve instantaneously at "subnational" (local in sociologese), national, regional, and global levels. By recognizing the engagement of the local component in societal processes, also those of global scope the proponents of both concepts considered here also acknowledge the role of individual and collective social actors in reconstituting the world they live in.

Although obviously related, the notions of globalization's multi-scalar scapes and glocalization have, however, different "interpretative capacities". The former, focused on the multi-level nature of globalization processes, offers a welcome antidote to the fixed (as in enduring) macrostructural emphasis of the classical globalization models by providing a heuristic guidepost for a more complex and flexible conceptualization of the *how* of these developments. In comparison, the notion of glocalization is, I believe, more capacious theoretically, in that it offers both insight into how globalization processes evolve and the proposition of *what* – new forms emerging from the mixing-and-blending of global and local influences – is the outcome of multi-scalarity of these phenomena. In addition, whereas the "object matter" of the notion of globalization's multi-scalar scapes are (different-level) localized global phenomena, the concept of glocalization encompasses, and thus invites empirical examination of, both that and the globalized local.

Having recognized globalization's multi-scalar scapes, but finding the notion of glocalization more challenging overall for the study of the effects of international migration, here, regarding the host society, I would like to propose three modifications to Giulianotti and Robertson's (2007) conceptualization of this process in relation to (im)migrants' activities in the receiver country. The first concerns the authors' typology of this phenomenon. Giulianotti and Robertson distinguish four kinds of glocalization projects: *relativization* or the preservation by social actors of their pre-existing ideas and practices, thus contributing to differentiation of the host culture; *accommodation* or the absorption by social actors of the meanings and practices associated with other societies; *hybridization* or the mixing-and-blending by social actors of their own and other sociocultural representations and habits to produce distinctive new forms; and *transformation* or the abandonment by social actors of their own traditions in favour of those associated with other sociocultural systems.

Assuming we agree that theoretical models produced by sociologists should be anchored in the social reality they are studying – here, (im)migrants' experience in the host society – and that the matter of concern is the relation of this experience to glocalization, I would suggest, first, that the first two of Giulianotti and Robertson's types are fused into one – *accommodation*. Whereas the retention by social actors of their group traditions in an ethnically plural society indeed contributes to its differentiation, it does not necessarily imply relativization if – as was the case examined in the section "The accommodation phase of the glocalization process" with regard to turn-of-the-20th-century America vis-à-vis new immigrants – such plural cultural patterns exist separately side by side rather than being "open" to reciprocal influences. I propose, therefore, to apply the term accommodation to two meanings corresponding to different situations. One mode of accommodation involves the coexistence of different but side by side sociocultural patterns, which implies heterogenization but no homogenization, and, therefore, cannot be treated as glocalization. This type of accommodation well illustrates the multi-scalarity of globalization processes: by settling in the host society and establishing foreign communities bustling with "foreign" sociocultural life and ideas, immigrants globalize the receiver country from below, but they do it on their own, as it were, without the active collaboration of native residents. The other situation and the precondition of interpenetration of coexistent modes of operation of groups or societies resulting in their simultaneous homogenization-and-diversification is the accommodation, likewise a multi-scalar process, which involves a reciprocal engagement.

Second, I suggest that hybridization *is* transformation as it involves the emergence of new sociocultural forms as the result of mixing-and-blending by immigrants of their home-country traditions and elements of host-country culture – the most common type both of immigrants' accommodation to the host society (for a review of existing studies, see Morawska, 2011) and of the receiver-country culture under the impact of immigrants' activities (see the section "The accommodation phase of the glocalization process"). As defined by Giulianotti and Robertson, transformation resembles the classical model of assimilation of Milton Gordon (1964), which posited the linear progressive disappearance of immigrants' cultural traits and social bonds, replaced by host society orientations and practices. It has since been effectively refuted by immigration scholars theoretically and, of concern here, empirically (see, e.g., Foner, 2001; Waters and Ueda, 2007; Portes and DeWind, 2008), although it can be defended as possible under a specific constellation of circumstances (Morawska, 1994). But what does this homogenization of sociocultural patterns through immigrants shedding their differences and assuming mainstream outlooks have to with glocalization defined by Giulianotti and Robertson as simultaneous differentiation and uniformization? The authors' reference to "location in global ecumene", and "critical reflexivity on new mediation" as definitional features of transformation-as-glocalization-project reflects the agenda of the recent vogue studies of "global cosmopolitanism" (see, e.g., Breckenridge, 2002; Fine, 2007; Archibugi, 2008) rather than the concerns of (im)migration studies.[3] As for the reverse effect or transformation-as-disappearance-of-native-features of the host society under the impact of immigrant activities, such alteration seems inconceivable at present (although one could imagine some such effect in the future in the American Southwest, for example, overcome by Mexicans and their offspring).

With the focus on the glocalization–(im)migration link, then, the second modification of Giulianotti and Robertson's conceptualization I would like to suggest is that we treat accommodation and transformation not as fixed types but as *phases* of glocalization or the processes of becoming. While recognizing varying durations of the accommodation and transformation processes, in the empirical analyses presented here I examine glocalization effects within the span of a generation.

The last adjustment of the concept of glocalization necessary, I believe, for it to serve as an effective interpretative tool for the examination of the interaction between (im)migrants and the receiver society, is to make it sensitive to societal contingencies embedded in this relationship. As it is, the concept of glocalization is devoid of any notion of potential differences in the operation of the processes of transformation-as-hybridization depending on its structural environment and the characteristics of the participant actors. Sociology offers different ways of accounting for such contingencies. I propose to do so in the mode of a historical-sociological analysis (see Abrams, 1982; Hall, 1999) whereby, in order to explain *why* things happen, an investigator demonstrates *how* they happen by identifying a constellation of relevant circumstances which have contributed to the specific outcome. In the case of (im)migrants' impact on the host society, this approach calls for incorporating the potentially relevant societal dividers, such as socio-economic position, racial membership, and gender of social actors; their group institutional completeness; and the receiver-country legal-institutional system, orientations, and practices regarding (im)migrants into a cluster of "variables", the effects of which are checked in the examined empirical material. This mode of accounting "from below" for the multiple context-dependency of societal processes requires the sustained alertness of a researcher to the potential influence of these circumstances, and yet allows for their absence in concrete situations.

The accommodation phase of the glocalization process: A comparison of the situations of turn-of-the-20th-century and contemporary immigrants in America

As proposed, accommodation may involve the side-by-side coexistence of different sociocultural patterns or – the precondition of interpenetration of coexistent modes of operation of groups or societies resulting in their simultaneous homogenization-and-diversification – the reciprocal readiness for such mutual engagement. Available studies of past and present immigrants' experiences in the United States suggest that three conditions are necessary (although not always sufficient) for the latter situation to emerge: (i) the host society's civic culture and practice of openness/inclusion vis-à-vis "others", and, in particular, acceptance of immigrants by the host society's native residents and institutions or, at a minimum, their pragmatically motivated interest in immigrant cultures; (ii) the existence of social spaces of contact between host society native residents and institutions; and (iii) a relatively low level of normatively (religiously, ideologically) prescribed sociocultural enclosure of the immigrant groups themselves. The temporal dimension of these circumstances creates further contingencies in the adaptation phase of the glocalization process: receiver society's and immigrants' openness vis-à-vis each other with regard to attitudes and everyday practices must constitute an enduring (rather than situational – now present now gone depending on current domestic or world developments) conditions; and contacts between native residents and institutions and immigrants must be regular (rather than sporadic).

I argue that the accommodation by the host, American society of turn-of-the-last-century immigrants, most of them peasants from South and East Europe, represented a side-by-side-coexistence type of adjustment, and even that was problematic for native residents, rather than a preparatory stage for the absorption of the newcomers' "profiles of cultural orientation" (Kluckhohn, 1950).[4] During the early decades of the 20th century public opinion of native-born Americans saw new immigrants as culturally inferior, uninteresting, and potentially dangerous, and there were neither laws nor civil organizations to protect immigrants' rights as foreign-born residents. Widely recognized "scholarly" racist theories represented South and East European groups defined today as white as racially differentiated by physical features, skin "hues", and genetically determined mental capacities. The "Nordic race" was considered superior to all others. In this scheme South and East Europeans – immigrants and their American-born children – were perceived as racially (and not just nationally or ethnically) distinct and inferior to the dominant Anglo-Saxon and other North-Western European groups: they are made of "germ plasm", "the Slavs are immune to certain kinds of dirt. They can stand what would kill a white man", Italians' "dark complexion... resembles African more than Caucasian hues", Jews or "furtive Yacoobs... snarl in weird Yiddish". Examples of such racist pronouncements about those "suspicious aliens of inferior species" by respectable public personae in respectable American institutions such as Congress, Harvard University, the US Bureau of the Census, the American Federation of Labor (AFL), and the like, were common. (On the American public opinion's and institutions' perceptions of South and East European immigrants and their offspring in racial terms, see Higham, 1972; Roediger, 1991; Kraut, 1994; Jacobson, 1998; Gutterl, 2000; Foner and Fredrickson, 2004; Gugliemo and Salerno, 2003.)

The exclusion of South and East Europeans from closer social relations with the natives, open discrimination against them at work, and their prolonged non-admission to the labour unions, resulted in part from these accepted perceptions and in part from the hierarchical and ethnic-divisive operation of industrial capitalism and, specifically, the employment of large numbers of foreign-origin workers assembled in nationality gangs in the mills and factories, whose contacts with native superiors were mediated through "gang leaders" or their fellow nationals with a longer duration of stay in the country. Immigrants' half-imposed/half-voluntary concentration in so-called "foreign colonies" isolated from native neighbourhoods, their unfamiliarity with English, and the sojourner, home-country-focused mentality of the majority, which endured for several decades after their arrival in America, further diminished their opportunities to influence the receiver society.

As a result, "old" immigrants were closet ethnics who lived their differences within their own communities. Turn-of-the-last-century American neighbourhoods, churches, schools, and workplaces were definitely multicultural – multi-scalar globalization as diversification from below of the American society was certainly taking place as immigrants established their communities and celebrated their traditions in the localities in which they settled, but it was segmented multiculturalism composed of ethnic niches. Hybridization processes did evolve at a slow pace as, within those niches, immigrants gradually incorporated American ways into their everyday lives, but it was a one-way glocalization, not accompanied by a parallel transformation of the receiver society.

The situation today is different on several counts. Prejudice and discrimination against newcomers by mainstream American society and its institutions have undoubtedly been enduring features of immigrants' experience then and now. But publicly sanctioned and openly proclaimed racist perceptions directed at the turn of the 20th century against basically defenceless South and East Europeans were an effective factor responsible for their exclusion from closer social relations with the natives and manifest discrimination against them at work and in public places. In comparison, the contemporary racism of Americans has been significantly tempered or potentially tempered by the shift in American civic-political ideology, accompanied by the institutionalization of practical measures to implement it, including weapons to fight racial discrimination. The official recognition of pluralism as the principle of American society and its trickle-down effect on its residents through the system of laws, education at schools and in the workplaces, and the media, have created a protective shield against discrimination for its potential victims and given the immigrants a sense of civic entitlement, including the encouragement to pursue their ethnic activities and make claims in the public sphere of mainstream society. Also, and of importance for the matter examined here, these development have opened the minds of a large segment of the native-born American population by making them view multiculturalism as a natural and welcome feature of society.

The restructuring of the American economy since the 1970s has produced a bifurcated labour market with a hardened barrier between the high-skilled, well-paid workforce very much in demand and the underclass, composed of low-educated, low-skilled residents, often of foreign birth, who, like their predecessors a century ago, live isolated from mainstream society. At the same time, however, the small-scale, informal, and decentralized mode of operation of post-industrial capitalism allows for much more contact among employees, especially higher-skill ones in primary and secondary sectors of the labour market.

Next, and related, has been the diversification of contemporary immigrants' human capital and their increased occupational and residential dispersion throughout the dominant society. Whereas the overwhelming majority of turn-of-the-century immigrants were unskilled manual labourers, today's arrivals match the native-born American population in the overall proportion of college and higher-educated persons (24 per cent), while the share of persons employed in professional and managerial positions (25 per cent) is only slightly lower than that among native-born employed residents (30 per cent). (Information about educational achievement and occupational position of the foreign-born population comes from the 2000 US Population Census; these proportions differ significantly, however, among particular immigrant groups, ranging from 70 per cent of college educated and 66 per cent in professional and managerial occupations for Asian Indians to 5 and 8 per cent, respectively, for Mexicans.) More than two-thirds of better-educated immigrants employed in high-skilled occupations live in residential dispersion among native-born Americans (see Iceland et al., 2002; Myles and Hou, 2004; Massey, 2008); as in the case of immigrants' socio-economic positions, group differences in rates of residential concentration are considerable, depending on the size and levels of institutional completeness of particular ethnic populations.

In such a context, inter-ethnic friendships and intermarriage as an important precondition for multicultural exchange from below have also significantly increased (although by no means become predominant, especially across racial lines). At the closing of the 20th century the rate of intermarriage was between 20 and 40 per cent depending on particular groups, as compared with 2–3 per cent for South and East Europeans combined in 1920. (Information about intermarriage between foreign- and native-born Americans then and now has been compiled from Perlmann and Waters, 2004, 2007.)

Last and important, the "spirit" of contemporary consumer capitalism relies on the constant updating and diversification of the supply of merchandise and services and, on the receiver side of the game, customers' needs and lifestyles. Interest in "other" people and their cultures by increasing numbers of native residents, especially in younger and better-educated groups, represents a form of this consumer culture. As we shall see in the section "The transformation phase of the glocalization process", this attraction to the "other" in contemporary mainstream American culture is capable of transgressing the structural barriers of socio-economic divisions.

The transformation phase of the glocalization process: contemporary immigrants' impact on the host society

The features of the contemporary immigrants and the receiver society identified in the section "The accommodation phase of the glocalization process" jointly contribute to the emergence of a considerably quicker pace of multiculturalism as mixing-and-borrowing rather than simply existing next to each other – within the newcomers' lifetime rather than over several generational cohorts as was the case with the impact of "old" immigrants.[5] We examine here the glocalization – transformation-as-hybridization – effects of present-day immigrants' presence in the United States in two areas: impact on the civic-political and the socio-cultural life of the host society. It is, of course, impossible to account for this influence by all immigrant groups, as they number, with documented and undocumented residents combined, 30-odd million people settled in different locations across the country. The few cases reported here demonstrating the transformative impact of immigrants on host society civic-political affairs and cultural orientations and practices have been selected not to make my account representative of this multiplicity, but to illustrate the diversity of glocalization effects contingent on the class, race/ethnicity, and gender position of those newcomers and the features of the locations where they settle.

Host society's civic-political affairs

We begin with the mainstream civic-political arena where two transformative developments can be noted. One of them has been the increase of anti-immigrant sentiments among native-born residents in response to the quickly growing numbers of (im)migrants. Interestingly, the mechanisms and transformative effects of the impact of this resentment on the lives of the native-born population have been different for middle-class white and lower-class black Americans. Los Angeles, which has attracted the largest numbers of immigrants during recent decades, well illustrates these processes.

"Unlike New York, Los Angeles is new to its present role as an immigrant mecca" – with this statement Roger Waldinger and Mehdi Bozorgmehr (1996: 9) open their reconstruction of the uneasy transformation of the city into a multicultural metropolis. Mostly still native-born (Anglo) white and parochial ("Iowa-on the Pacific") in the early 1960s, within a few decades Los Angeles had surpassed New York in its number of foreign-born residents. From a mere 10-odd per cent in 1960, the share of the foreign-born among Los Angelenos had quadrupled by 2000, and members of non-white ethnic minority groups (primarily Hispanics, and also Asians) have become, numerically, the majority population. The sudden change of the make-up of city neighbourhoods and workplaces caused by the rapidly growing numbers of foreigners, including an army of undocumented migrants from across the Mexican border, has generated increasing resentment among native-born residents, both white and black. (Information about the numerical growth of immigrants in Los Angeles and the resentful reaction of native-born residents can be gleaned from Chang and Leong, 1994; Bozorgmehr et al., 1996; Waldinger and Bozorgmehr, 1996; Johnson et al., 1997; Mollenkopf, 1999; Mollenkopf et al., 2002; US Census Bureau, *Current Population Survey*, 2006.)

The impact of the rapidly expanding presence of immigrants in the city, and in California in general, and of the shared sense of threat it poses to native-born residents, particularly middle-class white Americans, has been threefold. First, the increase of anti-immigrant sentiments in this population does not appear to have eradicated their general acceptance of multiculturalism, but has "hybridized" this attitude by introducing an element of ambivalence: immigrants are basically good for America and it is nice to have a multi-ethnic society, but there are too many of them where we live. The primary reaction of native-born white residents to this cognitive dissonance has been a flight farther and farther away from areas where Hispanic residents concentrate. It has been accompanied by the political mobilization of generally laid-back middle-class Californians, with white Los Angelenos at the helm of the lobbying, directed mainly at the local (state) authorities, for more restrictive action regarding social services to immigrants, especially undocumented ones.[6] (Information compiled from Hanson, 2003; Reitz, 2003; Zúñiga and Hernández-Leon, 2005; Gutierrez and Zavella, 2009.)

The main transformative effect of Hispanic and Asian immigrants' expanding presence in Los Angeles on the lives of the city's lower-class African American (the majority) residents has been different. Directly confronted with these newcomers in the neighbourhoods and at work, lower-class African Americans have lacked the resources available to middle-class whites to escape their situation in the form of either financial means to change their residence, sufficient training to obtain better employment, or the political know-how and influence to try to curtail the "foreign surge". Instead, they have experienced a sense of collective disenfranchisement and grievance regarding their group position vis-à-vis those immigrants and perceive them, adversely, as competitors for/encroachers upon the claimed resources. The shared feeling among Los Angeles blacks that, just when the Civil Rights Movement removed the formal institutions of racial segregation in the 1960s and opportunities appeared for the black minority, the massive arrival of immigrants set city development on a different track, stalling the African American progress, has made the sense of anger and disempowerment even more acute. This group aggravation has repeatedly led to open confrontations with immigrants since the 1990s. The most notorious among them have been black–Korean and black–Mexican conflicts – each of them, for that matter, generated by (inter)group-specific mechanisms. (This and the following information about African Americans' competition with immigrants in Los Angeles and its effect on the former has been compiled from Chang and Leong, 1994; Bozorgmehr et al., 1996; Sonenshein, 1996; Waldinger and Bozorgmehr 1996; Logan and Alba, 1999; Morawska, 2001; Mollenkopf et al., 2002; Min, 2008.)

An unusually large proportion, about 40 per cent, among the employed Korean immigrants in Los Angeles, most of whom arrived in the United States during the 1980s and 1990s, are self-employed in small business. The owners of these small establishments have their homes either in Koreatown, west of downtown Los Angeles, or in neighbourhoods outside of the city centre. But Korean businesses are disproportionately located in poor minority neighbourhoods: 60 per cent of the total, almost equally distributed between African American and Latino sections of South Central Los Angeles. The residents of such areas – here, African Americans – dissatisfied with what they perceived as discourteous service, non-employment of blacks in Korean businesses, and the lack of capital and social investment by Koreans in the African American community – the exploitation of which "they get rich on" – have frequently verbally abused Koreans and occasionally looted their stores. Koreans responded with racial slurs calling blacks "lazy", drug addicts, and good-for-nothings in general. Instigated originally by the anger of African Americans against a five-year probation sentence (much too lenient in their view) given in the autumn of 1991 to a Korean grocery owner who shot to death an African American girl while struggling with her over an unpaid bottle of orange juice, in the spring of 1992 anti-Korean hostility erupted into mass violence after a jury acquitted white police officers accused of beating black motorist Rodney King. During the burning and looting 1 Korean was killed and 46 injured, and over 2,000 Korean stores, worth more than $350 million, were destroyed, primarily in black neighbourhoods in the South Central section of the city but also in Koreatown four miles away. Although the conflict was eventually extinguished, "eruptive tension" between Korean shopkeepers and their black customers has persisted into the 21st century, making this one extra unpleasantness which was not there in the hopeful decades of the 1960s and 1970s, an enduring element of African Americans' everyday lives.

The local context of native-born black/Latino tensions in Los Angeles has differed from that fuelling African American/Korean hostilities. The massive entry of cheap Latino, mainly Mexican, labour into the Los Angeles economy between the 1970s and the 1990s has largely displaced black workers from several job concentrations, for example, certain manufacturing sectors, construction, services to dwellings, low-skill restaurant and hotel jobs (men), and textile production and domestic household service (women). In other fields, such as metal industries, furniture and fixtures, transportation, and higher-level manual jobs in hotel and restaurant services, the growing presence of immigrants and, in particular, the expansion of immigrant occupational niches based on in-group network recruitment has made it increasingly difficult for African Americans to compete successfully for jobs. In addition to the sheer mass of cheap and willing immigrants and a high-level ethnic nichification of the economy that has effectively excluded outsiders, a savage-capitalist open-shop labour market combined with native white and immigrant (Asian) employers' preference for Mexican (docile) over African American (finicky and too ambitious) workers even for jobs outside of ethnic occupational niches, makes job competition particularly tough for blacks.

African Americans' only occupational niche in the city has been in public-sector employment. As in the private sector, the competition between them and Hispanics/Mexicans, whose "fair share" demands for public jobs and political influence have intensified since the 1990s, has continued to generate mutual resentment and negative stereotyping. Mexicans see blacks as having been in power too long and not wanting to recognize the fact that they are no longer the majority. African Americans respond to these charges by pointing out that blacks struggled for years to win power in the civil service, while immigrants just arrived and expect to have everything. The Mexicans' upper hand in this conflict concerns the future. "Tom Bradley was not only L.A.'s first black mayor", as an observer of the Los Angeles political scene said half in jest, "he was also probably its last [African American mayor]. Power has shifted for good here, even though most people don't realize it yet" (after Rieff, 2002: 149). The disappointing realization that this may indeed be so among African Americans, who feel that, despite their difficult march towards equity in mainstream American society, which began in the 1960s, they are still a long way from their goal, cannot but add an angry element to their everyday lives.

The second transformative effect of immigrants' presence and, in this case, their engagement in the receiver society's civic-political affairs, has been the multiculturalization of concerns and issues informing civic-political processes in the cities/regions where immigrants live or their multi-scalar transformation through the incorporation of the global into the local. It is illustrated by the impact of Cubans on Miami's politics. I have selected this case to demonstrate the important role in facilitating glocalization of two circumstances: a high degree of institutional completeness of the immigrant/ethnic community including, in particular, the presence of the economically powerful elite active in the public forum and supported by group members, and the receiver society's political interests in the country/region of origin of the immigrants, which coincide with the latter's orientations.

The glocalizing influence of Cuban refugees on Miami's civic-political life represents an unusual – unique, really – case of "hybridization" of local public affairs, whereby the ethnic component prevails over the mainstream or native-born American one. Since the 1970s the intense "Cubanization" of Miami's politics has transformed the composition of political offices, imbued the local establishment with a staunchly conservative political orientation, and sustained its active preoccupation with the Cold War and Soviet influence in South America and, especially, efforts to undermine the Castro regime in Cuba.

A constellation of several conducive circumstances has made possible Miami Cuban immigrants' rise to such unprecedented prominence. Most of the 135,000-strong first wave of Cuban refugees were well-established businessmen and managers and their families, who came to Miami between January 1959 and mid-1961. Most of them had either already invested in the United States or managed to transplant their financial resources there as they fled the communist revolution which, combined with their entrepreneurial acumen, made it possible for this group to quickly re-establish their businesses in Miami and to gain positions of leadership in the growing Cuban community. Subsequent waves of lower-class Cuban immigrants into the Miami area – about 100,000 refugees followed first-wave families between 1962 and 1964 and another 250,000 had come by 1974 – supplied the same-language, same-culture workforce with the diverse skills needed for the formation of an extensive, residentially concentrated, thriving ethnic enclave as the mode of incorporation into the local economy. The generous support for Cuban refugees by the United States government, dictated by the priorities and preferences of its foreign policy in the Cold War era in the form of the Cuban Refugee Program and other federal initiatives, including direct loans, housing subsidies, and guaranteed health care, significantly helped the immigrants adapt to the new environment. (This and the following information about Cuban refugees' position in Miami has been compiled from Mohl, 1989; Portes and Stepick, 1993; Smith and Feagin, 1995; Perez-Stable and Uriarte, 1997; Becker and Dluhy, 1998; Bowie and Stepick, 1998; DeSipio, 1998; Garcia-Zamor, 1998; Grenier and Castro, 1998; Jones-Correa, 1998; Grenier and Perez, 2003; Eckstein, 2009.)

The solid presence of the powerful first-wave Cuban refugee businessmen and managers at the helm of the large Cuban economic enclave made this group a power to be reckoned with. In the secondary and informal sectors of the city's economy, in particular apparel manufacturing, construction, and hotel and restaurant services, Cuban immigrant businessmen have held an uncontested dominant position since the 1980s. The large size and good organization of the Cuban population and its elite's economic influence in Miami also enabled its leaders to gain central power in city politics. The appropriation by Cubans of the city political establishment was a prolonged process as it met with strong resistance – eventually ending in a concession – from the native white establishment, which saw itself increasingly set aside by the Cubans, who relied on their own ethnic organizations rather than, as native-born American leaders expected, integrating into the existing political system.

By the late 1980s the city of Miami and the surrounding townships all had Cuban-born mayors, and foreign-born Cubans controlled the City Commission and made up a majority of the county delegation to the state legislature. "Nowhere else in America, not even in American history" – Guillermo Grenier and Lisandro Perez comment on the long list of Cuban city and state officials in Miami – "have first-generation immigrants so quickly and so thoroughly appropriated political power" (Grenier and Perez, 2003: 368).[7] Characteristically, the agents of the Cubanization of Miami's political life have been exclusively men. Although more than one-third of the adult women refugees in the first-wave group of immigrants came to Miami with professional or managerial skills, and an equal proportion had training in sales and administrative jobs, after a brief period of outside employment when their families were putting down roots in the new environment, they withdrew into the homes as middle-class wives and mothers.

Host society's cultural orientations and practices

Another area of the operation of the receiver, American society upon which immigrants coming from other parts of the world exert a notable transformative impact is that of cultural orientations and practices. Two examples, one from the top and another the bottom of the receiver country's socio-economic structure illustrate the context-specific – here, class-specific – nature of the glocalization effects: the impact of Hong Kong global businessmen in the Los Angeles area on the local mainstream managerial culture, and that of undocumented Polish (im)migrants in Philadelphia on the practices of native-born Americans who employ them.

From among 80,000 Chinese immigrants from Hong Kong who reside in Los Angeles, most of whom have arrived in America since the 1980s, about 7 per cent are high-level employees of transnational companies and in global, mainly Asia-oriented, businesses. They reside – when they are in the United States, that is – in the suburban areas west of Los Angeles County called "Asian Beverly Hills", created by a Chinese real estate developer who launched the development of this residential area far away from the centres of Hispanic and African American concentration. Although as a (small) group they live there in residential dispersion among affluent native-born white Los Angelenos, individual families frequently buy homes in relative proximity to each other. (This and the following information about Hong Kong global businessmen in Los Angeles has been compiled from Skeldon, 1994; Dirlik, 1996; Waldinger and Bozorgmehr, 1996; Wong, 1998; Hamilton, 1999; Koehn and Yin, 2002; Ma and Cartier, 2003; Saxenian and Li, 2003; Saxenian, 2006; Holdaway, 2007; Yin, 2007.)

It has been primarily as powerful global traders and financiers with connections to Asia, sought after by American business and political leaders, that Hong Kong businessmen have integrated into Los Angeles society. Their entry into the United States has been facilitated from the start by a new "investor category" created in the receiver-country immigration system that guarantees permanent residence to 10,000 immigrants annually in exchange for a US $1 million investment by these newcomers that results in the creation of at least ten jobs in the United States. Native-born American leaders of the area's capitalist enterprises, American politicians, and the media all see this group as "bridge-builders" between the United States and South Asia, instrumental in the creation of the Pacific Century in the global economy. As studies indicate, Hong Kong immigrants' self-perceptions include this image as well. Their sustained contributions to the internationalization of the Los Angeles economy integrate them into the very core of mainstream American capitalism in the global era.

Hong Kong transnational businessmen's powerful economic position and their importance in expanding financial and trade connections between the United States and South-East Asia – nearly a half of American joint ventures and investments in that region in 2000 were sponsored either by Chinese immigrants alone or in partnership with all-American companies – also makes them important agents in the glocalization-as-hybridization of cultural habits among native-born (white) American leaders of transnational trade and finance in the Los Angeles area. The latter have been reported to learn and put into practice Chinese ways of conducting transnational business, such as an emphasis on a collective style of management and the protocol for interpersonal relations. As they do so, these modes of behaviour from a faraway part of the world are integrated into an important segment of the American mainstream economic cultural system.

Like male Cuban refugees in the transformation of Miami, the agents of glocalization of the managerial culture in Los Angeles have been Hong Kong transnational business*men*. A small number of women – known in the Chinese community as "strong women" – have independently engaged in transnational entrepreneurship as managers of global hotel chains, high-tech investment companies, and export/import firms, and, like their husbands or fathers, have travelled back and forth between the United States and Hong Kong. But these women have been an exception. The vast majority of the wives of wealthy global businessmen and financiers have been housewives. As we shall see in the next case, however, such strictly gendered hybridization of host-country practices through the involvement of immigrants has by no means been the rule.

This illustration comes from the opposite end of the receiver society's socio-economic spectrum and concerns the incorporation of what I call beat-the-system/bend-the law coping strategies used by low-skilled, especially undocumented, immigrants, men and women alike, into the practices of native-born American operators of the mainstream small-scale production and service sectors which employ such people. To the extent that such transformation of the pursuits of native-born Americans involves evading/corrupting the law, this particular instance of glocalization can be classified not only as cultural but also a civic-political transformative effect of the engagement by immigrants of host-country residents.

Empirical evidence for this case is provided by my ethnographic study of Polish *Arbeitstouristen* or (im)migrants on tourist visas who extend their stay in the host country and undertake undocumented employment in Philadelphia (Morawska, 2004; also in Berlin – Morawska, 2003a) and by recurrent media reports about native-born Americans seeking – and finding – labourers for home construction and repairs, house cleaning, and baby-sitting through informal connections in immigrant colonies.

Breaking the law as "an American way of life" (Bell, 1953) has been an enduring tradition in the United States. The novelty here is the way it happens. Rather than by individual or organized transgressions, as described by Daniel Bell more than a half century ago, the opportunistic *debrouillard* strategies of evading the existing laws and regulations employed by contemporary immigrants who come from un(der)developed countries with ineffective and often corrupt civic-legal systems and find themselves in economically or politically disadvantaged situations in the host country imperceptibly penetrate its structures through informal everyday interactions with the natives. A bottle of Polish vodka offered by émigré men or an amber brooch produced by a tourist-worker woman in exchange for a "connection" to the employer – "as a token of my appreciation for your kindness, it is customarily done in my culture" – is accepted without the recipient being aware that they are being subtly drawn into a nepotistic *potlatch* chain of exchanges of services. In a few instances when I asked native-born Philadelphians whether they were aware of what was happening when they were offered and accepted such "small gifts" (a bottle of home-made schnapps and an amber brooch) by Polish tourist workers in exchange for assistance with finding better-paying employment, the replies were puzzled looks. A similar implantation of beat-the-system/bend-the-law coping strategies used by immigrants into the practices of their native-born American employers has also been reported on the West Coast, where Mexicans in situations similar to those of Philadelphia Poles look for and find jobs outside of their ethnic niche (Hondagneu-Sotelo, 1997; Hanson, 2003; Gutierrez and Zavella, 2009).

In this case two major circumstances have created the space for this effect to emerge. Post-industrial restructuring of the host-country economy has created a large informal sector specializing in small-scale manufacturing, construction, and service industries offering low-paid and expendable jobs detached from the "official" legal-institutional infrastructure. And the receiver-country restrictive immigration policies, including, especially, regulations of the duration of sojourn and permission to work, have created an army of undocumented (im)migrants whose structural – here, civic-political – position channels them into the informal sectors of the receiver-country labour market where they are eagerly awaited by native employers seeking to lower the cost of their operations.

While polymorphization of the host society's economic culture, as in the case of the impact of Hong Kong global businessmen or Polish tourist, workers, requires a considerable accommodation period – the actors involved must collaborate with each other for a certain amount of time in order for the glocalization to occur – the permutation of present-day mainstream consumer culture occurs at a much quicker pace. In addition to a greater openness of the contemporary receiver society, guaranteed by the system of laws and sustained by the public discourse, another important circumstance responsible for this acceleration has been the cultural logic of consumer capitalism (Jameson, 1991) and, especially, its high-speed principle. The same principle may well contribute – the matter awaits empirical investigation – to the shallow reach and the short-span endurance of the incorporated fragments of outside consumer cultures, which come and go with the whims of fashion.

The last illustration of the glocalization of receiver-country cultural preferences and practices is the incorporation into mainstream American consumer culture – or cultures, more accurately, as these effects vary from city/region to city/region – of ethnic elements: Mexican, Jamaican, Korean, Chinese, and Indian food, music, dress, articles of clothing and jewellery, and different forms of entertainment such as films and street festivals. Some of these implantations into the host society's consumer culture have been the outcome of the activities of immigrant men and women alike, while the agents of others are gender-specific. For example, maid services commonly performed by documented and undocumented lower-class (im)migrant women in middle-class native-American homes have been reported to involve the transfer into these habitats of their home-country dishes which the employers, usually women, learn how to prepare and their family members begin to enjoy as part of their regular diet. Available studies on the contributions of immigrants' presence in the receiver society to new developments therein also report an increased interest in, often followed by intensified international tourism to, faraway regions of the world – most commonly noted among middle-class native-born Americans have been South and East Asian destinations. (Information about the glocalization of American consumer culture under the impact of immigrants has been compiled from Hu-DeHart, 1999; Hondagneu-Sotelo, 2003; Peterson, 2007; Parreñas, 2008; see also Ehrenreich and Hochschild, 2003; Reitz, 2003.)

One more interesting phenomenon should be noted in this context. Paradoxically, the implantation of elements of Mexican traditions such as food, music, and public festivals into mainstream American culture in the Southwest seems to have occurred quicker and to a considerably greater extent than the incorporation of Mexican immigrants themselves into the local American society. It is apparently easier, especially in the era of global consumer capitalism, to accommodate another culture and thus transform one's own than to accept and integrate its human carriers, especially when they are perceived as racially other and positioned at the bottom of the host society's socio-economic structure.

Conclusion

I hope my elaboration of Giulianotti and Robertson's (2007) conceptualization of the link between glocalization and (im)migration has been convincing and the empirical illustrations thereof persuasive, and, at the least, that the foregoing discussion would invite further rethinking of this relationship. The parallel purpose of this chapter has been to use the notion of glocalization for the examination of immigrants' activities as a way of remedying what I perceive as an unfortunate parochialization of international migration studies or their growing enclosure within narrow field-specific conceptual apparatus and research agendas. I do not believe one essay can accomplish this task, but perhaps it can serve as a reminder that the explicit linking of these subdisciplinary concerns with those currently debated in the mainstream social sciences is not only possible but also intellectually stimulating.

I have focused here on a dimension thus far neglected in (im)migration studies of the encounters between the newcomers and the country they settle in, namely, the glocalizing impact of (im)migrants on the host society. The traditional foci of research in this field, the modes of adaptation of immigrants into the receiver societies, and the patterns of the accompanying transformation of their home-country identifications, cultural practices, and social and civic commitments, can also be conceptualized in terms of glocalization-as-hybridization (or polymorphization) processes.

My underlying hope, again, is that this brief analysis could serve as an invitation to launch a new direction of research in the field of (im)migration studies. It could, of course, move in different empirical directions conceptualized in different theoretical frameworks. Conceptualized within the fashion proposed here, the most immediate task for empirical research should be, as I see it, to identify the patterns in the contexts – or the constellations of macro-, mezzo-, and local-level circumstances – that contribute to the specific outcomes (composition, endurance) of the transformation. Particularly promising for probing different mechanisms and forms of the relationship between glocalization and (im)immigrants' activities are comparative studies across time and/or space of the same groups in different locations or different groups residing in the same city or country.

Notes

1. In the meantime, mainstream social scientists take up the issues central to (im)migration research and, based on skewed and truncated readings of the literature in this field, construct theories of immigrants' assimilation, transnationalism, and generally, multicultural society. A good example of this development is a recent book by Jeffrey Alexander, *The Civil Sphere* (2006; for a critical review pointing to the author's lack of familiarity with (im)migration/ethnic studies, see Kivisto, 2007).
2. See Morawska (2003b, 2011) on contemporary immigrants; Morawska (1993, 1996) on turn-of-the-last-century arrivals; and Morawska (2001, 2005, 2013) on a comparison of these two waves.
3. The session of the Research Committee on International Migration held at the meetings of the International Sociological Association in Yokohama, July 2014, organized by myself and devoted to new avenues of immigrants' integration into the host society generated by the spread of cosmopolitan and multi-glocal interests and identities, may signal an emerging trend in scholarly reflection in this field of study.
4. Although it lies beyond the scope of this chapter, it is interesting to note that, while their transformative impact on the receiver American society was non-existent or minimal, turn-of-the-last-century South and East European immigrants exerted a considerable influence, noted by historians, on their home-country local cultures and, especially, on the rise of the modern national consciousness which began to replace local, village-scope identities, and on the formation of labour unions and agricultural cooperatives (see Greene, 1975; Nelli, 1979; Morawska, 2001).
5. It was only in the third+ generation of the descendants of turn-of-the-20th-century immigrants that the absorption of their ethnic cultures into the mainstream society became visible, such as, for example, the incorporation of Yiddish words into New York English, or of Italian food into mainstream American supermarkets in the form of all-American pizzas and Italian-American tortellini.

6. A successful state-wide action in 1994 for the passage of the Proposition 187 to add a constitutional amendment denying all but emergency aid to illegal immigrants and placing an obligation on public employers to report the suspects has been the most prominent instance of these activities, but more numerous have been local- (state-)level initiatives aiming at curbing immigration.
7. It has been, we should add, political power of a distinctly exclusionary bent, reluctant to accommodate other resident groups' aspirations for a share, which, combined with the Cuban establishment's conservative persuasion, has understandably aggravated the city's ethnic minorities, primarily African Americans. The enduring discontent among Miami's blacks caused by the pervasive barriers to competition and advancement opportunities for racial/ethnic outsiders posed by Cuban dominance is yet another instance of a transformative impact of immigrants on the quality of native-born, here, minority, Americans' everyday lives.

References

Abrams, Philip. (1982) *Historical Sociology,* Shepton Mallet: Open Books.

Alexander, Jeffrey. (2006) *The Civil Sphere,* New York: Oxford University Press.

Appadurai, Arjun. (1996) *Modernity at Large: Cultural Dimensions of Globalization,* Minneapolis, MN: University of Minnesota Press.

Archibugi, Daniele. (2008) *The Global Commonwealth of Citizens: Toward Cosmopolitan Democracy,* Princeton: Princeton University Press.

Becker, Fred and Milan Dluhy. (1998) "Fragmentation and the Erosion of Municipal Planning in Miami", *Research in Urban Policy,* 7: 101–120.

Bell, Daniel. (1953) "Crime as an American Way of Life", *The Antioch Review,* 12 (summer): 131–54.

Bowie, Stan and Alex Stepick. (1998) "Diversity and Division: Ethnicity and the History of Miami", *Research in Urban Policy,* 7: 19–32.

Bozorgmehr, Mehdi, George Sabagh and Ivan Light. (1996) "Los Angeles: Explosive Diversity", in Silvia Pedraza and Ruben Rumbaut (eds.) *Origins and Destinies: Immigration, Race, and Ethnicity in America,* Belmont, CA: Wadsworth, pp. 346–359.

Breckenridge, Carol. (ed.) (2002) *Cosmopolitanism,* Durham, NC: Duke University Press.

Chang, Edward and Russell Leong. (eds.) (1994) *Los Angeles: Struggles Toward Multiethnic Community,* Seattle: University of Washington Press.

DeSipio, Louis. (1998) "Building a New Foreign Policy among Friends: National Efforts to Construct Long-term Relationships with Latin American Émigrés in the United States", Unpublished paper.

Dirlik, Arif. (1996) "Asians on the Rim: Transnational Capital and Local Community in the Making of Contemporary Asian America", *Amerasia Journal,* 22: 1–24.

Eckstein, Susan. (2009) *The Immigrant Divide. How Cuban Americans Changed the US and Their Homeland,* New York: Routledge.

Ehrenreich, Barbara and Arlie Russell Hochschild. (2003) *Global Woman: Nannies, Maids, and Sex Workers in the New Economy,* New York: Metropolitan Books.

Fine, Robert. (2007) *Cosmopolitanism,* London: Rutledge.

Fitzgerald, David. (2004) "Beyond 'transnationalism': Mexican Hometown Politics at an American Labour Union", *Ethnic and Racial Studies,* 27 (2): 228–247.

Foner, Nancy. (ed.) (2001) *Islands in The City. West Indian Migration To New York,* Berkeley: University of California Press.

Foner, Nancy and George Fredrickson. (eds.) (2004) *Not Just Black and White. Historical and Contemporary Perspectives on Immigration, Race, and Ethnicity in the United States,* New York: Russell Sage Foundation.

Garcia-Zamor, Jean-Claude. (1998) "Social Service Delivery for Immigrants in Southeast Florida", *Research in Urban Policy,* 7: 185–200.

Giulianotti, Richard and Roland Robertson. (2004) "The Globalization of Football: A Study in the Glocalization of the 'Serious Life,'" *British Journal of Sociology,* 55 (4): 545–568.

Giulianotti, Richard and Roland Robertson. (2007) "Forms of Glocalization: Globalization and the Migration Strategies of Scottish Football Fans in North America", *Sociology,* 41 (1): 133–152.

Gordon, Milton. (1964) *Assimilation in American Life,* New York: Oxford University Press.

Greene, Victor. (1975) *For God and Country: The Rise of Polish and Lithuanian Ethnic Consciousness in America, 1860–1910,* Madison: State Historical Society of Wisconsin.

Grenier, Guillermo and Lisandro Perez. (2003) *The Legacy of Exile: Cubans in the United States,* Boston: Allyn and Bacon.

Grenier, Guillermo and Max Castro. (1998) "The Emergence of an Adversarial Relation: Black-Cuban Relations in Miami, 1959–1998", *Research in Urban Policy,* 7: 33–56.

Guglielmo, Jennifer and Salvatore Salerono. (eds.) (2003) *Are Italians White? How Race is Made in America,* New York: Routledge.

Gutierrez, Ramon and Patricia Zavella. (eds.) (2009) *Mexicans in California: Transformations and Challenges,* Urbana, ILL.: University of Illinois Press.

Gutterl, Matthew Pratt. (2000) *The Color of Race in America, 1900–1940,* Cambridge, MA: Harvard University Press.

Hall, John R. (1999) *Cultures of Inquiry. From Epistemology to Discourse in Sociohistorical Research,* New York: Cambridge University Press.

Hamilton, Gary. (ed.) (1999) *Cosmopolitan Capitalists: Hong Kong and the Chinese Diaspora at the End of the Twentieth Century,* Seattle: University of Washington Press.

Hanson, Cictor Davis. (2003) *Mexifornia: A State of Becoming,* San Francisco: Encounter Books.

Higham, John. (1972) *Strangers in the Land. Patterns of American Nativism, 1860–1925,* New York: Atheneum.

Holdaway, Jennifer. (2007) "China: Outside the People's Republic of China", in Mary Waters and Reed Ueda (eds.) *The New Americans: A Guide to Immigration since 1965,* Cambridge, MA: Harvard University Press, pp. 355–370.

Hondagneu-Sotelo, Pierette. (ed.) (1997) *Gendered Transitions: Mexican Experiences of Immigration,* Berkeley: University of California Press.

Hondagneu-Sotelo, Pierette. (ed.) (2003) *Gender and U.S. Immigration: Contemporary Trends.* Berkeley, CA: University of California Press.

Hu-Dehart, Evelyn. (ed.) (1999) *Across the Pacific. Asian Americans and Globalization,* Philadelphia: Temple University Press.

Iceland, John, Daniel Weinberg and Erika Steinmetz. (2002) "Racial and Ethnic Segregation in The United States: 1980–2000.", Paper presented at the annual meeting of the Population Association of America, Atlanta, Georgia, 9–11 May.

Jacobson, Matthew Frye. (1998) *Whiteness of a Different Color. European Immigrants and the Alchemy of Race,* Cambridge, MA: Harvard University Press.

Jameson, Fredric. (1991) *Postmodernism or The Cultural Logic of Late Capitalism,* London: Verso.

Johnson, James, Walter Farrell and Chandra Guinn. (1997) "Immigration Reform and the Browning of America: Tensions, Conflicts, and Community Instability in Metropolitan Los Angeles", *International Migration Review,* 31 (4): 1055–1095.

Jones-Correa, Michael. (1998) *Between Two Nations: The Political Predicament of Latinos in New York City,* Ithaca, NY: Cornell University Press.

Kivisto, Peter. (2007) "Comment on Jeffrey C. Alexander, *The Civil Sphere", Perspectives. Newsletter of the ASA Theory Section,* 30 (1): 5–7.

Kluckhohn, Florence Rockwood. (1950) "Dominant and Substitute Profiles of Cultural Orientations: Their Significance for the Analysis of Social Stratification", *Social Forces* 28 (2): 376–393.

Koehn, Peter and Xiao-huang Yin. (eds.) (2002) *The Expanding Roles of Chinese Americans in U.S.-China Relations: Transnational Networks and Trans-Pacific Interactions,* New York: M.E. Sharpe.

Kraut, Alan. (1994) *Silent Travellers: Germs, Genes, and the "Immigrant Menace",* New York: Basic Books.

Logan, John and Richard Alba. (1999) "Minority Niches and Immigrant Enclaves in New York and Los Angeles: Trends and Impacts", in Frank Bean and Stephanie Bell-Rose (eds.) *Immigration and Opportunity. Race, Ethnicity, and Employment in the United States,* New York: Russell Sage Foundation, pp. 172–193.

Ma, Lawrence and Carolyn Cartier (eds.) (2003) *The Chinese Diaspora: Space, Place, Mobility, and Identity,* New York: Rowman and Littlefield.

Massey, Douglas. (ed.) (2008) *New Faces in New Places: The Changing Geography of American Immigration,* New York: Russell Sage Foundation.

Min, Pyong Gap. (2008) *Ethnic Solidarity for Economic Survival,* New York: Russell Sage Foundation.

Mohl, Raymond. (1989) "On the Edge: Blacks and Hispanics in Metropolitan Miami since 1959", *Florida Historical Quarterly,* July: 37–56.

Mollenkopf, John. (1999) "Urban Political Conflicts and Alliances: New York and Los Angeles Compared", in Charles Hirschman, Philip Kasinitz and Josh De Wind (eds.) *The Handbook of International Migration.* New York: Russell Sage Foundation, pp. 412–422.

Mollenkopf, John, David Olson and Timothy Ross. (2002) "Immigrant Political Participation in New York and Los Angeles", in Michael Jones-Correa (ed.) *Governing American Cities: Interethnic Coalitions, Competitions, and Conflict,* New York: Russell Sage Foundation, pp. 17–70.

Morawska, Ewa. (2013) "Structuring Immigrants' Civic-Political Incorporation Into the Host Society", in Jennifer Hochschild et al. (eds.) *Outsiders No More? Models if Immigrant Political Incorporation,* New York: Oxford University Press, pp. 137–161.

Morawska, Ewa. (1993) "From Myth To Reality: America in the Eyes of East European Peasant Migrant Laborers", in Dirk Hoerder and Horst Rossler (eds.) *Distant Magnets: Expectations and Realities in the Immigrant Experience, 1840–1930,* Holmes & Meier, pp. 241–263.

Morawska, Ewa. (1994) "In Defense of the Assimilation Model", *Journal of American Ethnic History*, Winter 1994: 76–87.

Morawska, Ewa. (1996) "The Immigrants Pictured and Unpictured in the Pittsburgh Survey", chapter in Maureen Greenwald (ed.) *The Pittsburgh Survey Revisited,* Pittsburgh: University of Pittsburgh Press, pp. 221–241.

Morawska, Ewa. (2001) "Immigrants, Transnationalism, and Ethnicization: A Comparison of this Great Wave and the Last", in Gary Gerstle and John Mollenkopf (eds.) *E Pluribus Unum? Contemporary and Historical Perspectives on Immigrant Political Incorporation,* New York: Russell Sage Foundation, pp. 175–212.

Morawska, Ewa. (2003b) "Immigrant Transnationalism and Assimilation: A Variety of Combinations and a Theoretical Model They Suggest", in Christian Joppke and Ewa Morawska (eds.) *Integrating Immigrants in Liberal States,* Basingstoke: Palgrave Macmillan, pp. 133–177.

Morawska, Ewa. (2003a) "National Identities of Polish (Im)Migrants in Berlin, Germany: Four Varieties, Their Correlates, and Implications", in Willfried Spohn and Anna Triandafyllidou (eds.) *Europeanisation, National Identities and Migration: Changes in Boundary Constructions Between Western and Eastern Europe*. London: Routledge, pp. 173–192.

Morawska, Ewa. (2004) "Exploring Diversity in Immigrant Assimilation and Transnationalism: The Case of Poles and Russian Jews in Philadelphia", *International Migration Review,* 38 (4): 232–264.

Morawska, Ewa. (2005) "Sociology and History of (Im)Migration: Reflections of a Practitioner", in Michael Bommes and Ewa Morawska (eds.) *International Migration Research: Constructions, Omissions, and Promises of Interdisciplinarity,* Aldershot: Ashgate Press, pp. 203–242.

Morawska, Ewa. (2011) *A Sociology of Immigration. (Re)Making Multifaceted America,* Basingstoke: Palgrave Macmillan.

Myles, John and Feng Hou. (2004) "Changing Colours: Spatial Assimilation and New Racial Minority Immigrants", *Canadian Journal of Sociology,* 29 (1): 29–50.

Nelli, Humbert. (1979) *Italians in Chicago,* New York: Oxford University Press.

ParreñasRhacel Salazar. (2008) *The Force of Domesticity. Filipina Migrants and Globalization.* New York: New York University Press.

Perez-Stable, Marifeli and Miren Uriarte (1997) "Cuban and the Changing Economy of Miami", in Darrell Hamamoto and Rodolpho Torres (eds.) *New American Destinies. A Reader in Contemporary Asian and Latino Immigration,* New York: Routledge, pp. 141–162.

Perlmann, Joel and Mary Waters. (2004) "Intermarriage Then and Now: Race, Generation, and the Changing Meaning of Marriage", in Nancy Foner and George Fredrickson (eds.) *Not Just Black and White: Historical and Contemporary Perspectives on Immigration,* New York: Russell Sage Foundation, pp. 262–277.

Perlmann, Joel and Mary Waters. (2007) "Intermarriage and Multiple Identities", in Mary Waters and Reed Ueda (eds.) *The New Americans. A Guide to Immigration Since 1965,* Cambridge, MA: Harvard University Press, pp. 110–123.

Peterson, Marina. (2007) "Chinese Modern Dance at Downtown Los Angeles Public Concerts", in Saskia Sassen (ed.) *Deciphering the Global. Its Scales, Spaces, and Subjects*, New York: Routledge, pp. 41–58.

Portes Alejandro and Alex Stepick. (1993) *City on the Edge. The Transformation of Miami*. Berkeley: University of California Press.

Portes, Alejandro and John DeWind. (eds.) (2008) *Rethinking Migration. New Theoretical and Empirical Perspectives*. New York: Berghahn Books.

Reitz, Jeffrey. (ed.) (2003) *Host Societies and the Reception of Immigrants,* La Jolla, CA: Center for Comparative Immigration Studies, University of California-San Diego.

Rieff, David. (2002) *Los Angeles Capital of the Third World,* New York: Simon & Schuster.

Robertson, Roland. (1994) *Globalization: Social Theory and Global Culture,* London: Sage.

Robertson, Roland and K.E. White. (2005) "Globalization: Sociology and Cross-Disciplinarity", in Craig Calhoun and Brian Turner (eds.) *The Sage Handbook of Sociology*, London: Sage, pp. 345–366.

Roediger, David. (1991) *The Wages of Whiteness: Race and the Making of American Working Class* London: Verso.

Sassen, Saskia. (ed.) (2007) *Deciphering the Global. Its Scales, Spaces, and Subjects,* New York: Routledge.

Saxenian, AnnaLee. (2006) *The New Argonauts. Regional Advantage in a Global Economy,* Cambridge, MA: Harvard University Press.

Saxenian, AnnaLee and Chuen-Yueh Li. (2003) "Bay-to-Bay Strategic Alliances: Network Linkages between Taiwan and U.S. Venture Capital Industries", *International Journal of Technology Management,* 25 (91 and 2), entire issues.

Skeldon, Ronald. (ed.) (1994) *Reluctant Exiles? Migration from Hong Kong and the New Overseas Chinese*, Armonk, NY: M.E. Sharpe.

Smith, Michael and Joe Feagin. (eds.) (1995) *The Bubbling Cauldron: Race, Ethnicity, ad the Urban Crisis,* Minneapolis: University of Minnesota Press.

Sonenshein, Raphael. (1996) *Politics in Black and White. Race and Power in Los Angeles,* Princeton: Princeton University Press.

US Census Bureau. (2006) *Current Population Survey,* Washington, DC: Government Printing Office.

Waldinger, Roger and Mehdi Bozorgmehr. (eds.) (1996) *Ethnic Los Angeles,* New York: Russell Sage Foundation.

Waters Mary and Reed Ueda. (eds.) (2007) *The New Americans*, Cambridge, MA: Harvard University Press.

Wong, Bernard. (1998) *Ethnicity and Entrepreneurship. The New Chinese Immigrants in the San Francisco Bay Area,* Boston: Allyn and Bacon.

Yin, Xiao-huang. (2007) "Outside the People's Republic of China", in Mary Waters and Reed Ueda. (eds.) *The New Americans. A Guide to Immigration Since 1965*, Cambridge, MA: Harvard University Press, pp. 340–354.

Zúñiga, Victor and Ruben Hernández-Leon (eds.) (2005) *New Destinations. Mexican Immigration in the United States*. New York: Russell Sage Foundation.

6

From *Football* to *Futebol*

A Glocal Perspective on the Influence of Europe on Brazilian Football (and Vice Versa)

Paolo Demuru

Introduction

Since the 1938 World Cup, the Brazilian style of football has increasingly become textualized and stereotyped (Leite Lopes, 2000). Journalistic, marketing, even historical (Soares, 2001) and anthropological discourses (cf. Barba, 2007) all contributed to naturalize Brazilian's performances on the football fields, either relating them to some assumed Afro-Brazilian's "innate" bodily skills or to other Afro-Brazilian bodily practices – such as samba or *capoeira*. This to the point that, nowadays, the Brazilian way of playing football is an explicit form of cultural life, which internationally reflects the global image of Brazil, especially in Europe.

Two of the many examples of this narrative construction can be quoted: the first an article by the Italian writer, poet, and film director Pier Paolo Pasolini; the second a book by the British journalist Alex Bellos. In January 1971 – seven months after Italy's defeat against Brazil in the Mexican final – Pasolini published an article about the difference between the Italian and Brazilian style of football in the Milanese newspaper *Il Giorno* (Pasolini, 2010). Pasolini argued that football is an authentic semiotic system, which frames and expresses culture as a whole – so that different cultures play football in different ways – and he concludes with the following literary equation: Brazilian football is to poetry what Italian football is to prose. Likewise, Bellos' book *Futebol: The Brazilian Way of Life* (Bellos, 2002), suggests – even from its title – how important football is in defining the totality (or the globality) of Brazilian culture.

However – and this is one of the central issues that I explore in this chapter – the naturalization of the style not only concerns the "European" construction of the Brazilian stereotype. It also – no less importantly – underlies the "self-description process" (Lotman and Uspenskij, 1973; Lotman, 1990, 1993) of the Brazilian culture itself, which involves the selection of distinctive traits of a cultural identity and their narrative consolidation. In Lotman's words: "self-description is a necessary response to the threat of too much diversity within the semiosphere (...) this is the stage when grammars are written, customs and laws codified" (Lotman, 1990: 128). Normally, this involves the structuring of a "local grammar" and its progressive extension to the whole cultural system. In other words, this is a dynamic process of glocalization, in which what is "local" becomes "global" (and vice versa), assuming the function of "the metalanguage of description for culture as such" (Lotman, 1990: 128). In the same way, the Florence dialect "became during the Renaissance the literary language of Italy (...) and the etiquettes of the Parisian court of Louis XIV became the etiquettes of all the courts of Europe" (Lotman, 1990: 128).

The examples provided by Lotman are not so far from the Brazilian case. After the 1938 World Cup especially, football became a privileged arena in which to discuss and negotiate the position – and the weight – of different ethnic characters within the global identity of Brazil. As Gilberto Freyre – one of the most important Brazilian sociologists and anthropologists of the 20th century – wrote in his *Brazil, an Interpretation*:

> I have suggested also a study of the characteristic Brazilian way of playing the very Anglo-Saxon game of association football, or soccer. The Brazilians play it as if it were a dance. This is probably the result of the influence of those Brazilians who have African blood, or who are predominately African in their culture, for such Brazilians tend to reduce everything to dance – work and play alike – and this tendency is apparently becoming more and more general in Brazil and is not solely the characteristic of an ethnic or regional group.
>
> (Freyre, 1945: 88–89)

But Freyre is not simply observing a widespread process of generalization: he is actually shaping it – and we will see how in the rest of this chapter. There is a word in Brazilian Portuguese that accurately summarizes the general tendency described (and shaped) by Freyre – and also the weight of football in "framing" Brazil: *ginga*. Originally indicating the basic *capoeira* move, the use of the term – first reshaped through the practice of samba and then through the football discourses – provides a linguistic example of how a local sphere inside the Afro-Brazilian culture has increasingly assumed a global role in the building of Brazilian national character.

Two definitions extracted from two important stores of common sense can be initially compared: the Houaiss dictionary of the Portuguese language and the international advertising campaign of the Brazilian beer Bhrama – *Bhrama brings ginga to our consumers* – sponsor of the Brazilian national football team.

According to the Houaiss dictionary of the Portuguese language, "ginga" means:

(i) the act or effect of "gingar"; the swinging of the body;
(ii) the movement with which the *capoeirista* tries to deceive and confuse his opponent, both for defence and attack;
(iii) in football, a series of body movements designed to deceive the opponent.

Similarly, the verb "gingar" – derived from the noun "ginga" – is defined as follows:

(i) while walking, bending from one side to the other (with the whole body or with a part of it); to rock;
(ii) swinging the hips; to sway;
(iii) to shake; to dangle;
(iv) in football, "make ginga".

As we can easily see, the Houaiss dictionary of Brazilian Portuguese suggests that *ginga* is a body movement centred over the hips and pelvis, performed in *capoeira*, football, and also in daily walking. It is the expression of some sort of bodily intelligence or cunning.

Likewise, the international advertising campaign *Bhrama brings ginga to our consumers* stresses and reaffirms this sensory motor know-how. Even here, *ginga* represents "the way in which Brazilians walk, move; the way in which they play football".[1] This campaign does not seem to say anything new. Yet, on a closer look, it reveals an additional element: "the way in which *Brazilians* walk and move". Thus, *ginga* is not characterized here as a simple body movement, but as a collective attribute, as the style of a people. Indeed, the ad goes on:

> Brhama was created by Joseph Villager in 1888. Ever since it has flowed through Brazil, adding to the energy, passion and creative spirit called "Ginga". A Brazilian philosophy and approach to life fusing creativity and ingenuity and living life with effortless flare.[2]

The term gains here a value that goes beyond the kinesic meaning of the gesture. Rather, *ginga* – far from simply being a way of walking or playing football – becomes a real way of being: a national "way of life", as Bellos wrote.

Some questions have now to be addressed: What is the missing link between the Houaiss dictionary of Brazilian Portuguese and Bhrama's campaign? How has *ginga* moved from *capoeira* to samba, from samba to football, and from football to life? How and why has an element – once restricted only to the memory of the Afro-Brazilian culture – now become a global symbol – or, in Lotman's words, a "stereotyping device" (Lotman and Uspenskij, 1973) – of the entire Brazilian nation? And – last but not least – what is exactly the role of football in this process?

In an attempt to answer these questions, I aim to present in this chapter a glocal perspective of the history of Brazilian football and its relations with Europe through the articulation of a socio-cultural approach to glocalization (Robertson, 1992, 2003; Robertson and Giulianotti, 2007, 2009) and a cultural semiotics inspired by Lotman's work. If glocalization is intrinsically relational – since it involves the constitutive interdependency of the global and the local, between homogenizing and heterogenizing tendencies (Robertson and Giulianotti, 2007) – cultural semiotics – understood both as "the study of the correlation between systems and processes of meaning and of the systems and processes of correlation" (Sedda, 2006: 38) – may provide a theoretical and methodological framework within which to explore its complexity. While the first "registers the real world endeavours of individuals and social groups to ground or to recontextualize global phenomena or macroscopic processes with respect to local cultures" (Robertson and Giulianotti, 2009: 46), the second employs the tools of textual and discursive analysis (Greimas and Courtés, 1979; Greimas, 1983), both to reconstruct the dynamic evolution of the historical configurations of meaning and to explain how local and global cultural formations emerge and sedimentize in time and space (Lotman, 1990, 2006).

More specifically, I will track and identify here the global–local relationship that underlies the dynamic of formation and discoursivization of the Brazilian style of football. As we shall see, European culture and football played a crucial role in this process. Principally through the analysis of different texts (football guides and rules, journalistic articles, sociological essays) and practices (football and sociocultural habits), I will seek to describe how this has been the result of the interplay among different *glocal* layers: (i) the rise and the fall of amateur football, played by the elites of São Paulo and Rio de Janeiro and marked by the assumption of European trends and habits; (ii) a local interpretation and application of the European rules of the game, particularly the *charge rule*, which was strictly interpreted as a foul (favouring the development of a less physical way of playing); (iii) the reconfiguration of the social and ethnic tension – that pervaded Brazil after the abolition of slavery – inside (and then outside) the football fields; (iv) the discursive *globalization* – via football – of Afro-Brazilian characters (such as *ginga*) in the entire Brazilian culture.

Once described, I will be able to advance some theoretical conclusion on the semiotic specificity of this process of glocalization, discussing its temporal and spatial dimensions.

From Europe to Brazil: Brazilian football in the early 20th century

We want to be Europeans: the game of social distinction

At least until 1938, Brazilian football fields represented the ground of a great sociocultural conflict (Murad, 2007). Developed in the last decade of the 19th century within the elites of São Paulo and Rio de Janeiro, football quickly became a sign of social distinction. It became a sport for young men of European descent, often sporting long moustaches and fashionable clothes – like Charles Miller and Oscar Cox (Neto, 2002). In 1906, the uniforms of Botafogo were still imported from England, while Fluminense – for purely aesthetic reasons – played with a thin red belt tied at the waist, the ends of which dangled down (Pereira, 2000). *O malho* – a popular carioca magazine of the period – defined this football fever as follows:

> This kind of sport has attracted the cream of Brazilian youth, who considers it as one of the best entertainments and healthiest exercises. Football teams continue to grow in Bahia, São Paulo, Rio de Janeiro and wherever in Brazil. Each game that takes place is an animated party, frequented by the finest society.
>
> (*O malho*, 13 October 1906)

Games frequently ended with imported cigars and with whisky tasting and it was absolutely forbidden to offend or ridicule the players of the opposing team (Toledo, 2002; Franzini, 2003). The footballers took tea at five o'clock, shaved at the Rio's "Salão Naval" (Naval Salon), dined at the "French Rotisserie" (Silvares, 1915). Playing football was a practice within a universe of practices, in which the values of the European aristocracy were translated and reproduced (Leite Lopes, 2000).

The first manuals of football published in Brazil properly reflect the peculiarities of this process. The 1903 *Guia de Football* (*Football Guide*), by the journalist Mario Cardim, translated, for the first time, the rules of the International Football Association Board (IFAB). The *Guia* contained a small section entitled "The physical and moral qualities of football players", which, aside from describing the main tricks of the game, listed a series of attitudes to assume when on and off the football fields. An elitist image of football was also widespread in advertising and journalism, which portrayed the consumption of imported luxury goods – like cigars, wine, and whisky – as closely connected to this sport (see Cardim, 1906).

We can thus observe the first degree of glocalization of Brazilian football through the flow of European habits, trends, and ways of life – which slowly pervaded every other aspect of Brazilian social life, characterizing Rio de Janeiro and São Paulo as cosmopolitan (cf. Sevcenko, 1998).

From a semiotic point of view, this tendency happened through a continuous interplay between texts and practices. Several – old and recent – semiotics studies have shown how texts act as "modeling systems" (Lotman and Uspenskij, 1973), meaning-generating devices which impose models of behaviour and configure actions and passions (Sedda, 2006; Pezzini, 2007). For instance, analysing Decabrist behaviours in 9th-century Russia, Lotman observed how young officers imitated – in their daily life – the gestures and deeds of Byron's, Pushkin's, and Lermontov's characters, thus reading these texts as manuals for practical behaviour (Lotman, 2006: 208–209). Likewise – analogously to the etiquette guides analysed by Elias in his *The Civilizing Process* (1969) – Brazilian football manuals were no simple user manuals. Rather, they offered a model for behaviour – and at the same time, a model for the world – to the players of the early 20th century, contributing to the formation of an amateur ethos, or, rather, to the sedimentation of a specific form of life: the *sportsman's* form of life. Football players were indeed called *sportsmen,* men of good principles, good manners, and good habits. The use of this English expression – and, generally, the use of the English language in early Brazilian football discourse – is an example of the – locally grounded – "thick cosmopolitanism" (Robertson and Giulianotti, 2007, 2009) which spread in those years through the Brazilian metropolis.

We want to stay Europeans: the spread and the whitening of Brazilian football

In any case, the elitist image does not provide a complete map of early 20th-century Brazilian football. Indeed, the new sport was also very successful in factories and suburbs. The *lei áurea* (golden law) had just abolished slavery on 13 May 1888. The country was facing great migrations. Hundreds and thousands families of ex-slaves flowed to São Paulo and Rio de Janeiro searching for jobs and for better conditions, settling in the hills close to city centres and other places of difficult access. The first *favelas* appeared in Rio at that time and some teams, such as the Bangu – the team of the textile factory called Companhia Progresso Industrial, located in the north district of Rio – began to employ their workers and labourers, a major portion of whom were blacks and mulattos, in official matches.

As is easy to imagine, the increasingly popularization of football was frowned upon by the old promoters of this Anglo-Saxon sport. Taking a look at the magazines of the period, it is possible to outline the socio-cultural tensions provoked by the rapid spread of the sport. In 1915, Alberto Silvares – vice-director of the Rio Metropolitan League – wrote in his magazine, called *Sports*:

> We think – together with those who consider sincerity as a religion: football is a sport that can be practiced only by people of the same education and culture. People like us – who attend the academy, have a position in society, shave at the Rio Salão Naval, have dinner at the Rotisserie, attend literary conferences, go to five o'clock. Though, when we decide to practice sport and enter the Icarahy Club's field – distinguished team from the third metropolitan division – we are forced to play with workers, filers, postmen, mechanics, chauffeurs – and who knows what other professions – people who have nothing to do with the entourage in which we live. In that case, the sport becomes a torture, a sacrifice, and never a fun.
>
> (Antonio Silvares, alias Joffre, *Sports*, 6 August 1915)

To safeguard the amateur spirit, the sportsmen of the elites began to ban from the league illiterate players and labourers and to demand exorbitant registration fees. Furthermore, in 1907 the statute of the Liga Metropolitana de Football forbade "colored people" from playing (see Pereira, 2000: 66). Faced with this prohibition, the teams who included blacks and mulattos founded, in the same year, a suburb league (Liga Suburbana de Football), starting a new competition and thus increasing the tensions.

Throughout, the ethnic question remained, at least until the late thirties, the real issue in Brazilian football. Due to space constraints, I cannot give here an exhaustive description of this phenomenon (other studies persuasively showed its evolution: Pereira, 2000; Franzini, 2003; Murad 2007). Yet it is worth focusing on one historical event which summarizes both its premises and consequences well: the fifth South America League that took place in Buenos Aires in 1921.

On that occasion, members of the Liga Suburbana claimed that the Confederação Brasileira de Desportos (the governing body of football in Brazil) did not want to include in the Brazilian national team "colored players", such as Luis Antonio da Guia (Pereira, 2000: 177), who played for Bangu. Moreover, the carioca newspaper *Correio da Manhã* wrote that the president of the Brazilian Republic, Epitácio Pessoa himself, had requested that "players who were not rigorously white" not be sent to Buenos Aires (Pereira, 2000: 176). In spite of the objections, the appeal was accepted and the national team playing in Argentina was exclusively white.

This example both outlines the role of the international sporting events in defining national identities – particularly during the take-off phase of globalization (Robertson, 1992) – and helps us to understand how glocalization is enacted through these events. Indeed – paraphrasing Appadurai (1996) – the 1921 Brazilian national team is the (glocal) result of the interactions between a local *ethno-ideoscape* and a global *sportscape*. As Robertson and Giulianotti (2009: 32) wrote, "major international tournaments provide lively cultural arena for the (re)production and interplay of national-societal particularities". This is exactly what happened in our case: a *global event* – such as the South America League – forced Brazil to deal with its cultural diversity and produce a *global image* of the nation. In this international arena – even before the other participating nations had taken a stance – Brazil chose to describe itself as white. That is: the national team worked as a meta-model (Lotman, 1985, 1990) of the self-description, that *translated* and *globalized* only a portion of the cultural universe, while leaving out others – such any Afro-Brazilian element. Now, if we relate this event to the ethnic and ideological flows that pervaded

Brazil since the beginning of the 20th century we could probably understand why blacks and mulattos were excluded from the team. It is not a coincidence, indeed, that Brazil – searching for a new national identity after the failure of the indigenous models (Schwarcz, 1993) – witnessed the emergence of whitening theories. According to these theories – as João Baptista de Lacerda said at the first Congress on Race,[3] which took place in London on July 1911 – Brazil would have become white in, at most, a century (Schwarcz, 1993: 11). Thus, football was, at one and the same time, a local expression of and a catalyst for the social and ethnic tensions that globally affected Brazil.

The glocal formation of the Brazilian style of football: between Europe and Brazil

The translation of ethnic and social tensions onto the football field

To really understand the glocal essence of the history of Brazilian football it is important to highlight the consequences of these ethnic and cultural tensions on the style of play. In this regard, two further issues have to be addressed: the Brazilian application of the rule number nine of the IFAB (that covered fouls and misconducts) and the violence suffered by blacks and mulattos during the games.

First, it was precisely through rule number nine of the IFAB – particularly, through the *charge rule* – that the pattern of social distance and distinction was reflected in and practised on the football field. Unlike other nations, in which the rule went almost unnoticed, Brazil made it into an authentic "private matter" that played a crucial role in the development of the game. Let's take a look at the definition given by Mario Cardim: "a charge é permitida mas não de modo violento ou perigoso" (Cardim, 1906: 40). Cardim's version is practically identical to the IFAB's one, which says: "charging is permissible but it must be not violent or dangerous".[4] Apparently, a transparent sentence. Yet its consequences were anything but obvious. The dilemma – that is still an unsettling actuality – is in defining what exactly "violent" and "dangerous" mean: a semiotic problem of interpretation, or rather, of negotiation of meaning. In other words, while we can easily agree with the fact that the shoulder charge must be not violent or dangerous, it is not so simple to perfectly agree on what is really "violent" or "dangerous" and on what is not. On the contrary, it is an "agonistic" practice – even more so in its incarnation on a football field. Thus, if the term is intrinsically vague, what counts are power relations. Put differently: if the "what" and the "how" were unknown, it was certainly easier to define the "who": blacks, mulattos, mestizos, workers, labourers, illiterates were violent and dangerous. Such a stigmatization originated from and took root through journalist discourse. Since the second decade of the 20th century it has been quite common to find negative descriptions of such listed football players in the most influent sport magazines of Rio de Janeiro. As I said in *We want to stay Europeans: The spread and the whitening of Brazilian football* football underwent, in those years, a rapid process of diffusion. It was played in suburbs and also in the streets of some central districts, like Catete (Pereira, 2000: 132). Criticizing this widespread popularization and denouncing the loss of the noble spirit of the game, magazines and newspapers frequently related football to marginality. In order to bring out the presumed violence of the suburban football players, they often used expressions and words – such as *malta* – which were usually used to indicate groups of *capoeiras* (people who practised *capoeira*). Thus, suburban football was highlighted as an illegal black practice – *capoeira* would remain illegal until 1937 – a practice that induced "violence" and "chaos" all over the city (Pereira, 2000: 132–133). Umberto Eco wrote in *Semiotics and the Philosophy of Language:* "the power consists in possessing the key of the right interpretation or (which is the same) in being acknowledged by the community as the one who possess the key" (Eco, 1984: 152).

Second – as a result both of the interpretation of the charge rule and of the marginality discourse outside – it was not uncommon for blacks and mulattos to suffer violence during the games. I quote here two statements which summarize this topic:

> I thought about advancing, pushing the ball and helping *Prego* (...). Maybe we could even drew the game (...). Then I remembered that I was the only black in the team. And if we suffered a goal without my defensive help.... They didn't beat anymore, but the guilt was all over me.
>
> (Fausto dos Santos, *A noite*, 28 July 1930)

> When I was still a kid I was scared to play football, because I often saw black players, there in Bangu, get whacked on the pitch, just because they made a foul, or sometimes for something less than that... my elder brother used to tell me: "the cat always falls on his feet... aren't you good at dancing?" I was and this helped my football... I swung

my hips a lot . . . that short dribble I invented imitating the *miudinho*, that type of samba.

(Domingos da Guia, video interview, Nucleo de Sociologia do Futebol/UERJ)

There is no ambiguity in these declarations: blacks or mulattos who were guilty of a foul suffered punishments that went far beyond the yellow and red cards: they were simply "whacked on the pitch" – sometimes even by the police.

I can now make a hypothesis about the background of the Brazilian style of football, openly discussing the presumed naturalness of the *ginga*. Along the lines proposed by Toledo (2002), I argue here that the most plausible perspective on its formation involves a *glocal standpoint* on the interplay between the Brazilian interpretation of the rules of the IFAB and the translation of the sociocultural tensions into the football field.

Summing up, I have a frame composed by the following layers: (i) a set of moral norms and etiquettes that prohibited or advised against the cohabitation between people of different social extraction and different "colour"; (ii) a "global" rule which – to comply the "local" hierarchies – is, as it were, strictly interpreted; and (iii) physical assaults against suspected subversions of the order of the game – a game which is also a scale model of the social order. In other words, the social distance was translated into the field as a rejection of physical contact. Hence, it does not seem risky to assume that the taste for dribbling – which developed within this system of norms and restrictions – became entrenched because of the need to avoid hard physical contact (to not commit fouls and then not suffer the consequences), and not from some presumed inborn Afro-Brazilian physical skill.[5]

Such a stigmatization perpetuated over time, to the point of creating problems in international competitions. Ademir Pimenta, Brazilian coach in 1938 – Domingos da Guia's and Leônidas da Silva's team – considered the lack of the physical elements of the game, in particular the shoulder charge, as one of the main problems with the Seleção (the Brazilian national team) when matched with European teams, who were used to playing much more violently (Toledo, 2002). This seems to us a wonderful example of how social practice and meanings – even the most normative ones – are always *locally* situated, defined, and redefined. Moreover, we can notice that this process of translation involves a constant interplay between homogenizing and heterogenizing tendencies

(Lotman, 1985, 1990; Robertson and White, 2003; Giulianotti and Robertson, 2007, 2009). As the history of football demonstrates, the homogenization of the rules coincides with a heterogenization of the styles of play (Robertson and Giulianotti, 2009).

We have never been Europeans: discourses on Brazilian and European identities

We have seen how the formation of the Brazilian style of football must be framed within the glocal interplay between the national ethno-ideoscape and the European sportscape – particularly marked by the local interpretations of the IFAB's rules. However, from a cultural semiotic standpoint this process cannot be separated from the *stories* told about it. This is not about deconstructing a discursive formation. Rather, it is about highlighting the constitutive interdependence between *experience* and *narration* (Ricoeur, 1983), between *world* and *models of the world*. In other words, the Brazilian style – real or not, it doesn't matter – would not have existed independently of its narrative models (Lotman and Uspenskij, 1973). For reason of space, I cannot thoroughly sketch out the complex and dynamic evolution of the process of discursive sedimentation of the Brazilian style of football. It is, though, worthwhile to briefly highlight some key issues.

Probably the first euphoric description of the Brazilian style was given by the journalist of the *Estado de São Paulo*, Américo Netto, in 1919. Against those that were in favour of the "English way" (Cardim, 1906; Figueredo, 1918; Sant'Anna, 1918), he defended the peculiarity of the individualistic play – "so typical of our nature and of our sporting formation" (Netto, 1919: 7–8).

However – as mentioned in the introduction to this chapter – the most influent discourse about the national character of football is certainly Gilberto Freyre's one. In 1938, during the world championships in France, the Brazilian sociologist published an article in the *Diario de Pernambuco* entitled "Football Mulato", turning on its head the dysphoric relation between football and *capoeira* credited by the carioca magazines of the previous decade. If it is true that identity is defined only through its interdependences (Clifford, 2001), a world competition is obviously the best chance to reflect on what is *properly* Brazilian. As Freyre wrote:

> One of the premises of our triumphs seems to be the absolute courage – that we finally had – to send in Europe a strongly Afro-Brazilian team (...). Our mulatto football (...) is an expression of

> our social formation, such a democratic and rebel against the excess of internal and external orders, against the excesses of standardization (...) against totalitarianism that make disappear the individual variation or the personal spontaneity (...). Our style of playing football contrasts with the Europeans because of a combination of qualities of surprise, malice, astuteness and agility, and at the same time brilliance and individual spontaneity (...). Our passes (...) our dummies, our flourishes with the ball, the touch of dance and subversiveness that marks the Brazilian style (...) seem to show psychologists and sociologists in a very interesting way the roguery and flamboyance of the mulatto that today is in every true affirmation of what is Brazilian (...). The Brazilian mulatto de-europized football by giving it round curves and dancing graces. It is possible to feel in that contrast the shock between the European albinism and the Brazilian mulattism (...) psychologically, being Brazilian means to be mulattos.
>
> (Freyre, 1938)

Freyre's article is a real "mythology" of the Brazilian way of playing football. Through a lyrical and visionary prose, the author draws a network of relations and oppositions through which he defines Brazilian and European ways of being and feeling in the world: Dionysian versus Apollonian, sweet versus angular, spontaneous versus artificial, democratic versus authoritarian. A dissolution of adjectives, a cobweb of opposites in which he traps the discourse on identity. First, Freyre praises the decision to send to Europe a strongly Afro-Brazilian national team. Second, he compares the Brazilian style of football to the political style of Nilo Peçanha – a mulatto of humble origins who became president of the republic and foreign minister. Then, from politics he goes on to the dance, weaving parallels between the Afro-Brazilian players' dribbling and the graceful movement of the dancers. At this stage, the reader will have noticed that, in just a few lines, Freyre has already put forward three distinct cultural spheres: football, politics, and dance. And there is more: colours, mulattism as a defining psychological condition: "psychologically, being Brazilian means to be mulattos". Vice versa, being European means to be albino. Here is defined – in two pages – the ethos and the deep structure of what is Brazilian and what is European.

From Gilberto Freyre onwards, the discourses on football assumed a central role in constructing modern Brazilian identity, "through mass media, education, language and popular culture" (Giulianotti and Robertson, 2009: 36). Historical-journalistic works – like the Mário

Rodrigues Filho's book *O negro no futebol brasileiro* (*The Black in Brazilian Football*, 1947) – anthropological studies (DaMatta, 1994), romances, and novels (Rodrigues, 1993, 1994) all contributed to shape Brazilian football as a national form of life. More precisely, Afro-Brazilian football narratives support and increase the fall of the whitening and racial theories and the global rise of the positive miscegenation as the new meta-model of the nation (Schwarcz, 1993),[6] a concept which was also endorsed by the populist ideology of Vargas' government in 1938 and by the military dictatorship with the Brazilian victory in the 1970 Mexico World Cup. As Freyre's article perfectly summarizes, this process coincides with the "resignification" of some Afro-Brazilian characters – such as *capoeira* and *malandragem* (the artful rogue way of life) – through the narratives about the style and its progressive "globalization" into the semiosphere of Brazilian culture (DaMatta, 1979; Schwarcz, 1995). Thus, we came back to *ginga*: a *capoeira* move, a way of playing, walking, and, finally, a form of life. To become an imperishable form is always a matter of good expression.

Conclusions

Applying a cultural semiotic approach to the history of Brazilian football and its relationship with Europe, we can thus sketch some general conclusions about glocalization.

As Robertson and Giulianotti (2007: 60) argued, glocalization registers the simultaneous "co-presence of sameness and difference, and the intensified interpenetration of the local and the global, the universal and particular, and homogeneity and heterogeneity". In line with this model, Lotman's theory of culture highlights the constitutively tension between: (i) "structural heterogeneity" – the continuous reformulation of its internal structures – and (ii) "meta structural self-descriptions" – the creation of *hubs* structuring the connections between its *nodes*, through specific modelling discourses and parameter text (Lotman, 1985: 66) – as we saw in the previous paragraph.

In the light of the analysis of the history of Brazilian football, it seems possible to add that this strong interdependence is reproduced and translated at the same time on multiple levels and on different spatial and temporal scales. Indeed, my case study provides some basic illustrations of this progressive dynamic of integration and superimpositions between global and local movements. Here, it is possible to highlight:

(i) a range of *global* flows – basically, European etiquette and trends, rules and international tournaments – which spread in Brazil;
(ii) a series of specific *local* tensions – essentially social and ethnic.

As we saw, the overlap between these two scapes results in some consequences. First – in a very local sphere, represented by the football field – it leads to the production of a specific style of play, which tends to stigmatize physical contact. Second – if we move to a higher level – it also favours the construction of a new *globality*, that is, Brazil as an "imagined community" (Anderson, 1991; Lechner, 2007). More precisely, it requires Brazil to produce, from time to time, *global models* of the nation – the "whitening" model in 1921 and the "miscegenation" model in 1938. Within this globality we can register, third, the dynamic process of glocalization that leads – via football – to the affirmation of the Afro-Brazilian characters as national forms of life. Indeed – despite the fact they were relegated in the first two decades of 20th century to the "periphery" of the Brazilian culture – those cultural forms of life start to "explode" (Lotman, 1993) and suddenly move to its centre, extending their norms to the whole semiosphere. Put differently, the local style becomes the global image of the nation.

Thus, following and developing Sedda's reasoning on Lotman's theory of the semiosphere, we may talk of a *glocal device* that underlies the history of culture, sketching two basic dimensions of glocalization:

(i) a spatial dimension, "in which each entity is at one level a globality and, at another level, a locality" (Sedda 2006: 45). For instance, the Brazilian style of football is clearly a local style of play if we remain in the sporting discourse (either in the early 20th century or nowadays). Conversely, *when* and *where* the international *sportscape* crosses the national and international *ideoscapes*, it becomes, undoubtedly, a "globality", which embodies Brazil as whole;
(ii) a temporal dimension, in which what is local can turn into global and vice versa – as shown by the global rise of Afro-Brazilian characters (Freyre, 1943).[7]

In that sense, glocalization has a purely semiotic identity: the global and local have *topological* and *relational* dimensions, that is, they are always determined by their *position* and *relationship* with other elements inside and outside a given world, culture, discourse, practice, and so on. Nevertheless, glocalization is also a dynamic process of translation *among* and *within* cultures, in which elements are constantly reconfigurated (Clifford, 1997). In this regard, I can conclude by highlighting the double glocal tension of Brazilian football: on one hand, indeed, Brazil translates European football into the languages of its cultural system; though, on the other hand, the irruption of European football deeply reconfigures Brazilian culture. This is not a "unidirectional path" nor a "liquefaction" process where every reconfiguration is possible. Rather, it is a complex dynamic of interaction between homogenizing and heterogenizing tendencies.

Notes

1. See http://www.estadao.com.br/arquivo/economia/2005/not20050322p6852.htm.
2. See http://www.brahma.com/about.
3. Lacerda was a Brazilian physician, author of *Sur le metis au Bresil* (1911).
4. See http://ssbra.org/html/laws/IFABarc/pdf/1905/1905min.pdf.
5. It also should be taken into account that, since its early beginning, Brazilian football seems to have be characterized by a dribbling style. Football manuals and social histories denounced from the beginning the individualistic abuse of this technique (Cardim, 1906: 60), claiming that it killed the social essence of the game as it was played in the United Kingdom (Figueredo, 1918; Sant'Anna, 1918). A few isolated voices, on the contrary, praised this difference (Netto, 1919). The relationship between this first phase and the subsequent development of Brazil's individualistic style of play have yet to be demonstrated. In any case, it is strongly attested that, while in daily life Brazilian sportsmen followed European routines, different *habits* seem to have emerged on the field since the first years of the 20th century.
6. Miscegenation has always been the big issue of Brazilian social science. However, before the publication, in 1933, of Gilberto Freyre's book *Casa Grande e Senzala*, it was mostly described negatively. For an exhaustive analysis of its role in Brazilian culture and scientific discourse see Schwarcz (1993) and Skidmore (1976).
7. Reaffirming this reversibility between the global and the local, Hannerz (1990) claimed that what was cosmopolitan in the 1940s is now a form of localism.

References

Anderson, B. (1991) *Imagined Communites: Reflections on the Origin and Spread of Nationalism*, London and New York: Verso.

Appadurai A. (1996) *Modernity at Large. Cultural Dimensions of Globalization*, Minneapolis and London: University of Minnesota Press.

Barba, B. (2007) *Un antropologo nel Pallone*, Rome: Meltemi.

Bellos, A. (2002) *Futebol: The Brazilian Way of Life*, London: Bloomsbury.

Cardim, M. (1906) *Guia de Football*, São Paulo: Casa Vanordem.

Clifford, J. (1997) *Routes. Travel and Translation in the Late Twentieth Century*, Cambridge, MA; London: Harvard University Press.

Clifford, J. (2001) "Indigenous articulations", *The Contemprary Pacific State*, 13 (2), University of Hawaii Press.

DaMatta, R. (1979) *Carnavais, Malandros o Heróis: Para uma Sociologia do Dilema Brasileiro*, Rio de Janeiro: Zahar Editores.

DaMatta, R. (1994) "Antropologia do óbvio. Notas em torno do significado social do futebol brasileiro", *Revista USP*, n 22.

Eco, U. (1984) *Semiotica e filosofia del linguaggio*, Torino: Einaudi.

Elias, N. (1969) *The Civilizing Process. Vol I. The History of Manners*, Oxford: Blackwell.

Figueredo, A. (1918) *História do foot-ball em São Paulo*, São Paulo: Secção de obras d'O Estado de S. Paulo.

Franzini, F. (2003) *Corações na ponta da chuteira: cápitulos iniciais da história do futebol brasileiro*, Rio de Janeiro: DP&A.

Freyre, G. (1933) *Casa grande e senzala*. Rio de Janeiro: José Olympo.

Freyre, G. (1938) "Foot-ball mulato", *Diário de Pernambuco*, Recife, 17 jun. 1938.

Freyre, G. (1945) *Brazil: An Interpretation*, New York: Knopf.

Giulianotti, R. and Robertson, R. (2007) *Globalization and Sport*, Oxford: Balckwell.

Giulianotti, R. and Robertson, R. (2009) *Globalization and Football*, London: Sage.

Greimas, A. J. (1983) *Du Sens II – Essais sémiotiques*, Paris: Éditions du Seuil.

Greimas, A. J. and Courtés, J. (1979) *Sémiotique – Dictionnaire raisonné de la théorie du langage*, Paris: Hachette.

Hannerz, U. (1990) "Cosmopolitans and Locals in World Culture", in M. Featherstone (ed.) *Global Culture: Nationalism, Globalization and Modernity*, London: Sage Publications Ltd.

Lechner, F. J. (2007) "Imagined Communities in the Global Game: Soccer and the Development of Dutch National Identity", in R. Giulianotti and R. Robertson (2007) *Globalization and Sport*, Oxford: Blackwell.

Leite Lopes, J. S. (2000) "Successes and Contradictions in Multiracial Brazilian Football", in G. Armstrong and R. Giulianotti (eds.) *Entering the Field. New Perspective on World Football*, New York, Oxford.

Lotman, J. M. (1985) *La semiosfera*, Venice: Marsilio.

Lotman, J. M. (1990) *Universe of the Mind. A Semiotic Theory of Culture*, London-New York: Tauris.

Lotman, J. M. (1993) *Kul'tura i vryz*, Gnosis, Moskva (Ital. trans., 1993, *La cultura e l'esplosione. Prevedibilità e imprevedibilità*, Milan: Feltrinelli).

Lotman, J. M. (2006) *Tesi per una semiotica delle culture*, Franciscu Sedda (ed.), Rome: Meltemi.

Lotman, J. M. and Uspenskij, B. A. (1973) *Tipologia della cultura*, Milan: Bompiani (1975).

Murad, M. (2007) *A violência e o futebol*, Rio de Janeiro: Editora FGV.

Neto, J. M. d. S. (2002) *Visão do jogo: primórdios do futebol no Brasil*, São Paulo: Cosac Naify.

Netto, A. R. (1919) "Football: inovação brasileira", in *Sports*, ano 1, n. 1. São Paulo.

Pasolini, P. P. (2010) "Il calcio è un linguaggio con I suoi poeti e prosatori", in Franciscu Sedda, Leonardo Romei and Pierluigi Cervelli, *Mitologie delle sport: 40 saggi brevi*. Rome: Edizioni Nuova Cultura.

Pereira, L. A. de M. (2000) *Footballmania: uma história social do futebol no Rio de Janeiro, 1902–1938*, Rio de Janeiro: Editora Nova Fronteira.

Pezzini, I. (2007) *Il testo galeotto: la lettura come pratica eficace*, Roma: Meltemi.

Ricoeur P. (1983) *Temps et récit, Tome I*, Paris: Éditions du Seuil.

Robertson, R. (1992) *Globalization: Social Theory and Global Culture*, London: Sage.

Robertson R. and K. White (2003) "La glocalizzazione rivisitata ed elaborata", in F. Sedda (ed.) *Glocal, sul presente a venire*, Rome: Luca Sossella Editore.

Rodrigues, N. (1993) *À sombra das chuteiras imortais*, São Paulo: Companhia das Letras.

Rodrigues, N. (1994) *A patria em chuteiras*, São Paulo: Companhia das Letras.

Rodrigues M. F. (1947) *O negro no futebol brasileiro*, Rio de Janeiro: Irmãos Pongetti Editores.

Sant'Anna, L. (1918) *O football em São Paulo. Notas crítico-biográficas dos principais jogadores paulistas antigos e modernos*, São Paulo: TYP Piratininga.

Schwarcz, L. K. M. (1993) *O espectaculo das raças: cientistas, instituições e questão racial no Brasil, 1870–1930*, São Paulo: Companhia das Letras.

Schwarcz, L. K. M. (1995) "Complexo de Ze Carioca. Sobre Uma Certa Ordem da Mesticagem e da Malandragem", *Revista Brasileira de Ciencias Sociais*, São Paulo, 29 (10): 17–30.

Sevcenko, N. (1998) "A capital irradiante: técnica, ritmos e ritos do Rio", in Sevecenko, N. (ed.) *História da vida privada no Brasil*, vol. 3, São Paulo: Companhia das Letras.

Sedda, F. (2006) "Introduzione", in J. Lotman (ed.) *Tesi per una semiotica delle culture*, Roma: Meltemi.

Silvares, A. (1915) "A nossa Campanha", *Sports*, 6 August.

Skidmore, T. (1976) *Preto no Branco: raça e nacionalidade no pensamento brasiliero*, Rio de Janeiro: Paz e Terra.

Soares, A. J. (2001) "História e invenção de tradições no futebol brasileiro", in Ronaldo Helal, Antonio Jorje Soares and Hugo Lovisolo (eds.) *A invenção do pais do futebol: mídia, raça e idolatria*. Rio de Janeiro: Mauad.

Toledo, L. H. de. (2002) *Lógicas no futebol*, São Paulo: Hucitec-Fapesp.

7

Exploring the Glocal Flow of Beauty

From Euro-America to the World?

Debra Gimlin

While long a focus of feminist protest, "beauty" is today becoming an increasingly central theme within mainstream political discourse. This trend is apparent in, for example, the 2012 formation of an All Party Parliamentary Group in the UK, which was organized to investigate the sources of body image anxiety in that nation and to propose policy solutions to what is now deemed a serious social problem (see www.ymca.co.uk). At the level of international politics, the United Nations' 2012 Commission on the Status of Women featured the psychoanalyst, Susie Orbach, who likened "the viscous body practices" required of contemporary Western women to the "appalling forms of violence" targeted at females in other parts of the world, such as forced marriage, rape as a tactic of war, and female genital mutilation. According to Orbach, "beauty" has become so dangerously powerful due to two simultaneous global forces; that is, at the same time that "beauty has been democratised" – or extended across national contexts – "the ideal of what beauty is" has grown increasingly narrow (see AnyBody's Vent, 2012).

Such claims draw attention to the perceived threat of Euro-American beauty ideals, particularly when they are conceptualized as a homogenizing force worldwide (Chapkis, 1986; Wolf, 1991). Indeed, phenomena such as the rising popularity of US-style beauty pageants, the increasing prevalence of aesthetic plastic surgery, and the rapidly growing cosmetics industry have all been cited as both contributing to and reflecting a broader trend in which Euro-American, white values and perceptions are imposed on the rest of the globe, while local identities and understandings are suppressed (Banet-Wiser, 1999; Halberstam, 1999). In the following pages, I argue that this perspective massively oversimplifies the processes involved in the globalization of beauty. In so doing, my work resembles that of scholars who have used examples as diverse as McDonald's fast food (Watson, 1997), bridal photography (Adrian, 2003), and American hip-hop (Condry, 2000) to demonstrate that cultural encounters are neither unidirectional nor predictable in their outcomes.

Here, I make a similar claim with regard to shared notions about the dimensions of beauty and how it can be judged. Like Appadurai's (1990) master term, "democracy", "beauty" has a global meaning that is somewhat homogeneous. Yet it also has important heterogeneous, local elements that differ by context. As Meredith Jones (2008: 32) writes:

> Perhaps a Claudia-Schiffer-style beauty is close to something perpetuated as a global ideal: long legs, large breasts, thin body, fair hair and skin, delicate features, big blue eyes. People from Poland to Pakistan may well . . . recognise and accept Schiffer as a "universal beauty". But attractiveness is also inflected and varied according to local context.

In essence, global culture flows everywhere but its morphology differs according to its host (Jones, 2008). Thus, I will examine both the instruments of beauty's homogenization and the ways that these are "absorbed into local political and cultural economies, only to be repatriated as heterogeneous dialogues" (Appadurai, 1990: 307).

Drawing on illustrations from beauty pageantry, aesthetic plastic surgery, and the cosmetics industry, I explore four interrelated patterns through which beauty is diffused globally, each of which represents a challenge to the trope of straightforward Euro-American emulation. The first pattern I discuss involves practices that appear superficially to reflect the simple acceptance of Western beauty ideals, but which are enacted in ways that are sufficiently local and, in some cases, non-Western, as to make them distinctive. Homogenization occurs, but its associated practices differ according to national setting. I next examine how local structures (such as the availability or dearth of transportation networks and, thus, channels for the distribution of beauty-related products) and cultures (e.g. notions of femininity, sexuality, and respectability) shape processes of diffusion. Local circumstances necessarily give form to the global flow of beauty: enabling it, constraining it, and, at times, causing it to be rejected outright.

I will also outline several ways in which national context is relevant to the *meanings* associated with global beauty ideals. Features such as large breasts, "double" eyelids,[1] and pale skin are considered desirable in many parts of the world, yet the reasons underlying their perceived desirability vary significantly with their cultural relevance (which is itself the product of distinctive historical, political, and economic circumstances). Finally, I will explore instances in which local beauty ideals and practices are diffused globally. In some cases, such as the recent prominence of Indian and East Asian contestants in beauty pageants like Miss World and Miss Universe, non-Western beauty is itself reformulated as the global standard. In concluding, I will argue that while beauty may be subject to processes of "glocalization" (Robertson, 1995), in which particularizing and universalizing forces operate simultaneously, a consistent theme spanning beauty practices worldwide is the increasingly prevalent view of the body as "unfinished" – that is, as a series of flexible surfaces ready to be inscribed with new meaning (Featherstone, 1991). At the same time, such meanings are themselves both local and global, as are the practices used to express and revise them.

Homogenizing beauty

One need not search for long to identify numerous ways that European and North American nations have shaped global understandings of beauty and its performance. One of the more frequently cited examples of such influence is the proliferation of US-style beauty pageants around the world, including huge global contests like Miss Universe (owned by Donald Trump and NBC, which also own Miss USA and Miss Teen USA) and Miss World (owned by Rupert Murdoch and his News Corporation). Each of these pageants reaches an audience of over 2 billion viewers and has franchise holders in over 150 countries (Wilk, 2004). Pageant owners run the national competitions, which serve as pathways to global contests; all levels are controlled through an elaborate set of contracts and rules that specify the physical, social, and moral qualities of contestants (Rhode, 2010).

Many authors have characterized beauty pageantry as a form of Euro-American neocolonialism that commodifies and essentializes women, while defining female expectations and aspirations (see Cohen et al., 1996). Critics charge these contests with giving people in poor countries only the illusion of real participation in a global sorority where all nations are on an equal footing, as well as promoting a distinctively Western ideal of physical beauty in parts of the world where this can never be achieved (Gundle, 2008). In many ways, these criticisms are justified. The paler skin and wider eyes historically favoured in Miss World and Miss Universe have arguably reflected and reinforced the pre-eminence of Western looks. Scandinavian women were the first winners of both contests (Jones, 2010). The first nine winners of Miss World included six Europeans and three pale-skinned contestants from Venezuela, Egypt, and South Africa, while the early winners of Miss Universe were overwhelmingly pale-skinned contestants from the USA, Europe, and Latin America (Rhode, 2010). Even when non-whites began winning beauty pageants, as did Miss Japan and Miss Thailand in the Miss Universe contests in 1959 and 1965, respectively, those contestants largely conformed to a so-called "Miss Universe Standard of Beauty" in terms of face, figure, proportions, and posture. Miss India for 1966 became the first darker-skinned winner of Miss World (van Esterik, 1996: 215).

Similar charges have been made against local "ethnic" contests held by immigrant communities, such as the Nisei Week Japanese Festival and Pageant in Los Angeles and the Miss Chinatown USA Beauty Pageant in San Francisco (King-O'Riain, 2006). Such contests were originally organized to foster pride in immigrants' communities and raise their stature in relation to the larger city; most claimed that their queen would be selected based on her ability to represent the feminine qualities most valued by both her ethnic and American cultures (Reiko Yano, 2006). Yet numerous questions have been raised about the standards of beauty which govern even these "ethnic" contests. Chinese American feminists from the late 1960s through the 1970s claimed that the Miss Chinatown USA Pageant had beauty standards which reinforced the notion that "the closer you look to the Whites, the prettier you are" (Wu, 1997: 15). Some contestants too have argued that taller candidates and, particularly those with larger double- rather than single-lidded eyes, are unfairly advantaged in these competitions. Indeed, the souvenir book from the 1970 Miss Chinatown USA Pageant featured an advertisement for a surgeon who claimed to have a special technique for converting "Oriental eyelids" to "Caucasian eyelids" and a clientele of "movie actresses, singing stars and participants in beauty contests" (Wu, 1996, cited in Haiken, 1997: 207).

A related critique levelled against beauty pageantry derives from such associations with aesthetic plastic surgery, which has itself been characterized as a powerful force in the global spread of Euro-American beauty ideals (Kaw, 1993). Historical accounts of cosmetic surgery's development show that many of its early applications were intended to diminish the physical signs of ethnicity among immigrants to the USA (Haiken, 1997; Gilman, 1999). For example, surgeons working in the late 19th century developed techniques for "correcting" the "pug" noses of Irish immigrants to allow "the unregenerated 'Celt' to 'pass' as American" and, more specifically, as Anglo-Saxon (Gilman, 1999: 95). Racial anthropologists of the era saw the Irish as direct descendants from Cro-Magnon man, defined by his "big ears" and a "nose, oftener concave than straight" (Stepan, 1982: 103, quoted in Gilman, 1999: 94). In the context of late 19th-century physiognomy and popular caricatures, the snub-nose of the Irish was taken to represent "weakness", "lack of development", servility, "bad temperament", and a "poor character", marking the Irish through animal analogies as "doglike, which is why the nose itself was labelled 'pug' " (Gilman, 1999: 93–97). In turn, the so-called "Jewish nose", identifiable by its "considerable length and height", "convexity of profile, a depressed tip with a downward sloping septum, and thick, flared alae or wings", was thought to reflect "commercialism or desire for gain" and "considerable shrewdness in worldly matters"; in its departure from the idealized Anglo-Saxon nose, the Jewish nose was also thought to signal the bearer's racial closeness to "inferior" groups – that is, Africans and other darker-skinned races (Gilman, 1999: 120–121).

The "big and protruding" ears of Jewish immigrants, too, were taken as a "visible and repugnant" sign of racial difference, which was ascribed to the character as well as the body (Gilman, 1999: 126). Accordingly, early operations to "normalize" ears considered "too Jewish" were justified based on the professional and social disadvantage that they engendered. In 1910, the prominent New York surgeon William H. Luckett reported that one of his young patients suffered "constant harassing by classmates", which was "the cause of so much distress as to produce a very bad mental condition in the child as well as his parents, and to warrant our surgical intervention" (quoted in Gilman, 1999: 127). By altering the feature that gave offence, surgery could eliminate the reaction it inspired, thereby mitigating the damaging psychological effects of prejudice (Haiken, 1997).

Examples of similar experiences among other immigrant groups are readily available (Davis, 2003). Asian American and Asian men living in the USA and Europe have, for many years, undergone nose jobs and eyelid surgery to appear "less ethnic", "more Caucasian", and, as Gilman (1999: 99) notes, "more erotic, because Asian men are generally viewed as unerotic" in Western societies; Asian women living in Europe and North America too have used these and related procedures to avoid the "dullness, passivity, and lack of emotion" associated with their looks. During the latter half of the 20th century, the numbers of African Americans having surgery to narrow the nose and lips increased and, even more recently, Middle Easterners living in Western nations have undergone nose jobs to remove any resemblance to the stereotypical "Islamic Fundamentalist" associated with terrorism in popular media imagery (Gilman, 2005: 131–135; Jones, 2008).

Beauty pageantry and cosmetic surgery are only two elements of a much larger "fashion-beauty complex" (Bartky, 1990: 42), comprised of numerous body-related industries. One of the largest is composed of manufacturers and sellers of the $160 billion in fragrances and cosmetics purchased annually by consumers around the world (Orbach, 2010: 90). Like cosmetic surgery and beauty pageantry, the fragrance/cosmetics industry has received considerable criticism, much of which centres around its homogenizing effects on global beauty ideals via advertising and other media (Wolf, 1991; Jeffreys, 2005). For example, Orbach (2010: 88) argues that the beauty industry today contributes to an "almost worldwide dissemination of common imagery. Globalism brings uniformity to visual culture so that what I see in London is not so different from what the billboards display in Rio, Shanghai or Accra." That imagery, according to Orbach, is neither random nor globally representative, but rather "narrows yearly as globalism promotes the idealised thin western female body as *the* body to possess" (2010: 137, emphasis in original).

The diffusion of Western beauty ideals is closely associated with the historical development of the beauty industry itself. The industry's emergence in the late 19th century was driven largely by manufacturers in Paris and New York, who understood beauty primarily as a characteristic of Caucasian females (Rhode, 2010). The imagery employed in these firms' efforts to expand their markets was disseminated around the world, thereby encouraging the global association of beauty with Western countries, white people, and women (Peiss, 2002). Those associations reflected broader social changes. During this period, Western understandings of masculinity and femininity became more and more disparate, such that clothing choice and employment patterns grew increasingly gendered. This was also an age of Western imperialism. The beauty industry capitalized on the dominance of Western nations by marketing brands based on their affiliations with Euro-American wealth and modernity, thereby creating aspirations to drive the growing consumption of their products, particularly among the social elites of large cities around the world (Allen, 1981).

In recent decades, the beauty business has remained highly concentrated (Jones, 2010: 1). Many of the best-selling products still identify themselves with either Paris or New York and even brands owned by companies which are neither French nor American lay symbolic claim to these locales (e.g. the most expensive skin cream sold by Shiseido, Japan's largest cosmetics manufacturer, is named Clé de Peau Beauté). The ten biggest companies in the industry account for over one-half of sales throughout the world, with the two largest (L'Oréal and Proctor & Gamble) together earning over one-fifth of total global sales (Jones, 2010: 2). The worldwide popularity of "mega" and "celebrity" brand cosmetics also speaks to the impact of the global beauty industry. The consumption of beauty products in China is a case in point. Only three decades ago, there were virtually no cosmetics in China, largely because the communist regime of Mao Zedong regarded their use as bourgeois decadence (Peiss, 2002). Today, China constitutes the world's fourth largest market for beauty products, many of which are the same as those purchased by westerners (Jones, 2010: 3; Orbach, 2010). Indeed, the largest skincare and colour cosmetics brands in China – Olay and Maybelline New York, respectively – hold the same market positions in the USA (Jones, 2010: 310).

The above discussion outlines various instances that contribute to the view that beauty ideals are being "flattened out" over time. But the homogenization of beauty is only one element in its story of globalization. As briefly outlined in the introduction, the remainder of this chapter will focus on other aspects of that process. In the first instance, I will examine attitudes and ideals that appear superficially to be a straightforward emulation of Euro-American beauty, but which differ so significantly in practice as to make them distinctively local.

The global as diverse practice: breasts and beauty pageantry

Breasts have long been a central feature in European and Northern American notions of female attractiveness (Hollander, 1993). Since the turn of the last century, and particularly from the late 1940s, the Western emphasis on large breasts has intensified into what can today be characterized as a "hypermammary fixation" (Miller, 2006: 71–72). Large breasts are similarly eroticized in contemporary Japanese society, though the association of breasts with sexual desire is a relatively recent phenomenon there. Prior to the 20th century, the female breast in Japan was linked to motherhood and maternal nurturance, with celebrations of mothers' breasts regularly appearing in Japanese plays, poems, songs, and folklore (Lebra, 1976). Few, if any, restrictions were placed on public breastfeeding, suggesting that the bare bosom was not inconsistent with notions of feminine modesty; the chest-flattening kimono de-emphasized breasts relative to more highly eroticized parts of the female body, such as the nape of the neck; and sexual imagery in art and popular culture focused predominantly on the genitalia, with the breasts playing only a subsidiary role (Levy, 1971; Bornoff, 1991).

The shift from maternal to erotic understandings of the breast in Japan has many of its roots in the American occupation of the country following the Second World War (Rhode, 2010). During these years, the American "strip show" was first introduced to Japan, such that the public viewing of unclothed women's bodies, with a corresponding emphasis on female breasts, was popularized as a common form of entertainment. The influx of Western films, magazines, television, and, especially, pornography, in subsequent years, further reinforced the now deeply entrenched Japanese eroticization and commodification of female breasts (Jeffreys, 2005), giving rise to an enormous range of products and services – both surgical and non-surgical – intended to alter breast size and shape. In this sense, then, Japanese beauty ideals, with their focus on a large chest combined with "an ultraslim, smooth, and youthful-looking" body (Miller, 2006: 81) appear little different from those of Western societies.

Yet crucial differences exist in the ways that Japanese women pursue such ideals, at least compared to those in the USA, where breast augmentation is currently the most common form of plastic surgery (according to the American Society of Aesthetic Plastic Surgery Statistics, over 300,000 such procedures were performed in 2011, more than three times the total figure from 1997). Surgical augmentation of the breast is readily available in Japan as well and, in fact, many of the early techniques for breast enlargement were first developed there (Haiken, 1997). Japanese rates of breast augmentation remain relatively low, however, a difference that Miller (2006) attributes to the cultural influence of Confucian beliefs, which conceptualize the body as an inheritance from ancestors. In that context, altering the body surgically is marked as a sign of disrespect for one's forebearers, such that most Japanese women instead opt for topical breast treatments offered by "aesthetic salons". Growing increasingly popular from the 1990s, these procedures typically involve "manual massage, the application of creams or packs, and mechanical stimulation with some type of appliance or apparatus" (Miller, 2006: 87). Most importantly, they are non-surgical and therefore acceptable to a Confucian understanding of embodiment (see also Jones, 2008). In effect, then, even as Japanese women engage with an ideal that is Euro-American in origin, they do so in ways that reflect a unique set of cultural values and beliefs.

The Miss Heilala Beauty Pageant, held in the Kingdom of Tonga in Western Polynesia, provides a rather different illustration of practices that appear, superficially, to be a straightforward westernization of beauty. The Miss Heilala Pageant is the official forum for selecting the Tongan contestant for Miss South Pacific, who then goes on to compete for Miss World and Miss Universe (Teilhet-Fisk, 1996). As the gateway to international pageants, the Miss Heilala contest is necessarily subject to their rules and guidelines, including those pertaining to the format of the competition, the panel of judges, and contestants' age and marital status. Significantly, the pageant is also the main event in Tonga's annual Miss Heilala Festival and, as such, serves as an important means for maintaining links with (the more than half of all) Tongans who live overseas (Campbell, 1992); many expatriates return to attend the festival, including a handful who do so explicitly to participate in the beauty contest.

As the centrepiece of the Heilala Festival, the pageant allows Tongans living at home and abroad to enact their culture via the practice of distinctively Tongan values, including those pertaining to the nature of "beauty" itself (Teilhet-Fisk, 1996). The local Tongan community has its own perception of beauty, *faka' ofo' ofa*, that "goes far beyond the surface of physical attributes and is deeply entrenched in social and moral values that uphold and emphasize the family, kinship, church, and a nationalist ideology" (Teilhet-Fisk, 1996: 186). This notion of beauty is most clearly expressed in the pageant's Miss *Tau'olunga* evening, which is the highlight of the event. The *Tau'olunga* is the traditional solo dance of Tongan culture. In it, every "aspect of the presentation – the costume, the set-piece movements, the ... art of their execution, the charm and beauty of the dancer – are strictly marked" (Teilhet-Fisk, 1996: 192). Contestants' performances are judged primarily as expressions of Tongan cultural values pertaining to kinship, respect, and modesty; accordingly, they are meant to convey a conceptualization of beauty that is relational rather than individual (in contrast to more explicitly Western notions of beauty, which tend to view it as an individual possession).

While Tongans consider *Tau'olunga* the most important part of the Miss Heilala competition, international pageant guidelines require that the contest winner be selected based on her performance in several events, including one featuring "beach wear". This round of competition is, however, potentially problematic in the Tongan context due to long-held avoidance taboos which forbid males from viewing the upper thighs and lower torso of their female relatives (Teilhet-Fisk, 1996).

Consequently, traditional Tongan swimwear for women includes a sarong that covers these "forbidden" regions. While pageant contestants who reside in Tonga universally opt for this relatively conservative garb, expatriate contestants have, on occasion, appeared in Western-style bathing suits (Teilhet-Fisk, 1996). These women's decision to adopt Western beach attire (and, by implication, Western notions of beauty), while flouting Tongan avoidance taboos, has at times caused significant uproar, both during the competition and among the Tongan public more generally. During one year, numerous men in the pageant audience rushed from the venue and fights broke out as some males attempted to block the view of others (Teilhet-Fisk, 1996). The contestants' behaviour was condemned as immoral and "un-Tongan"; in some cases, it resulted in their disqualification, with the title of Miss Heilala being awarded to a candidate who more clearly embodied a Tongan sense of beauty – one which is based on respect for community values and notions of propriety, and personified in the ritual of the *Tau'olunga* rather than the display of female flesh. In effect, by selecting a more traditional model of the feminine ideal, pageant judges used what would otherwise be an instance of homogenization (here, in the spread of global pageantry) to reject Western understandings of beauty as an individual quality in favour of a distinctively Tongan notion of beauty as social practice.

The global's local acquiescence: cosmetics and fragrances worldwide

Orbach (2010) and others have emphasized the beauty industry's impact on beauty ideals and practices cross-culturally, arguing that, as cosmetics and fragrance manufacturers have extended existing markets and created new ones, they have also contributed to the rapid spread of Euro-American notions of physical attractiveness. Given that the beauty industry's history is clearly one of increasing internationalization, such claims are not wholly inaccurate. They are, however, somewhat simplistic, in so far as they pay too little attention to the ways that the beauty industry's expansion necessarily takes shape within particular national and regional settings, all of which involve local distribution channels, forms of advertising, tastes and preferences, regulations on product content, and government restrictions on foreign ownership of enterprise. These and other local features exert a powerful influence on the shape of beauty's global flow: on its reach, form, content, and timing (Jones, 2010). For example, television has long been one of the primary means for firms within the beauty industry to advertise their products. This tendency began with the US market, where television first became available in the 1930s. In the post-war years, television service spread rapidly in the USA, albeit with only local broadcasting until 1951, when coast-to-coast transmission became possible (Blaszczyk, 2009: 234–238; McCraw, 2009: 101–102). The spread of television followed elsewhere, although unevenly and with a time lag – for example, colour television was launched in the USA in the mid-1950s but did not reach many European countries until the following decade (Feldenkirchen and Hilgen, 2001: 264).

The increasing availability of television did not mean that access to local consumers became uniformly open to the sellers of beauty products. In Europe, governments often controlled broadcasting and allowed little or no advertising (Jones, 2010). In 1955, the UK was one of the first European countries to permit television advertising (notably, for a toiletry product), if only to a minimal extent; the country's main provider of television services, the British Broadcasting Corporation (BBC), is publicly funded and shows no commercial advertising (Frost and Sullivan, 1983). In Sweden, television commercials were barred until 1990, while in France even advertising on the radio was initially prohibited; the beauty industry responded to this restriction by trying to sell its products through the privately owned Radio Luxembourg, which was located just outside France (Jones, 2010: 160). Government restrictions on advertising necessarily determine local exposure to many kinds of beauty imagery and, thus, its diffusion. In some non-European nations, state policies have prohibited the introduction of Western beauty products altogether. As noted in the section on beauty's homgenization, this was long the case in China (Peiss 2002; Brownell, 2005). In South Korea, high levels of government protection against foreign investment, demanding and idiosyncratic health regulations, and a limited infrastructure combined to exclude foreign companies from the marketplace for many years, with the effect that a locally owned beauty industry emerged (Ghemawat et al., 2006). From the 1950s, that industry was dominated by a single firm, Amore-Pacific, which not only produced the country's most popular face cream, but also launched Korea's first beauty magazine in 1958 and co-hosted the first Miss Korea Pageant in 1978 (Jones, 2010).

In other cases, state policies have shaped the local diffusion of Euro-American beauty by *encouraging* its adoption. For example, during the late 19th century, Japan reacted to Europe's growing colonial power by attempting to modernize the nation (Horne, 2000). Such efforts involved building institutions deemed necessary for an internationally competitive economy and increasingly adopting "western standards for corporeal deportment" (Allison, 1996: 163). These changes were partly a reaction to foreign visitors' reported perceptions of late-19th-century Japan as "a land of 'nudity, rudity and crudity' " (Dore, 1958: 159). The government responded by striving to alter the nation's image; it discouraged customary behaviours such as mixed bathing and breast feeding in public, as well as traditional body practices like tooth blackening and shaving eyebrows, both of which had nearly disappeared in urban areas by 1924. In the interest of implementing Western-style gender distinctions in appearance, the government also banned the whitening of male faces, restricting this form of adornment to women (Jones, 2010). Norms for bodily behaviour in Japan thus changed dramatically within the space of 50 years, as did cultural notions of facial beauty. According to Ashikari (2003), the long face with narrow eyes and thin eyebrows that had long been idealized by the Japanese gave way, during these decades, to a more rounded face with thicker eyebrows and wider eyes. The resulting ideal is arguably more Western and less explicitly "Japanese", but its emergence is not so much a product of consumerism and corporate media (to which the West's cultural imperialism is often attributed), but a result of the Japanese state's selective incorporation of ideas and practices from Europe and North America since the Meiji restoration at the end of the 19th century.

The global's local meanings: plastic surgery in Brazil and South Korea

Much has been written about aesthetic plastic surgery performed on non-white bodies (Haiken, 1997; Kaw, 1993; Davis, 2003). Authors in the field typically focus on immigrants and ethnic minority populations in Western nations, arguing that procedures such as double-eyelid surgeries, nose reshaping, and skin lightening represent efforts to avoid racism by accommodating to the appearance norms of dominant white groups (Kaw, 1993: 75). There also exists a smaller, but growing, literature on cosmetic surgery practices in non-Western countries, much of which emphasizes the globalization of Western appearance norms and subsequent homogenization of bodies (Gilman, 2005). With few exceptions, then, studies of "ethnic" cosmetic surgery have failed to examine the local meanings of such procedures, including the complex and, at times, competing discourses (pertaining to national identity, tradition, class, religious belief, ageing, gender, and self-care) that inform them (Holliday and Elfving-Hwang, 2012; see also Jones, 2008).

Cosmetic surgery is becoming increasingly commonplace around the world, although few regions have embraced it more enthusiastically than Brazil (ISAPS, 2010), where per capita rates are higher than in much wealthier European countries. In fact, Brazil is one of the only nations in the world to offer cosmetic surgery (or *plástica*) through its nationalized health-care system, thus making it available to large segments of the population who would not otherwise be able to afford it (Edmonds, 2007a). While *plástica* in Brazil shares many features with the global practice, its meanings are nonetheless highly local. Most significantly, they are deeply informed by "the experience and 'management' of motherhood and sexuality" in Brazil, as these have been transformed alongside the nation's rapid modernization (Edmonds, 2009: 154). Changes in Brazilian conceptualizations of motherhood and sexuality can be traced to national policies, and particularly to the state's retreat from a previous pro-natalist position during the 1970s and eventual provision of contraception through the public health-care system. According to Edmonds (2009: 160), the spread of birth control in subsequent decades helped to "culturally legitimate interference in biological processes, rational control over the body and the separation of sexuality from reproduction". That change has, in turn, contributed to rising rates of sterilization and caesarean section, two procedures which have become conceptually and practically linked in the state's management of reproduction and sexuality. As Edmonds (2007a) argues, these widespread practices familiarize Brazilian women with surgical interventions and their associated scarring as a "normal" part of the reproductive process. And, like *plástica*, both may be undertaken for "sexual-aesthetic" reasons: sterilization because it ensures that stretch marks, weight gain, and other bodily changes associated with pregnancy will never occur, and caesarean section because it avoids the distensions caused by vaginal birth which can make sexual relations difficult. In essence, the "erotic" body in Brazil is maintained through surgery which is tied explicitly to reproduction.

Conceptualizations of beauty and sexual desirability in Brazil – and, thus, the practice of *plástica* – are also deeply informed by the country's history of racial mixing among Indian, African, and Portuguese inhabitants. As Edmonds (2007b, 2009) describes it, during the 20th century the racially mixed body took on a key role in the re-imagination of hybridity (or *mestiçagem*) which is central to modern Brazilian identity. The paradigm of *mestiçagem* is, moreover, represented by a single body type for women (including large hips, thighs and buttocks, a narrow waist, and small chest) which is marked as both erotic and distinctively Brazilian (Edmonds, 2007b). Not surprisingly, popular magazine articles and advertisements train the Brazilian reader in the forms of *plástica* best suited to achieving the eroticized body of *mestiçagem*. Notably, that body departs in significant ways from the "Claudia-Schiffer-style beauty" of "long legs, large breasts, thin body, fair hair and skin... [and] big blue eyes", which is often characterized as the "global ideal" (Jones, 2008: 32). Thus, in Brazil, plastic surgery is not best understood as a simple exercise of "medical imperialism" that inscribes European or North American beauty ideals on the female body. Instead, both the practice's meanings and goals are deeply informed by Brazilian culture, which imbues them with the significance of a unique historical tradition of the body in which sensuality and racial mixing stand as key symbols of modern national identity (Edmonds, 2009: 165).

As in Brazil, the meanings of cosmetic surgery in South Korea are thoroughly bound up with matters of national identity and patriotism. Holliday and Elfving-Hwang (2012: 71) argue:

> The most important aim of cosmetic surgery [in South Korea] is to create a natural look that 'enhances' the body without losing the 'Koreanness' of the subject who undergoes surgery.

Importantly, looking "Korean" is understood largely in terms of *not* looking Chinese or Japanese. Korean aesthetics are also informed by the country's strong physiognomic tradition, such that cosmetic surgery is seen as a way to improve not only one's features in line with accepted Korean beauty ideals, but also the "auspiciousness" of those features and, thus, one's fortunes (Zane, 2003). Indeed, many Koreans who consider undergoing aesthetic surgery even consult a physiognomist before having an operation.

According to Holliday and Elfving-Hwang (2012), the Korean practice of altering appearance in order to have a more "auspicious" face has little to do with enhancing one's looks vis-à-vis Western models of beauty. For example, one popular procedure involves removing moles or blemishes from the skin around the eyes, as these are seen to resemble tears which symbolize the individual's predestined life of sorrow (Lee, 2006). The "right face" is one with no such inauspicious features, signifying upper-class status, youth, and vitality; it is also an increasingly important factor in gaining employment in the highly competitive Korean job market, where nearly 80 per cent of young people now attend further education college or university and where photographs (which are frequently assessed based on physiognomic principles) are required in all job applications (Holliday and Elfving-Hwang, 2012). Even more commonplace in Korea is eyelid surgery. The popularity of this operation among Asians has been explained in terms of westernization (Kaw, 1993), but Holliday and Elfving-Hwang (2012) assert that the wider eyes produced by blepharoplasty are understood less as a reflection of Euro-American emulation than of characteristics valued by Koreans themselves: youth, energy, and alertness. Such meanings are, however, subject to transformation over time and alongside other social changes. Historically, round eyes were taken to represent lasciviousness in Korea, while a large moon face connoted fertility and thus value for females. Yet procedures for widening eyes and narrowing faces are prevalent among Korean women today, for whom employment opportunities and choices regarding marriage and reproduction have risen dramatically in recent decades (Kim, 2003). In that context, Korean women's cosmetic surgery practices suggest that they are distancing themselves from the maternal body – that is, the moon face associated with fecundity – and embracing signs of overt sexuality, such as wide eyes, thereby resisting earlier models of propriety (Holliday and Elfving-Hwang, 2012). Again, the appearance resulting from such procedures may seem to align with European and North American ideals; however, its meanings for Korean women can be understood only in relation to their country's distinctive history and traditions, and their own experiences of femininity and sexuality.

Diffusing the local: Indian beauty queens and (globalized) niche products

The final pattern I will explore involves the international diffusion of local beauty ideals and practices, such that non-Western beauty – often in a revised and at least partially "globalized" form – is established as a worldwide standard. One illustration of this process is the increasing dominance of non-Western and, especially Indian, contestants in pageants such as Miss World and Miss Universe. This trend became marked in 1994, when the then Miss India, Sushmita Sen, became the first Indian woman ever to win the Miss Universe title. Some months later, the Miss India runner-up, Aishwarya Rai, earned the same honour in the Miss World Pageant (Dewey, 2008). Just one year before, India's most popular women's magazine and Miss India sponsor, *Femina*, began holding a month-long training programme for pageant participants. Each year, 23 contestants are housed, fed, and instructed with one goal in mind: to create a Miss World or a Miss Universe (Banet-Weiser, 1999).

Miss India winners are subsequently groomed for months in preparation for international contests.

Femina's efforts have been strikingly successful: Indian women have since won Miss World in 1997 and 1999. In 2000, the Miss India winner and runners-up were crowned Miss Universe, Miss World, and Miss Asia-Pacific. (The only other country to have won all three major titles in one year was Australia in 1972.) India is currently tied with Venezuela for having the highest number of Miss World winners; in most years, Indian women place as runners-up in at least one global competition (Dewey, 2008). India's success in international beauty pageants has been interpreted as evidence that Indian women (and, by implication, Indian notions of beauty) have global "currency" (Banet-Weiser, 1999). Following the 1994 successes of Sen and Rai, a *Los Angeles Times* article (Dahlburg, 1994) claimed that the citizenry of India was as jubilant about the wins as it would be about Nobel Prizes or Olympic medals. Central to popular commentary was what the victories signaled about India – e.g. its international image, the place of women in its society and its attitudes towards sex.

While many segments of the Indian population were apparently thrilled about Sen's and Rai's accomplishments, though, it became clear in 1996 than not all citizens were committed to participation in international beauty pageantry. In November of that year, feminist and nationalist groups picketed the Miss World Pageant, which was being held in Bangalore. Protesters went so far as to threaten mass suicide, claiming that beauty pageantry was not only demeaning to women but also threatened the nation's 2000-year history via the introduction of corrupt Western standards and values (Banet-Weiser, 1999: 183). Thus, while pageants may provide a means for poorer nations to secure their place in an imagined "global community", they also serve as a stage for the enactment of struggles over both national and international gender identity. As Wilk (1996: 218) notes, "Pageants as an institution can serve the state's goals of 'domesticating difference'", by "channeling potentially dangerous social divisions into the realm of aesthetics and taste. But they can also fail in getting this message across" and end up emphasizing "the very divisions they are meant to minimize and control". In the case of India, Wilk's point is relevant to the political protests of nationalist and feminist groups as well as to long-standing divisions of "race" and class. The latter point is particularly apparent in *Femina*'s practice of selecting pageant contestants, all of whom are drawn from a relatively narrow range of Indian females – that is, from tall and slender urbanites with fair skin and, usually, light eyes.

Also dating to the 1990s, the global beauty industry witnessed a surge in products associated with the local, traditional, and "authentic" (Jones, 2010). Brands became increasingly distinct during the late 1990s and early 2000s; by 2007, "niche" brands (associated with environmentally friendly practices, fair trade, and the like) took one-quarter of the $8 billion US prestige beauty market, compared to only 2 per cent in 1997 ("L'Oreal Finds Buzz in Niche Beauty", *Wall Street Journal*, 2007). Numerous entrepreneurial start-ups in the beauty industry contributed significantly to the development of new niche brands. One example is the Korres Natural Products Company in Greece, which began from a homeopathic pharmacy in Athens (Korres Natural Products USA, 2010). George Korres, a pharmacist and the company's owner, began selling herbal cosmetics and skincare products from his store in the early 1990s. The reputation of these products grew by word of mouth, and in 1996, Korres and his wife, Lena Philippou, a chemical engineer, launched their own company (Korres Natural Products USA, 2010).

Korres' cosmetics are based on herbs and flowers, and claim to draw on "traditional knowledge of their efficacy" (Jones, 2010: 331). By 2008, 350 different herbs – many of which were unique to Greece – were used in making the products. For instance, a yoghurt and honey aftersun cream was based on the centuries-old Greek tradition of using yoghurt to relieve sunburn (Katsikis, 2009). Other components included honey, rose, sage, hibiscus, fig, watermelon, and mint. Within a decade, Korres had edged past much larger cosmetics manufacturers like L'Oreal, Pierre Fabre, and Johnson & Johnson in Greece. In 2000, the firm started selling in high-end department stores in New York, and in 2003 it opened its first store in Britain. Four years later, Korres owned 18 stores with sales of $50 million annually; 16 of the stores were outside Greece and two were in Beijing (Katsikis, 2009).

Large multinational firms helped to orchestrate this trend towards the local. In 2000, L'Oreal purchased the New York pharmacy brand Kiehl's, a family-owned product line that had emerged and flourished as a single store in Manhattan's East Village since 1851 (Kiehl's, 2010). Kiehl's products were sold in simple packaging and never advertised; their appeal was based in large part on the store's attachment to the local community (Godin, 2005). Much of the shop's inner space was devoted to local activities, including an entire wall covered in pictures of customers' children. After its purchase, L'Oreal expanded Kiehl's to other US cities and then internationally; by 2009, the brand was sold in 33 countries in Europe, Latin America, the Middle East, and Asia (Jones, 2010: 329). In each city, the company replicated features of the original store, while "forging links with the local community and seeking relevance to local consumers" (Jones, 2010: 329).

The globalization of local practices also involves the incorporation of traditional herbal and craft knowledge, as well as the use of natural ingredients, in the production of cosmetics sold primarily, although not exclusively, in Western markets. In 1978, Aveda launched a line of plant- and flower-based beauty treatments based on Ayurvedic philosophy and principles of aromatherapy; the company's products and policy of environmental sustainability quickly became popular throughout the USA (Aveda, 2010). In 1990, Estée Lauder began selling its Origins Natural Resources line, which uses recycled paper and includes make-up shades that emphasize natural skin tones, while avoiding animal products and petroleum-based active ingredients (Jones, 2010: 330). In 1992, the Western-educated biochemist, Vinita Jain, created Biotique, an Indian herbal cosmetics company; by 2000, it had sales of $13 million annually, 80 per cent of which were outside India (Jones, 2010: 332). Each in their own way, these examples testify that the globalization process works not only to homogenize, but also to facilitate the diffusion of different beauty practices around the globe. That is, beauty products which represent particular regions, peoples, and traditions circulate globally, taking diversity around the world and legitimizing the local in the process.

Conclusion

The global flow of beauty is not a simple or straightforward phenomenon. Instead, it involves multiple, complex, and even seemingly contradictory forces. In the preceding pages, I have outlined four such patterns of beauty's flow. In closing, however, I would like to move to the discussion of a phenomenon that bridges such patterns – namely, the increasingly prevalent view of the body as "unfinished", a collection of malleable surfaces ready to be inscribed with new meaning (Featherstone, 1991). While all cultures require their members to perform work on their bodies to transform them from a "natural" state to one that it more obviously "social", over time such requirements have grown increasingly invasive and apply to an ever-greater number of physical features. Indeed, numerous social critics have argued that fewer and fewer areas of the body remain free from the mandate for modification (Bartky, 1990; Wolf, 1991; Morgan, 1991). Thus, to the list of bodily regions long deemed in need of alteration (like breasts, bellies, and thighs), can be added newly "legitimate" targets of adornment (as in the "vagazzling" of women's pubic regions, in which crystals are applied to skin following the removal of pubic hair; see http://www.vajazzling.com/) and cosmetic surgical transformation of the genitalia and reproductive structures (e.g. labiaplasty, hymenoplasty, and vaginoplasty). Such mandates also apply to ever larger groups of people, independent of factors such as age. For instance, by the early 21st century, nearly half of 6 to 9-year-old girls in the USA were wearing lipstick, some two-thirds of preteens wanted to lose weight, and the number of adolescent girls receiving breast implants had quadrupled since the preceding decade (Rhode, 2010).

In the context of high modernity, beauty routines and reworkings are naturalized via commercial and media exposure. As one illustration, a *Wall Street Journal* article from 2009 announced recent trends in liposuction with the lead: "For the Body-Conscious, It's now the Ankle that Rankles" (Chozick, 2009). These processes are spurred by ever more creative marketing strategies such as "surgeon and safari" getaway vacations and girls' night out Botox parties (Cognard-Black, 2007: 47–48). As another example, the Aesthetica Salon in Los Angeles offers:

> the "perfect" "Say it with Liposuction" Valentine's Day gift "for the woman who has everything". This "ultimate cosmetic surgery experience" comes complete with stretch limousine travel, a twenty-four-hour private nurse, Dior robe, Godiva chocolate, and the "fixative" of her choice.
>
> (*Harper's Magazine*, August 1990: 31, cited in Rhode, 2010: 50–51)

One excellent illustration of the media's influence is the introduction of television to Fiji in the 1990s. Prior to that time, beauty ideals in Fiji had favoured plump bodies, while eating disorders were practically non-existent. Both changed dramatically, however, as television became commonplace. In fact, within only three years of the first broadcast, adolescent girls had started to reshape their bodies in the image of the super-slim female stars they admired; the incidence of eating disorders had also risen dramatically (Becker, 2004).

Such processes accompany the shift within modernity from birth-determined identity to self-fashioned identity; in that context, the role of appearance has taken on critical meanings, and thus "we find the movement of subjectivity more frequently deflected from placement in a social matrix and onto the surface of the body" (Miller, 2006: 11). Miller's statement suggests that the "somatic shift" may allow for greater social equality, at least in the sense that identities and statuses are achieved rather than ascribed. Indeed, various authors have lauded the opportunities provided by the ever-growing capacity to alter the body, particularly when such efforts are intended to subvert the normative (see, for example, Morgan, 1991). This position presents bodily practices that challenge contemporary beauty ideals as subverting certainties, unsettling comfortable expectations about the "natural" body (Pitts, 2003), and upsetting normative conceptions of appropriate femininity (Grosz, 1995). While such work has been accused of being "distressingly at one with the culture in celebrating the creative agency of individuals and denying systemic patterns" (Bordo, 1993: 31), it is an exaggeration to suggest that authors like Pitts (2003) ignore the structural and cultural obstacles to bodily self-narration and self-creation. In fact, Pitts (2003: 34) acknowledges that "self-invention is an *ideology* that informs body projects as much as it is a practice that constitutes them" (emphasis in original). She recognizes, moreover, that while the production of body and self may appear to be a uniquely individual endeavour, it is an endeavour that is located within a specific cultural and historical context and shaped by existing power relations.

The conditions of late modernity may well allow for new expressions of the embodied self (Giddens, 1991), but these expressions are undeniably shaped by the standardizing effects of commodity capitalism. In the logic of capitalism, everything may be transformed into a product or consumer good with worth, including beauty (Bordo, 1993; Shilling, 1993). Accordingly, the closer the body comes to prevailing ideals, the higher its exchange value (Featherstone, 1991). The meanings of the body and its modification are certainly not free-floating. Yet they are multiple, operating as a form of self-definition and differentiation (Miller, 2006), both within cultures and between them. The body's importance as the representation of selfhood is increasingly commonplace throughout the world. At the same time, the particular nature of the body–self relationship in any context is inherently local, the product of not only global capitalism but also the distinctive histories, traditions, and social relations of particular groups.

Note

1. Eyelids in which there are two folds rather than a single one, which is common among some groups of Asians.

References

Adrian, Bonnie. (2003) *Framing the Bride: Globalizing Beauty and Romance in Taiwan's Bridal Industry*, Berkeley: University of California Press.

Allen, Margaret. (1981). *Selling Dreams: Inside the Beauty Business*, New York: Simon and Schuster.

Allison, Anne. (1996) *Permitted and Prohibited Desires: Mothers, Comics and Censorship in Japan*, Boulder, CO: Westview Press.

AnyBody's Vent. (2012) "Susie Orbach speaks at the UN Commission on the status of Women", available at http://anybody.squarespace.com/anybody_vent/2012/3/6/susie-orbach-speaks-at-the-un-commission-on-the-status-of-wo.html.

Appaduri, Arjun. (1990) "Disjuncture and Difference in the Global Cultural Economy", *Theory, Culture & Society*, 7: 295–310.

Ashikari, Mikiko. (2003) "The memory of the women's white faces: Japaneseness and the ideal image of women". *Japan Forum*, 15: 55–79.

Aveda. (2010) "History of Aveda since 1978". http://www.aveda.co.uk/aboutaveda/history.tmpl.

Banet-Weiser, Sarah. (1999) *The Most Beautiful Girl in the World: Beauty Pageants and National Identity*, Berkeley: University of California Press.

Bartky, Sandra Lee. (1990) *Femininity and Domination: Studies in the Phenomenology of Oppression*, New York: Routledge.

Becker, Anne E. (2004) "Television, Disordered Eating and Television in Fiji: Body Image and Negative Identity during Rapid Social Change". *Culture, Medicine, and Psychiatry*, 28: 533–559.

Blaszczyk, Regina Lee. (2009) *American Consumer Society, 1865–2005*, Wheeling, IL: Harlan Davidson.

Bordo, Susan (1993) *Unbearable Weight: Feminism, Western Culture and the Body*, Berkeley: University of California Press.

Bornoff, Nicholas. (1991) *Pink Samurai: Love, Sex and Marriage in Contemporary Japan*, New York: Pocket Books.

Brownell, Susan. (2005) "China Reconstructs: Cosmetic Surgery and Nationalism in the Reform Era", in Joseph A. Alter (ed.) *Asian Medicine and Globalization*, Philadelphia, PA: University of Pennsylvania Press, pp. 132–150.

Campbell, Ian. (1992) *Island Kingdom, Tonga Ancient and Modern*, Christchurch: Canterbury University Press.

Chapkis, Wendy. (1986) *Beauty Secrets: Women and the Politics of Appearance*, New York: Women's Press.

Chozick, Amy. (2009) "For the Body-Conscious, It's Now the Ankle that Rankles", *The Wall Street Journal*, 23 July A1.

Cognard-Black, Jennifer. (2007) "Extreme Makeover, Feminist Edition: How the Pitch for Cosmetic Surgery Co-opts Feminism', *Ms.*, Summer, pp. 46–49.

Cohen, Colleen Ballerino, Wilk, Richard and Stoeltje, Beverly (1996) "Introduction: Beauty Queens on the Global Stage", in Colleen Ballerino Cohen, Richard Wilk and Beverly Stoeltje (eds.) *Beauty Queens on the Global Stage: Gender, Contests and Power*. New York and London: Routledge, pp. 1–12.

Condry, Ian. (2000) "The Social Production of Difference: Imitation and Authenticity in Japanese Rap Music", in U. Poigner and H. Fehrenback (eds.) *Transactions, Transgressions, Transformations: American Culture in Western Europe and Japan*, New York: Berghan Books, pp. 166–184.

Dahlburg, John-Thor. (1994) "Pageant Victories Inspire Debate Over Women's Roles", *The Los Angeles Times*, 25 November.

Davis, Kathy. (2003) *Dubious Equalities and Embodied Differences: Cultural Studies on Cosmetic Surgery*, Lanham, MD: Rowman & Littlefield.

Dewey, Susan. (2008) *Making Miss India Miss World: Constructing Gender, Power and Nation in Postliberalization India*, Syracuse: Syracuse University Press.

Dore, Ronald. (1958) *City Life in Japan*, London: Routledge and Kegan Paul.

Edmonds, Alexander. (2007a) " 'The Poor Have the Right to be Beautiful': Cosmetic surgery in Neoliberal Brazil", *Journal of the Royal Anthropological Institute*, 13(2): 363–381.

Edmonds, Alexander. (2007b) "Triumphant Miscegenation: Reflections on Race and Beauty in Brazil", *Journal of Intercultural Studies*, 28 (1):83–97.

Edmonds, Alexander. (2009) " 'Engineering the Erotic': Aesthetic medicine and modernization in Brazil", in Cressida Heyes and Meredith Jones (eds.) *Cosmetic Surgery: A Feminist Primer*, Aldershot: Ashgate, pp. 153–169.

Featherstone, Mike. (1991) "The Body in Consumer Culture", in Mike Hepworth, Bryan Turner, and Mike Featherstone (eds.) *The Body: Social Process and Cultural Theory*, London: Sage Publications, pp. 170–196.

Feldenkirchen, Wilfried and Hilger, Susanne. (2001) *Menschen and Marken: 125 Jahre Henkel 1876–2001*, Dusseldorf: Henkel KGaA.

Frost and Sullivan. (1983) *Marketing Strategies for Selling Cosmetics and Toiletries in Europe*, New York. April.

Giddens, Anthony. (1991) *Modernity and Self-Identity: Self and Society in the Late Modern Age*, Stanford: Stanford University Press.

Gilman, Sander. (1999) *Making the Body Beautiful: A Cultural History of Aesthetic Surgery*, Princeton: Princeton University Press.

Gilman, Sander. (2005) "Ethnicity and Aesthetic Surgery", in Angelika Taschen (ed.) *Aesthetic Surgery*, Cologne, London, Los Angeles, Madrid, Paris, Tokyo: Taschen Books, pp. 112–135.

Ghemawat, Pankaj, Kiron, David and Knoop, Carin-Isabel. (2006) "AmorePacific: From Local to Global Beauty", *Harvard Business School Case no.* 9–706–411, 21 November.

Godin, Seth. (2005) *All Marketers Are Liars: The Power of Telling Authentic Stories in a Low-Trust World*, New York: Portfolio Hardcover.

Gundle, Stephen. (2008) *Glamour: A History*, Oxford: Oxford University Press.

Grosz, Elizabeth. (1995) *Space, Time, and Perversion: Essays on the Politics of Bodies*, London: Routledge.

Haiken, Elizabeth. (1997) *Venus Envy: A History of Cosmetic Surgery*, Baltimore: The Johns Hopkins Press.

Halberstam, Judith. (1999) "F2M: The Making of Female Masculinity", in J. Price and M. Shildrick (eds.) *Feminist Theory and the Body*, New York: Routledge, pp. 125–133.

Hollander, Anne. (1993) *Seeing Through Clothes*, Berkeley: University of California Press.

Holliday, Ruth and Elfving-Hwang, Jo (2012) "Gender, Globalization and Plastic Surgery in Korea", *Body and Society*, (forthcoming).

Horne, John. (2000) "Understanding Sport and Body Culture in Japan". *Body & Society*, 6 (2): 73–86.

International Society of Aesthetic Plastic Surgeons (2010) "ISAPS Biennial Global Survey 2009. Worldwide Plastic Surgery Statistics Available for the

First Time", http://www. isaps. org/uploads/news_pdf/BIENIAL_GLOBAL_ SURVEY_press_release.pdf.

Jeffreys, Sheila. (2005) *Beauty and Misogyny: Harmful Cultural Practices in the West*, New York: Routledge.

Jones, Geoffrey. (2008) "Blonde and Blue-Eyed?: Globalizing Beauty, C.1945–1980", *Economic History Review*, 61: 124–154.

Jones, Geoffrey. (2010) *Beauty Imagined: A History of the Global Beauty Industry*, Oxford: Oxford University Press.

Jones, Meredith. (2008) *Skintight: An Anatomy of Cosmetic Surgery*, New York: Berg Publishers.

Katsikis, Ioannis N. (2009) "Market Demand and New Industry Formation: Eco-Products and Entrepreneurship in the Natural Cosmetics Sector in Greece", paper presented at the DIME Workshop on Environmental Innovation, Industrial Dynamics and Entrepreneurship, Utrecht University, 10–12 May 2009, Hotel Mitland, Utrecht, The Netherlands, http://www.dime-eu.org/files/active/0/Katsikis_Utrecht_2009.pdf.

Kaw, Eugenia. (1993) "Medicalization of Racial Features: Asian American Women and Cosmetic Surgery", *Medical Anthropology Quarterly*, New Series 7 (1): 74–89.

Kiehl's Since 1851. (2010) "About Us: Our Humble Beginnings . . . ", http://www.kiehls.com/About-Us/about-us,default,pg.html.

Kim, Taeyon. (2003) "Neo-Confucian Body Techniques: Women's Bodies in Korea's Consumer Society", *Body & Society*, 9 (2): 97–113.

King-O'Riain, Rebecca Chiyoko. (2006) *Pure Beauty: Judging Race in Japanese American Beauty Pageants*, Minneapolis: University of Minnesota Press.

Korres Natural Products USA. (2010) "Our Founders", http://www.korresusa.com/all-about-korres/our-founders.

Lebra, Takie Sugiyama. (1976) *Japanese Patterns of Behavior*, Honolulu: University of Hawaii Press.

Lee, E-Wha. (2006) *Korea's Pastimes and Customs: A Social History*, translated by J.-H. Park, Paramus, NJ: Homa and Sekey Books.

Levy, Howard. (1971) *Sex, Love and the Japanese*, Washington, DC: Warm-Soft.

'L'Oreal finds buzz in Niche Beauty', *Wall Street Journal*, 25 April 2007.)

McCraw, Thomas K. (2009) *American Business Since 1920: How it Worked*, Wheeling, IL: Harlan Davidson.

Miller, Laura. (2006) *Beauty Up: Exploring Contemporary Japanese Body Aesthetics*, Berkeley: University of California Press.

Morgan, Kathryn Pauly. (1991) "Women and the Knife: Cosmetic Surgery and the Colonization of Women's Bodies", *Hypatia*, 6 (3): 25–53.

Orbach, Suzie. (2010) *Bodies*, London: Profile Books, Ltd.

Peiss, Kathy (2002) "Educating the Eye of the Beholder: American Cosmetics Abroad", *Daedalus*, 131 (4): 101–109.

Pitts, Victoria. (2003) *In the Flesh: The Cultural Politics of Body Modification*, New York: Palgrave Macmillan.

Reiko Yano, Christine. (2006) *Crowning the Nice Girl: Gender, Ethnicity, and Culture in Hawaii's Cherry Blossom Festival*, Honolulu: University of Hawaii Press.

Rhode, Deborah L. (2010) *The Beauty Bias: The Injustice of Appearance in Life and Law*, New York: Oxford University Press.

Robertson, Roland. (1995) "Glocalization: Time-Space and Homogeneity-Heterogeneity", in Mike Featherstone, Scott Lash and Roland Robertson (eds.) *Global Modernities*, London: Sage, pp. 25–44.

"Say it with Liposuction" (1990) *Harper's Magazine*, August, p. 31.

Shilling, Chris. (1993) *The Body and Social Theory*, London: Sage.

Stepan, Nancy. (1982) *The Idea of Race in Science: Great Britain, 1800–1960*, London: Macmillan, in association with St. Anthony's College, Oxford.

Teilhet-Fisk, Jehanne. (1996) "The Miss Heilala Beauty Pageant: Where Beauty is More Than Skin Deep", in Colleen Ballerino Cohen, Richard Wilk and Beverly Stoeltje (eds.) *Beauty Queens on the Global Stage: Gender, Contests and Power*, New York and London: Routledge, pp. 185–202.

van Esterik, Penny. (1996) "The Politics of Beauty in Thailand", in Coleen Ballerino Cohen, Richard Wilk and Beverly Stoeltje (eds.) *Beauty Queens on the Global Stage: Gender, Contests, Power*, New York: Routledge, pp. 203–216.

Watson, James L. (ed.) (1997) *Golden Arches East: McDonalds in East Asia*, Stanford, CA: Stanford University Press.

Wilk, Richard. (1996) "Introduction: Beauty Queens on the Global Stage", in Coleen Ballerino Cohen, Richard Wilk and Beverly Stoeltje (eds.) *Beauty Queens on the Global Stage: Gender, Contests, Power*, New York: Routledge, pp. 1–11.

Wilk, Richard. (2004) "Miss Universe, the Olmec, and the Valley of Oaxaca", *Journal of Social Archaeology*, 4(1), 81–98.

Wolf, Naomi. (1991) *The Beauty Myth: How Images of Beauty Are Used Against Women*, New York: Vintage.

Wu, Judy Tsu-Chun. (1996) " 'Loveliest Daughter of Our Ancient Cathay': Representations of ethnic and gender identity in the Miss Chinatown USA Beauty Pageant", paper presented at Pacific Coast Branch, American Historical Association, San Francisco.

Wu, Judy Tsu-Chun. (1997) " 'Loveliest Daughter of Our Ancient Cathay': Representations of Ethnic and Gender Identity in the Miss Chinatown USA Beauty Pageant", *Journal of Social History*, 31: 5–31.

YMCA. (2012) "Parliament", available at http://www.ymca.co.uk/bodyconfidence /parliament, accessed 17 March 2012.

Zane, Kathleen. (2003) "Reflections on a Yellow Eye: Asian I(/eye\)cons and Cosmetic Surgery", in Amelia Jones (ed.) *The Feminist and Visual Culture Reader*, New York: Routledge, pp. 354–363.

8

Glocalization and the Simultaneous Rise and Fall of Democracy at the Century's End

Christopher Kollmeyer

Introduction

How has the intensification of globalization over the last few decades affected democracy at the national level? If one answers this important question by considering the circumstances in Europe's oldest democracies, then it appears that globalization is adversely affecting democratic governance. In general, two issues plague European democracy. The first is that, even before the onset of the current financial crises, globalization has been undermining the social model upon which European democracy rests. Emerging in the post-war era, this social model helped to consolidate democracy in Western Europe by successfully integrating the working class into mainstream society. This social integration was achieved politically by broadening participation in important decision-making processes (e.g. electoral politics and tripartite bargaining), and by equating democratic citizenship with a set of social rights that ensured decent living standards (e.g. universal health care and state pensions). In short, the European social model represented a historic compromise in which advocates of liberalism dropped their commitment to the laissez-faire market, and advocates of socialism dropped their commitment to the command economy (Hobsbawm, 1996: 268–286). What emerged was a system of hybrid institutions – such as the mixed economy, the regulated market, the welfare state, and corporatism – which were neither wholly capitalist nor wholly socialist. For decades, this model oversaw social stability, widespread prosperity, and democratic accountability in Western Europe, and later became a template for emerging democracies in Southern and Eastern Europe.

More recently, however, the viability of the European social model is being called into question. Here the main issue is that, in a world of heightened capital mobility, those controlling and managing capital can more easily sidestep the considerable expenses associated with the European social model by relocating their investments to other parts of the world. The ever-present threat of disinvestment, combined with a need to maintain economic competitiveness against low-cost producers in other parts of the world, is creating a situation in which public policy across Europe drifts ever towards the narrow interests of capital and further away from the general interests of society.

The second issue relates to a more general crisis of the nation-state and its capacities for effective governance. Increasingly, European electorates demand action across a range of pressing policy issues – for example, climate change, financial sector reform, immigration, tax avoidance by transnational corporations and European elites – but even well-intentioned officials lack the capacity to resolve these concomitant effects of globalization. This is the case because, by definition, globalization manifests as the spatial enlargement of many societal processes. This phenomenon, in turn, puts national officials in the unenviable position of having only limited influence over transnational processes, even though many of these transnational processes have considerable domestic effects. In short, globalization has unleashed social forces that are widening the mismatch between what European electorates demand of their governments and what their governments can actually achieve. In this way, the European democracies are experiencing a de facto loss of sovereignty.

Somewhat paradoxically, however, the view from many less-developed countries appears more sanguine. Despite the democratic malaise in Europe, many other parts of the world have been experiencing a democratic awakening. As recently as the mid-1970s, only a small minority of the world's countries were democracies, about 30 altogether, with the bulk of them being in Western Europe (Huntington, 1991; Markoff, 1996; Tilly, 2006). However, by the century's end, the situation had changed markedly, with new democracies not only taking root in Southern and Eastern Europe, but also Latin America, Southeast Asia, and sub-Saharan Africa. When this wave of democratization ended, the number of democracies in the world had trebled, bring the present total to about 90 (Freedom House, 2009). For some scholars, these events signalled not just a triumph for democracy, but a triumph for globalization as well. Such claims rest on the idea that globalization – by making commerce, civil society, and culture more transnational and hence less amenable to manipulation by political elites – tends to pushes authoritarian countries towards democracy.

The aim of this chapter is to explain this paradox. Put succinctly, the paradox is that globalization appears to promote democracy where it has never existed, but constrain democracy where it is highly developed. To help unravel this paradox, I draw on theoretical perspectives developed by two prominent British sociologists. The first perspective is associated with the work of Roland Robertson (1992, 1994, 1995) and centres on the idea that globalization-induced cultural change typically arises from an interplay between global and local forces, with neither of these forces reigning supreme. Robertson calls this process *glocalization*. From his perspective, globalization is not a juggernaut that obliterates national differences, although homogenizing tendencies clearly exist, but rather a force that interacts with local traditions and social structures, creating geographically distinct forms of social and cultural change. As I will endeavour to show in this chapter, this concept can help explain the paradoxical nature of contemporary democracy, because it allows for the possibility that global forces can inspire different types of political change in different parts of the world.

The second theoretical perspective centres on the work of T. H. Marshall (1950) and his typology of citizenship rights. Famously, Marshall noted that democracy in Britain developed in gradual stages, with each stage being marked by the issuance of new rights of citizenship. In short, Britain's sequential march towards democracy began in the 18th century with the issuance of civil rights, advanced further in the 19th century with the issuance of political rights, and culminated in the mid-20th century with the issuance of social rights. Drawing on this idea, some contemporary scholars note that cultural rights, broadly defined, are also an important aspect of citizenship, albeit these rights have not been fully enshrined in state policy (Pakulski, 1997; Stevenson, 2003). Despite some limitations with this paradigm, I will show that the Marshall original typology of citizenship rights can shed important light on the globalization–democracy paradox, largely because it allows for the possibility that globalization can strengthen some democratic rights but weaken others.

In what follows, I further elaborate on these theoretical ideas and use them to construct an overarching analysis of the political consequences of globalization. My general argument is that globalization creates pressure for political change almost everywhere (a universal tendency), but consistent with the premises of glocalization, these pressures bolster democracy in some countries but hinder it in others (a particularizing tendency). More specifically, what emerges is a pattern of political change in which globalization increases the democratic nature of many non-democratic countries, by prodding them to grant basic civil and political rights, but decreases the democratic nature of many long-standing democracies, by pressuring these countries to rollback social rights and by leaving elected officials without the proper means to control the domestic consequences of transnational processes. When combined, these dissimilar patterns of political change create a situation in which globalization has contributed to both the rise and fall of democracy at the same moment in history.

From globalization to glocalization

From the perspective of the social sciences, the concept of glocalization arose out of an attempt to better conceptualize the likely cultural consequences of globalization. Early scholarship on this topic tended to overemphasize globalization's capacity to induce cultural homogenization. Here, globalization was thought to facilitate a worldwide diffusion of undifferentiated consumer goods, ideas, and cultural practices, which, together, moved the world's diverse societies towards a common cultural banner. For example, in his early account of globalization, Barber (1992) pitted the highly powerful and culturally homogenizing forces of global capitalism against a myriad of disorganized and traditionally minded peoples fighting to retain their distinct ways of life. This implicitly depicted a world of binary opposites, in which the global forces of homogeneity were the primary agents of social change and the local forces of heterogeneity were at best, agents of resistance.

For Robertson (1992, 1994, 1995), such accounts of globalization under-appreciate what he sees as a fundamental aspect of globalization and sociocultural change. Following attempts within sociology to bridge the agency-structure and micro–macro dichotomies, Robertson maintains that any proper account of globalization must not only consider its homogenizing effects, but also its capacities to perpetuate heterogeneity. Nearly all commentators recognize that globalization involves the worldwide diffusion of similar products, cultural practices, and ideas, things that could potentially homogenize the world's national cultures, but, for Robertson, this is only half of the story. In addition to this aspect of globalization, he maintains that one must also recognize that local-level actors have the capacity to augment the effects of globalization by selectively adapting and partially incorporating globally diffused practices into their locally situated lives. He calls this process glocalization. For example, a recent study of American rap music in West Africa finds that, instead of embracing this type of music unchanged, local youths meld it with African rhythms, lyrics, and styles, with the outcome being a new musical genre known as "hiplife" (Oduro-Frimpong, 2009). Such findings are consistent with Robertson's larger point – namely that globalization tends to create cultural change worldwide, but that the resulting change is often locally distinct. In this way, globalization can be a force for heterogeneity as well as homogeneity, producing difference as well as sameness.

So far, the concept of glocalization has been associated almost entirely with the cultural dimension of globalization. This theoretical paradigm has proven useful in understanding the behaviour of Scottish football supporters in North America (Giulianotti and Robertson, 2004, 2006), the origins of Japanese cinematic styles (Yomota, 1999), and, as mentioned, new forms of popular music in West Africa (Oduro-Frimpong, 2009). For analytical purposes, it is important to note that each of these instances of cultural change arises from the same causal mechanism. Although not always explicitly noted, cultural glocalization occurs when local actors selectively adapt, partially incorporate, reinterpret, or recontextualize global cultural flows that emerge in their locales. This dynamic infers, in short, that cultural glocalization arises from the agency of local actors, who (to varying degrees) can modify globally diffused cultural practices, rendering them more consistent with their local traditions.

My interest in glocalization, however, rests not with its potential to understand cultural change, but with its potential to understand political change. To begin such an analysis, it is useful to note that the basic premise of glocalization – that the same global forces can create unique changes in different parts of the world – applies to other dimensions of society as well. For example, global production networks are contributing to the industrialization of less-developed countries, but also to the deindustrialization of affluent countries (Arrighi et al., 2003; Kollmeyer, 2009). In other words, the same global forces that are transforming countries like China and South Korea into industrial powerhouses are transforming countries across Europe into post-industrial societies.

In the case of the industrialization–deindustrialization nexus, the divergent patterns of economic change are propelled more by pre-existing structural differences across national economies than selective policy choices made at the local level. Here, the important structural difference is the large discrepancy between prevailing wages in developed and less-developed countries (see Kollmeyer, 2009, table 1). Attempting to generate large profits from these wage differences, many transnational firms locate their routine manufacturing jobs in less-developed countries (where wages are low), but sell most of the resulting products back in affluent countries (where consumer prices are much higher). The popularity of this global manufacturing strategy causes industrial employment to expand in less-developed countries, but contract in affluent countries. Again, pre-existing structural differences at the national level caused the same global process to produce different patterns of change in different parts of the world. As I will attempt to show in the remainder of this chapter, a similar story is unfolding in politics. Here it is my contention that globalization generally strengthens democracy in countries ruled by authoritarian regimes, but generally weakens democracy in countries with long traditions of democratic governance. To facilitate this argument, I briefly discuss the multiple dimensions of democracy by extending ideas developed by Marshall.

Multiple dimensions of democracy

In his now-classic book, *Citizenship and Social Class* (1950), Marshall developed what is arguably the most influential account of citizenship produced in the 20th century. Consistent with the tendency of Britons to see their modern country as the product of gradual reforms, rather than revolutionary changes, Marshall set out to explain how Britain transformed itself from a highly unequal and rigidly hierarchical society in feudal times, to one that had become much more inclusive and egalitarian by mid-20th century. His primary contention was that this transformation, which essentially represents the slow democratization of British society, can best be understood by examining how the rights of citizenship evolved in Britain over time. From this perspective, Britain took its first steps towards democracy during the 18th century when all citizens were granted basic civil or legal rights. These rights secured liberty for the individual by legally circumscribing the authority of the state, and by subjecting all citizens to the same set of laws, independent of their wealth and status. In the 19th century, the democratization of Britain advanced further when political rights were granted to the working class. These rights allowed all adult males, regardless of wealth or status, to run for public office, join political parties, and vote in free and fair elections – rights that were eventually extended to women in the early 20th century. Importantly, Marshall noted that the broadening of the franchise was not just beneficial in its own right. Rather, it also had the added effect of making pre-existing civil rights more meaningful for the working class, because now they could influence the nature of those rights through the legislative process.

Finally, Marshall argued that Britain entered its last phase of democratization when social rights were introduced in the mid-20th century. While the rule of law and universal suffrage had clearly made Britain more democratic – since they had abolished the feudal system of legally defined privileges and exclusions – barriers to a genuine democracy remained in place. In this regard, Marshall claimed that if all citizens have the same civil and political rights, yet some citizens cannot utilize these rights because of deep-rooted material deprivation, then for practical purposes the link between social class and citizenship that prevailed in feudal times had not been fully broken. For example, he states that "freedom of speech has little real substance if, from lack of education, you have nothing to say that is worth saying" (Marshall, 1950: 88). To remedy such problems, Britain and other modern democracies have sought, to varying degrees, to give their citizens social rights, which obligate the government to make real-world social and economic conditions more equal. This is accomplished by providing public services, such as free education and health care, and by setting minimum living standards beyond which citizens are not permitted to fall. However, social rights are difficult to entrench. Whereas civil and political rights can be indelibly codified in the constitution or other legal statues, social rights typically manifest in less durable forms, such as the annual budget for the welfare state. This makes them susceptible to retrenchment, a possibility that Marshall did not foresee.

Several caveats to Marshall's analysis are in order. First, it should be noted that democratization results neither from a natural process of social evolution, nor from the benevolence of the upper class, but rather from struggles surrounding the privileges of social class (Giddens, 1982, 1996; Turner, 1993). This implies, and I think Marshall would agree, that the broadening of citizenship has been the primary mechanism by which the excesses of capitalism and its attendant class system have been attenuated in democratic societies. Second, the sequence of development followed in Britain has not been followed by all European countries (Mann, 1993, 1996). For example, in Germany, the working class enjoyed many social rights, in the guise of the Bismarckian welfare state, well before they were granted full political rights (Mann, 1996: 133–135). Similarly, in Europe's formerly communist countries, social rights were well developed but civil and political rights were lacking. Such examples indicate that each dimension of citizenship can develop according to its own logic, and that the sequential order followed by Britain is by no means predetermined. Finally, beyond these omissions, Marshall's original analysis fails to consider gender, family, and cultural identity as salient categories around which struggles for rights have occurred (see, i.e., Vogel, 1994; Pakulski, 1997; Isin and Wood, 1999; Stevenson, 2003).

Despite its limitations, Marshall's typology of citizenship rights can be used to conceptualize democracy as having two dimensions, which can be combined to yield four ideal-types of political systems (see Figure 8.1). The *liberal dimension* forms one axis. It runs along a continuum with high levels of civil and political liberties at one end, and low levels of civil or political liberties at the other end. The *social democratic dimension* forms the other axis. It runs along a continuum with high levels of social rights and socio-economic equality at one end, and low levels of social rights and socio-economic equality at the other end. When combined, these two axes yield four ideal-types of political regimes: liberal democracies, social democracies, authoritarian regimes, and communist regimes, the latter often called "people's democracies".

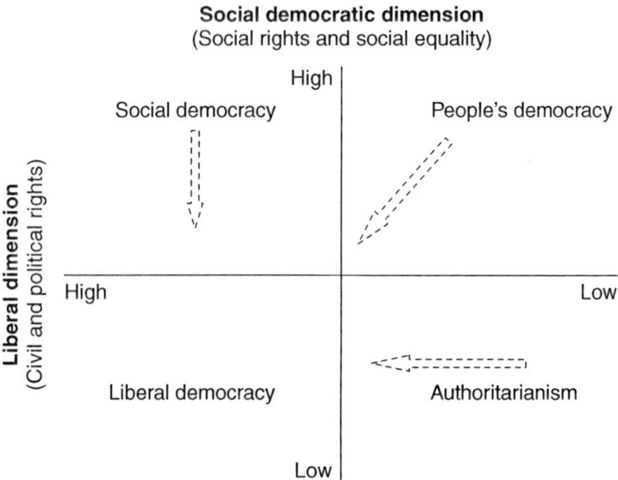

Figure 8.1 Two dimensions of democracy derived from Marshall's (1950) typology of citizenship rights

Note: Arrows represent direction of political change created by globalization.

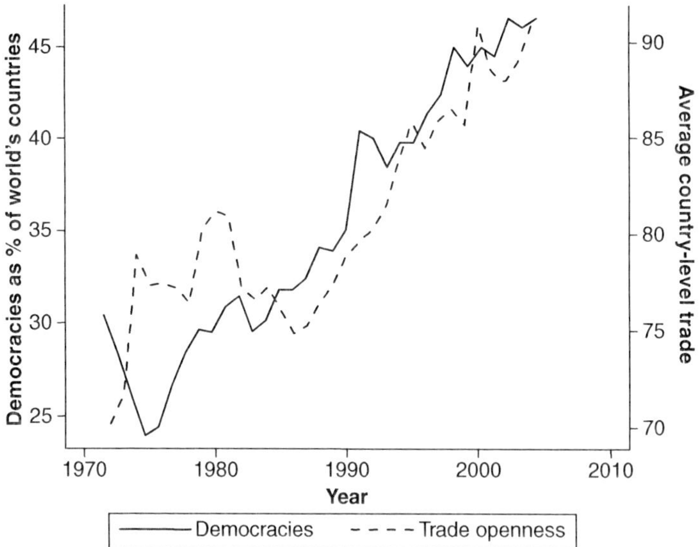

Figure 8.2 Correlation between global trade and the number of countries granting basic civil and political liberties to their citizens, 1972 to 2006

Note: Data on number of democracies in the world from Freedom House (2009), and data on average trade openness of the world's countries from United Nations (2009).

In what follows, I use this conceptual framework to argue that globalization is pushing the world's political systems towards the liberal model of democracy (a universal tendency), but resulting political changes increase the democratic nature of some countries and reduce the democratic nature of others (a particularizing tendency). Importantly, the concept of glocalization anticipates this pattern of political change.

Globalization spreads civil and political liberties

Many, but certainly not all, social scientists believe that globalization is having a positive effect on democracy. Such views are supported by the close historical congruence between the expansion of the global economy and the number of democracies in the world (see Figure 8.2). As discussed in the remainder of this section, several studies have examined this relationship by using quantitative measures of civil and political rights as proxies for liberal democracy.

The social science literature contains over 20 indices of what I call the liberal dimension of democracy. Perhaps the most widely used are the Freedom House (2009) indicators of political and civil liberties and the Polity IV indictors of political regime characteristics (Marshall and Jaggers, 2009). From 1972 onwards, the Freedom House index assesses civil and political rights in all countries of the world. Civil rights are measured by the presences and effectiveness of ten basic civil rights, including the right to free speech and association, the right to impartial application of the law, and the right to live without interference from the state. Political rights are measured by the presence and effectiveness of 15 basic political rights, including the right to vote and hold office, the right to join political parties, and the right to elect representatives who exercise power over public policy. Based on aggregate scores, countries are categorized as "free", "partly free", or "not free", with "free" countries being considered democracies. The other main index of democracy, Polity IV, operates on a similar logic but includes a much longer time frame and focuses only on political rights. Beginning with data from 1800, it assesses the competitiveness and openness of executive recruitment, constraints paced on executive power, and openness of political participation in countries where data is available. The resulting scores form the basis of a democratic–autocratic continuum.

The Freedom House and Polity IV indices have been used to assess various arguments about globalization's capacity to democratize authoritarian countries. Arguably, the most persuasive of these arguments contends that globalization, as a social and civil society phenomenon, exerts pressure on authoritarian rulers to adopt global norms for governance, which at this moment in history means adopting basic civil and political rights. This idea draws heavily upon "world polity" theory and its contention that the world is becoming an integrated social system, in which certain institutional forms and cultural practices have become de facto global standards (Meyer et al., 1997). Here, the main argument is that, due to the status and legitimacy bestowed upon democracy by the global community, less-developed countries can bolster their domestic and international credibility by adopting this form of governance. Using both Freedom House and Polity IV datasets, as well as measures of ties to the world polity, several scholars find that such "isomorphic" processes contribute to the diffusion and consolidation of democracy outside of the democratic West (Brinks and Coppedge, 2006; Gleditsch and Ward, 2006; Torfason and Ingram, 2010). Overall, this body of scholarship reaches the following conclusions: (1) international non-governmental organizations (INGOs), as important carriers of global norms, help to diffuse democracy; (2) authoritarian countries with democratic neighbours are more likely to become democracies than authoritarian countries without democratic neighbours; and (3) diffusion processes can work across geographically dispersed countries, if the affected countries are bound together by shared cultural traditions, strong diplomatic and civil society ties, or previous colonial linkages. Hence, for example, former British colonies are likely to be democracies.

Although poorly theorized, another argument contends that trade and capital account liberalization, two hallmarks of economic globalization, help create conditions conducive to democracy because they often disrupt and fragment the sources of power upon which authoritarian rulers depend (Rudra, 2005). Foreign investors may seek special privileges and concessions, which betray the ideals of democracy, but they also want governments to conduct their affairs in predictable, transparent, and legally abiding manners. In other words, they want to operate in countries where basic civil rights are respected. At the same time, economic globalization can also disrupt customary social arrangements, leading subordinate groups to become more politicized. Hence, with the business community becoming more powerful and subordinate groups becoming more politicized, authoritarian rulers may seek to appease critics by granting limited civil and political rights as concessions. Such compromises are believed to place affected countries on the path towards democracy. Using Freedom House and Polity IV data, along with measures of economic globalization, several scholars find empirical support for this theoretical argument (López-Córdova, et al., 2005; Rudra, 2005; Eichengreen and Leblang, 2008; cf. Reuveny, 2003; Milner and Mukherjee, 2009). This is not to say that basic liberties are secure everywhere. For multifaceted reasons, they are coming under pressure in numerous countries worldwide, including some European countries where democracy has been long established (see Robertson, 2007). The possibility of de-democratization is always present (Huntington, 1991; Markoff, 1996; Tilly, 2006).

Globalization undermines social rights and social equality

Paradoxically, just as democracy became the global norm for governance, many people began losing faith in its ability to produce fair and just societies. This view is particularly pronounced in Europe's oldest democracies, where many citizens feel that globalization reduces the democratic content of their political systems, even though the formal structures of their political systems are unchanged. Here, the general concern is that globalization, for reasons discussed in this section, tends to hamper the ability of democratically elected leaders to address pressing policy issues and to mitigate social inequality through the extension of social rights. Yet, unlike the literature on democratization in authoritarian countries, these contentions have not been subjected to same number of empirical tests, largely because measures of social citizenship and social equality are lacking. Nonetheless, there exists strong theoretical rational, and some empirical evidence as well, suggesting that globalization undermines what I call the social democratic dimension of democracy.

One prominent criticism of globalization is that it weakens and constrains the power of the nation-state, the very entity within which democracy has historically been embedded. As numerous scholars point out, the recent wave of globalization expanded the spatial mismatch between the territorial boundaries of the state and the far-reaching spatial configuration of many important social and economic processes (Held, 1995; Markoff, 1996, 1999: ch. 6; Sassen, 1996; Hirst and Thompson, 1999: 256–280; Fraser, 2008). This transformation leaves even the most powerful national governments with only limited control over the considerable domestic consequences of these transnational processes. For democracies, this outcome is particularly troublesome because it reduces the capacity of elected officials to achieve the policy objectives favoured by the electorate (Dryzek, 1996; Habermas, 1998; Cerny, 1999; Barber, 2000; Crouch, 2004). For instance, most of the British electorate want to rein in the risky business practices of the City, the British financial sector located in London. But, given that high finance operates at the transnational rather than national level, even the most sympathetic British officials will struggle to make this happen. In effect, the City has evaded some of the regulatory controls of the British state, and, in doing so, bypassed the democratic processes that hold them accountable to the British electorate. As this occurs in more and more areas of society, democracy becomes less meaningful to the lives of ordinary people.

Arguably, the greatest globalization-induced constraints arise in the area of economic and social welfare policy. During the immediate post-war period, when the scope of national economies and national political borders were more congruent, European governments could pursue a variety of strategies to promote stable economic growth and reduce socio-economic inequality (Ruggie, 1982, 2003; Hewitt, 1996; Habermas, 1998). Broadly speaking, these twin goals were achieved through some combination of Keynesian macroeconomic management and social welfare spending, which together allowed European governments to shield their citizens from undesired side effects of capitalism while maintaining robust economic growth. The European social model, which granted generous social rights to all citizens, sat at the centre of this system. However, in order to be effective, such strategies require that governments control the market conditions within their borders. Globalization, however, makes this increasingly difficult. Furthermore, due to greater geographic mobility of capital, European governments find themselves competing against each one another, and against low-wage countries, to attract capital investment. One ramification of this heightened competition for mobile capital is that policies favourable to the business community often trump policies supporting social rights – a significant change from the post-war era when these goals could be more evenly balanced. According to Habermas (1998), this routinely forces democratically elected officials to pursue policies that betray the desires of their electorates. At no time has this been more evident than during the recent sovereign debt crisis, which has propelled national governments in Europe (whether they be of the left, right, or centre) to push through the austerity measures demanded by international bond markets over the democratically voiced objections of their electorates.

Empirical research on this subject yields interesting results. One approach to answering this question centres on measuring the number and generosity of social rights offered to citizens of European democracies. Here, research by Korpi and Palme (2003, 2008) has been particularly influential. Their research measures the generosity of social citizenship rights granted in numerous Western European countries from 1930 onwards. The social rights are related to five potential areas of social need: old age, illness, unemployment, disability, and family change. Based on their data, they find that social rights in most European countries grew in number and generosity from 1930 until the late 1970s and early 1980s, at which time many European governments embarked upon a programme of retrenchment. This policy reversal, according to Korpi and Palme, was brought about by domestic political forces (the rise of neoliberal parties), and by global market forces (the need to accommodate global capitalism).

Another empirical approach to this question focuses on the overall level of social welfare spending in European countries. Here, important research conducted by Rodrik (1998) finds that, somewhat counterintuitively, the most globalized countries tend to have the largest welfare states. His explanation for this finding is not that proponents of globalization want generous welfare states, but rather that globalization exposes countries to greater amounts of economic insecurity, which in turn increases demand for social welfare spending. Integrating this view with Korpi and Palme's findings suggests that the retrenchment of the European welfare state manifests not as an outright reduction in social spending, but as a situation in which social need grows faster than social provision. For example, the unemployed in Europe today receive less generous benefits than their counterparts from decades past. Nonetheless, government budgets supporting this social right are expanding due to growth in unemployment.

Another prominent concern is that economic globalization disrupts the balance of class power upon which the entire notion of social citizenship rests. Since business activity is now territorially dispersed, highly flexible, but disproportionately controlled by transnational corporations and mega financial institutions, European workers have less political power than they enjoyed during the post-war era (Hewitt, 1996; Markoff, 1996: 127–141, 1999; Crouch, 2004: 31–52; Cowling and Tomlinson, 2005). The once impressive political power of the European working class has been eroded by the credible threat of capital flight, made possible by the ability of transnational corporations to relocate business activities across their globally dispersed production and distribution networks, and by the ability of financial investors to relocate their capital almost instantly.[1] These capacities leave European workers in precarious positions when bargaining for wages and social benefits, because instead of compromising on such issues, mobile capital can bypass the entire democratic process and relocate to more favourable business climates outside of Europe. This situation is compounded by the declining willingness and ability of European elected officials to aid workers and the general citizenry in their struggle for greater social equality. Combined, these changes have the following consequences: (1) market-generated socio-economic inequality is increasing, as, now, more of the wealth generated by economic activity manifests as profits rather than wages or taxes, and (2) many European governments are less inclined to mitigate these inequalities, as, now, political parties across the ideological spectrum embrace market competition, instead of universal social rights, as the preferred strategy for distributing scarce resources.

Elsewhere, I have attempted to test these broad claims with empirical evidence (Kollmeyer, 2003). Based on several indicators of social equality (running across 16 affluent democracies from 1960 to 1999), I find that social disparities have increased most notably in the United

States, and to a lesser extent in other English-speaking democracies including Britain. Conversely, in the countries of continental Europe and Scandinavia, social disparities have changed in less noticeable ways. The heterogeneity of experiences implies that national policies and institutions still exert considerable influence over the ultimate effects of globalization. Similar findings emerge from cross-national studies of income inequality (Alderson and Nielsen, 2002).

Conclusion and discussion

This chapter has sought to develop a theoretical account of the nature of political change brought about by contemporary globalization. Undoubtedly, growing connectivity among disparate parts of the world affects national systems of governance everywhere. Yet are these changes made making the world more or less democratic? The answer to this question is "both". This somewhat paradoxical answer makes sense, if we conceptualize democracy as having both a liberal dimension (comprised of civil and political rights fostering individual liberty) and a social democratic dimension (comprised of social rights fostering socio-economic equality). When viewed from this perspective, it becomes apparent that globalization induces the following political changes: (1) it increases the democratic quality of non-democratic countries, because here it pressures rulers to grant basic civil liberties and political rights, but (2) it decreases the democratic quality of Europe, because here generous social rights are threatened by the imperatives of global capitalism.

Importantly, the concept of glocalization anticipates the general thrust of these political changes. In his seminal essay on glocalization, Robertson (1995) points out that globalization-induced cultural change often embodies elements of "sameness" and "difference", "homogeneity" and "heterogeneity", "universalism" and "particularism". In short, globalization makes countries more similar and more different at the same time. At a general level, this is a reasonable depiction of how globalization affects democracy. On one hand, political systems worldwide are taking on common characteristics. In particular, manifesting as the worldwide spread of capitalism and as transnational isomorphic processes, globalization is prodding many non-democratic countries to grant their citizens basic civil and political freedoms. A few decades ago such freedoms were only found in a handful of countries, most of them located in Western Europe. Now these rights are much more widespread. Conversely, by constraining the policy options available to governments and by increasing the political power of capital, globalization is putting downward pressure on the generosity of social rights granted by European democracies. Consequently, in many European countries, class differences among citizens are widening.

There is another notable element of particularism in these changes. Given that globalization appears to make some countries more democratic but others less democratic, it logically holds that people around the world are experiencing these changes in qualitatively different ways. Generally speaking, people living in newly democratizing countries are clearly becoming better off because they are gaining rights they never had under authoritarian rule. Conversely, many people in Europe's oldest democracies are dissatisfied with these changes, because rights they long took for granted are being called into question. Hence, one's point of reference is key. After all, as Merton (1949) pointed out decades ago, people interpret their circumstances in reference to their immediate social world. Since the level of democratization varies worldwide, it follows that political changes brought about by globalization will induce qualitatively different experiences across the affected countries. Again, this pattern of global political change contains both elements of universalism and particularism, the hallmarks of glocalization.

Note

1. Oddly, some of the problems facing the European social model were brought about by its success. Decades of rising living standards, upward social mobility, and changing occupational structures have turned the traditional working class into a rump of its former self. This, in turn, leaves European societies with less of a counterweight to the interests of capital.

References

Alderson, Arthur S. and François Nielsen. (2002) "Globalization and the Great U-Turn: Income Inequality Trends in 16 OECD Countries", *American Journal of Sociology,* 107 (5): 1244–1299.

Arrighi, Giovanni, Beverly J. Silver and Benjamin D. Brewer. (2003) "Industrial Convergence, Globalization, and the Persistence of the North-South Divide", *Studies in Comparative International Development,* 38 (1): 3–31.

Barber, Benjamin R. (1992) "Jihad vs. McWorld", *Atlantic Monthly,* 269 (3): 53–65.

Barber, Benjamin R. 2000. "Can Democracy Survive Globalization?" *Government and Opposition,* 35 (3): 275–301.

Brady, David, Martin Seeleib-Kaiser and Jason Beckfield. (2005) "Economic Globalization and the Welfare State in Affluent Democracies, 1975–2001", *American Sociological Review,* 70 (6): 921–948.

Brinks, Daniel and Michael Coppedge. (2006). "Diffusion Is No Illusion: Neighbor Emulation in the Third Wave of Democracy", *Comparative Political Studies,* 39 (4): 463–489.

Bulmer, Martin and Anthony M. Ress. (1996) "Citizenship in the 21st Century", in Martin Bulmer and Anthony M. Rees (ed.) *Citizenship Today: the Contemporary Relevance of T.H. Marshall,* London: UCL Press.

Cerny, Philip G. (1999) "Globalization and the Erosion of Democracy", *European Journal of Political Research,* 36 (1): 1–26.

Cowling, Keith and Philip R. Tomlinson. (2005) "Globalisation and Corporate Power", *Contributions to Political Economy,* 24 (1): 33–54.

Crouch, Colin. (2004) *Post-Democracy,* Cambridge: Polity.

Dryzek, John S. (1996) *Democracy in Capitalist Times: Ideals, Limits, and Struggles,* Oxford: Oxford University Press.

Eichengreen, Barry and David Leblang. (2008) "Democracy and Globalization", *Economics & Politics,* 20 (3): 289–334.

Fraser, Nancy. (2008) *Scales of Justice: Reimagining Political Space in a Globalizing World,* Cambridge: Polity Press.

Freedom House. (2009) "Freedom in the World, 2009", New York: Freedom House.

Giddens, Anthony. (1982) "Class Divisions, Class Conflict, and Citizenship Rights", in Anthony Giddens and Fred Reinhard Dallmayr (ed.) *Profiles and Critiques of in Social Theory,* London: MacMillian.

Giddens, Anthony. (1996) "T.H. Marshall, the State, and Democracy", in Martin Bulmer and Anthony M. Rees (ed.) *Citizenship Today: The Contemporary Relevance of T.H. Marshall,* London: UCL Press.

Giulianotti, Richard and Roland Robertson. (2004) "The Globalization of Football: A Study in the Glocalization of the 'Serious Life'", *British Journal of Sociology,* 55 (4): 545–568.

Giulianotti, Richard and Roland Robertson. (2006) "Glocalization, Globalization and Migration: The Case of Scottish Supporters in North America", *International Sociology,* 21 (2): 171–198.

Gleditsch, Kristian S. and Michael D. Ward. (2006) "Diffusion and the International Context of Democratization", *International Organization,* 60: 911–933.

Habermas, Jürgen. 1998. "Beyond the Nation-State?" *Peace Review,* 10 (2): 235–239.

Hadenius, Axel. (1997) *Democracy's Victory and Crisis,* Cambridge: Cambridge University Press.

Held, David. (1995) *Democracy and the Global Order: From Modern State to Cosmopolitan Governance,* Stanford: Stanford University Press.

Hewitt, Patricia. (1996) "Social Justice in a Global Economy", in Martin Bulmer and Anthony M. Rees (eds.) *Citizenship Today: the Contemporary Relevance of T.H. Marshall,* London: UCL Press.

Hirst, Paul and Grahame Thompson. (1999) *Globalization in Question, 2nd Edition.* Cambridge: Polity Press.

Hobsbawm, Eric. (1996) *The Age of Extremes: A History of the World, 1914–1991,* New York: Vintage Books.

Huntington, Samuel P. (1991) *The Third Wave: Democratization in the Late Twentieth Century*, Norman: University of Oklahoma Press.

Isin, Engin F. and Patricia K. Wood. (1999) *Citizenship and Identity*, London: Sage.

Kollmeyer, Christopher. (2003) "Globalization, Class Compromise, and American Exceptionalism: Political Change in 16 Advanced Capitalist Countries", *Critical Sociology*, 29 (3):369–391.

Kollmeyer, Christopher. (2009) "Consequences of North-South Trade for Affluent Countries: A New Application of Unequal Exchange Theory", *Review of International Political Economy*, 16 (5): 803–826.

Korpi, Walter and Joakim Palme. (2003). "New Politics and Class Politics in the Context of Austerity and Globalization: Welfare State Regress in 18 Countries, 1975–95", *American Political Science Review*, 97: 425–446.

Korpi, Walter, and Joakim Palme. (2008) *The Social Citizenship Indicator Program (SCIP)*, Swedish Institute for Social Research, Stockholm University.

López-Córdova, J. Ernesto and Christopher M. Meissner. (2005) "The Globalization of Trade and Democracy, 1870–2000", Washington, DC: National Bureau of Economic Research.

Mann, Michael. (1993) *The Sources of Social Power. Volume II: The Rise of Classes and Nation-States, 1760–1914*, New York: Cambridge University Press.

Mann, Michael. (1996) "Ruling Class Strategies and Citizenship", in Martin Bulmer and Anthony M. Rees (eds.) *Citizenship Today: the Contemporary Relevance of T.H. Marshall*, London: UCL Press.

Markoff, John. (1996) *Waves of Democracy: Social Movements and Political Change*, Thousand Oaks, CA: Pine Forge Press.

Markoff, John. (1999) "Globalization and the Future of Democracy", *Journal of World-Systems Research*, 2: 277–309.

Marshall, T. H. (1950) *Citizenship and Social Class and Other Essays*, Cambridge: Cambridge University Press.

Marshall, Monty and Keith Jaggers. (2009) "Polity IV Project: Political Regime Characteristics and Transitions, 1800–2007". George Mason University: Center for Systemic Peace.

Merton, Robert K. (1949) *Social Theory and Social Structure*, New York: Free Press.

Meyer, John W., John Boli, George M. Thomas and Francisco O. Ramirez. (1997) "World Society and the Nation-State", *American Journal of Sociology*, 103 (1):144–181.

Milner, Helen V. and Bumba Mukherjee. (2009) "Democratization and Economic Globalization", *Annual Review of Political Science*, 12: 163–181.

Oduro-Frimpong, Joseph. (2009) "Glocalization Trends: The Case of Hiplife Music in Contemporary Ghana", *International Journal of Communication*, 3: 1085–1106.

Pakulski, Jan. (1997) "Cultural Citizenship", *Citizenship Studies*, 1 (1): 73–86.

Robertson, Roland. (1992) *Globalization: Social Theory and Global Culture*, London: Sage.

Robertson, Roland. (1994) "Globalisation or Glocalisation?" *Journal of International Communication*, 1 (1): 33–52.

Robertson, Roland. (1995) "Glocalization: Time-Space and Homogeneity-Heterogeneity", in Featherstone, Mike, Scott Lash, and Roland Robertson (eds.) *Global Modernities*, London: Sage.

Robertson, Roland. (2007) "Open Societies, Closed Minds? Exploring the Ubiquity of Suspicion and Voyeurism", *Globalizations*, 4 (3): 399–416.

Rodrik, Dani. (1998) "Why do More Open Economies Have Bigger Governments?", *Journal of Political Economy*, 106 (5): 997–1032.

Rudra, Nita. (2005) "Globalization and the Strengthening of Democracy in the Developing World", *American Journal of Political Science*, 49 (4): 704–730.

Ruggie, John G. (1982) "International Regimes, Transactions, and Change: Embedded Liberalism in the Postwar Economic Order", *International Organization*, 36 (2): 379–415.

Ruggie, John G. (2003) "Taking Embedded Liberalism Global: The Corporate Connection", in Held, David and Mathias Koenig-Archibugi (eds.) *Taming Globalization: Frontiers of Governance*, Cambridge: Polity Press.

Sassen, Saskia. (1996) *Losing Control: Sovereignty in an Age of Globalization*, New York: Columbia University Press.

Stevenson, Nick. (2003) "Cultural Citizenship in the 'Cultural' Society: A Cosmopolitan Approach", *Citizenship Studies*, 7 (3): 331–348.

Tilly, Charles. (2006) *Democracy*, Cambridge: Cambridge University Press.

Torfason, *Magnus Thor and Paul* Ingram. (2010) "The Global Rise of Democracy: A Network Account", *American Sociological Review*, 75 (3): 355–377.

Turner, Bryan. (1993) "Contemporary Problems in the Theory of Citizenship", in edited by Bryan S. Turner (eds.) *Citizenship and Social Theory*, London: Sage.

United Nations. (2009) *UN Commodity Trade Statistics Database (COMTRADE)*. New York: United Nations Statistics Division.

Vogel, Ursula. (1994) "Marriage and the Boundaries of Citizenship", in Bart van Steenbergen (ed.) *The Condition of Citizenship*, London: Sage Publications.

Yomota, Inuhiko. (1999) "New Challenges for Japan: A Historical Look at Japanese Film in a Glocal Context", *Japan Review of International Affairs*, 134: 277–293.

Epilogue

The Provincialization of Europe?

Roland Robertson

In addressing the issues of the analysis and comparison of sociocultural entities on a global scale, Ulf Hannerz argues that nations – or national entities – appear to be part of the natural order of things, but "by now even larger-scale entities such as continents may seem most enduringly given, yet we are at least vaguely aware that these, too, are notions which made their appearance at some point in history" (Hannerz, 2009: 268). Even more relevant to this epilogue, Hannerz (2009: 268) shows that the concept of "Europe" emerged, as he puts it, about 300 years ago. However, with the changing boundaries and what Hannerz (2009: 268) calls the "two-steps-forward, one-step-backward integration of the European Union, we are again not quite sure what sort of entity it is". Hannerz (2009: 268) strengthens his argument by maintaining that the name West Indies was rapidly discovered to be a misnomer, while "the Near East, Middle East and Far East are obviously Eurocentric categories...".

Generally speaking, Europe has manifested a great "openness" (or vulnerability) to multiplicity; indeed, this very feature threatens to lead to its dissolution – more specifically the end of the European Union as we now know it. This has been expressed in one way or another in a few of the preceding chapters. In this epilogue I seek to show the significance of the shifting boundaries of Europe over a long period. As Hannerz states in the preceding quotations, Europe in the sense of the name, "Europe", emerged significantly more than a thousand years ago. What we call "Europe" at the present time is the outcome of a long succession of projects – for example, ecclesia, community, empire, church, and European Union (Guenoun, 2013). Guenoun claims that many of these conceptions have been constructed in contrast to an Oriental "other", although, of course, orientalism in the conventional "modern" sense has been in play throughout European history (Neumann, 1996, 1999). In this epilogue I attempt to sketch the history and the geo-cultural place of Europe in the world. As I emphasize at the outset, a rather glaring weakness is that most studies of Europe have tended to be Eurocentric (cf. Outhwaite, 2008). Of course, Eurocentric and Eurocentricity are highly contested words (Bhambra, 2007). I follow Bhambra in defining Eurocentrism thus: "Eurocentrism is the belief, implicit or otherwise, in the world historical significance of events believed to have developed endogenously within the cultural-geographical sphere of Europe." In *Rethinking Modernity* Bhambra (2007) seeks to contest Eurocentrism in various ways, being particularly concerned with the tendency of many to equate Europe with modernity.

One particular attempt to specify and explore the "origins of Europe" is that of Hodges and Whitehouse (1983) in their book, *Mohammed, Charlemagne and the Origins of Europe*. The latter carries the subtitle *Archaeology and the Pirenne Thesis*. Of course, it is clear that Hodges and Whitehouse were mainly concerned with the so-called Pirenne thesis that dominated thinking about Europe from the early 1930s until the early 1980s – or at least this was thought by many to be the history of the Middle Ages in Europe (e.g. Pirenne, 1925, 1939). However, it is not my concern here to assess the accuracy or worthwhileness of the thesis of Hodges and Whitehouse or other endeavours "of family resemblance", but simply to provide this as an exemplification of a Eurocentric view of European history.

Is it possible for there to be an Archimedean point from which to "gaze" upon Europe? Moreover, is such a vantage point desirable, let alone viable? These questions are necessary because there seems, for many, to be a need for an alternative to what is usually called Eurocentrism. In the last 30 years or so there have developed a number of overlapping alternatives to Eurocentrism. Some adopt the position that Europe can best be looked upon from a particular region or area of the world. Such is implied by the ancient Chinese view that China was/is the Middle Kingdom. In fact, in one way or another, many if not most societies or civilizations have considered their territory and culture to be central to the world as a whole and its history. In Japan a similar example is the concept of *Nihonjinron*, this meaning that Japan is considered to be the world's most sacred place and the beginning of life on earth. In fact, there is a special intellectual preoccupation with what can be translated as Japanology – basically the study of Japan's uniqueness and special significance. Some Japanologists take their views to extremes so as to promote ideas such that the Japanese language cannot be understood as just one language among others, that the metabolisms of Japanese people are entirely unique, and so on and so forth. To lesser or greater degrees most, if not all, societies have such beliefs, even though, in our highly compressed world, and with the global consciousness that we have, it becomes much less easy to sustain them. Here it should be stressed that, in speaking of global consciousness, I do not intend to convey the idea that such consciousness is consensual. By using this term I am simply stating that nearly all of the peoples in the world have some kind of conception of the world as a whole (Tsing, 1993, 2005; Robertson, 2011). In fact, the more compressed the world becomes and the more the contestation with respect to quotidian conceptions of the world as a whole increases, the more claims as to "ultimate origins" are intensified.

The principal contemporary analytical perspective that has explicitly involved the attempt to provincialize Europe has derived from the overlapping fields of subaltern and post-colonial studies (Bhambra, 2007; Spivak, 1999). It is Chakrabarty (2000) who has spoken most explicitly about the provincialization of Europe. However, in the title of this epilogue I have definitely placed a question mark after "Europe". The question mark denotes that I am not committed in a "militant" sense to arguing that Europe has been provincialized. A better concept to express my intentions is *relativize*. Relativization must be a key concept in any attempt to comprehend the world as a whole, or parts thereof. In speaking of relativization I mean merely that no global unit can stand, or should be considered, on its own, and that, in fact, world history has largely consisted of civilizations, regions, alliances, or societies attempting to outdo other such "units". The contemporary German historian, Jürgen Osterhammel (2014), eloquently puts it thus:

> Two or three decades ago, the history of the modern world could still blithely proceed on the assumption of "Europe's special path". Today, historians are trying to break with European (or "Western") smugness and to remove the sting of "special path" notions by means of generalization and relativization.

Linda Colley (2013: 18) says that Hans Kohn's *The Age of Nationalism: The First Era of Global History* (1962) was the first book published in English designed to address our increasingly global age. It is also appropriate here to state that relativization is as historical as it is geographical or spatial and this compels us to invoke Janet Abu-Lughod's *Before European Hegemony* (1989), a book that convincingly argues against Eurocentrism with respect to the making of the "world system".

Hannerz regards the concept of geo-cultural scenarios as a particularly helpful way of comprehending the world as a whole. The two parts of the word "geo-culture", in combination, bring together and cross the fault lines of, on the one hand, cultural continuities and, on the other, cultural discontinuities. In this epilogue I apply some of the insights of Hannerz to the foregoing chapters. This involves approaching the topic from two different, but complementary, directions. For example, I discuss the discourse of "triumphant Europe", comparing it with much less optimistic views of the "destiny" of Europe. I will also consider Europe as it is conceived by "outsiders", attending in particular to what is often called subaltern, or post-colonial, thinking. In these and other cases I bring into play much of what I have said before concerning glocalization. Obviously so-called subaltern thinking, for example, comes in a variety of forms, depending upon the national–cultural heritage of the writer (cf. Moyn, 2013). Moreover, a great deal of rival thinking about the West and the world as a whole has been accomplished by Amartya Sen (e.g. Sen, 2005).

In this concluding chapter I outline the basic requirements of such an endeavour and sketch some pivotal features of the regional aspects of such. I am particularly concerned to reduce, if not entirely obliterate, the triumphalism involved in much (European) academic-intellectual thinking about Europe. Having said this, it must be strongly emphasized that this attempt to *relativize* Europe has nothing to do with the anti-European sentiments so strongly expressed in recent years by militant, "extremist" movements; nor of the hostility towards Europe in Russia, other parts of the former Soviet Union, China, and, to a lesser extent, in Africa and Latin America (cf. Tsytankov, 2006). At the other extreme, an excellent example of what I call European triumphalism is expressed by Ulrich Beck in his statement that "the catch-phrase for the future might be 'Move Over America – Europe is back' " (quoted in Marquand, 2011: 24.) Marquand (2011: 1–26) invokes other such claims from writers in Western Europe, involving what might well be called the glocalization of European triumphalism.

There is a particular difficulty at this moment in dealing with such a problem in the sense that there is, in recent geo-cultural discourse, a frequent conflation of Europe and the USA (e.g. Judt, 2006; Kane,

2006).This is particularly ironic in the sense that much of Europe's self-identity has, in the recent past, consisted of opposition to, or distrust of, the USA. In any case there is now a strong tendency to refer simply to "the West" (e.g. Moyo, 2011); this in spite of significant tensions between the USA and the EU, particularly concerning trade and commerce.

Not so long ago it was quite common for the idea of a global triad to be employed as a depiction of the dominant portion of the world as a whole: the triad consisting of a Japan-centred East, a Germany-centred Europe, and a USA-centred western hemisphere (Robertson, 1992: 182–188, 1997). Obviously the "shape" of the world has changed a fair amount over the last three decades. We now find that there is much talk of the BRIC countries (Brazil, Russia, India, and China) with South Africa often being added (BRICS). Other blocs have also been suggested, such as the MINT bloc (Mexico, Indonesia, Nigeria, and Turkey.) On the other hand, after the fall of the Berlin Wall in 1989, there was much talk of the end of a bipolar world and the rise of the conception of a unipolar world, one dominated by the USA. There was also, on the other hand, much talk of a multipolar world. (As of mid-2014 it would be more accurate to speak of a world in disarray, or one of shifting configuration.)

The idea of a Japan-centred East has been heavily questioned by the relative decline of Japan in relation to its neighbour, China. Indeed, the considerable tension between China and Japan is one of the most significant global flashpoints at present; the tension between the two being centred upon their respective claims to islands in the East China Sea. (Other countries are, of course, involved in these disputes.) Undoubtedly, one of the most crucial issues in the contemporary world is the "rise" of China, although this relates in a much more general sense to the whole question of the relationship between Orientalism and Occidentalism. While the first of these terms is well known but often misused (Robertson, 1990), the second has only recently become adequately employed (e.g. Buruma and Margalit, 2004). As already stated, perhaps the most noteworthy aspect of this change in the Eastern part of the so-called triad is the rapid and highly impressive rise of China (Shambaugh, 2011; Fenby, 2014; Dyer, 2014; cf. Guthrie, 2012; Hutton, 2007) of which I will say more.

It should be noted that the attempt by Putin to place Russia firmly back on the "world map", and its tentative (and problematic) alliance with China, has greatly complicated the position of Europe (Arutunyan, 2014). Much of the remainder of this present chapter will be devoted not merely to the latter's changing position in terms of relations with other blocs, but also to its severe crises in the period beginning in 2008. Much of this has been centred on the Eurozone financial, economic crisis of 2010 and the fall-out from it. On occasion the Eurozone crisis has been characterized as a form of internal colonialism.

However, in spite of recent events that have raised the entire question of the identity, the cultural cohesion, the boundaries, or the general condition of Europe, it is, for the most part, the issue of Islam and the Middle East and adjacent regions that have caused the greatest concern. More specifically, it is the "war on terror" – as it is frequently called – that has been the symbolic pivot of most discourse about this region, at least from outside the latter. However, it has fairly frequently been used within the Middle East as a way of rhetorically distancing one state, or the dominant elite of that state, from other states in the region. For example, the "war on terror" has been "successfully" employed by the Assad regime in Syria against its alleged or declared enemies within, as well as by Russia, in an apparently pro-Assad sense, and by "the West", in an anti-Assad respect. In Israel it has been employed as a way of attempting to associate Israel with "the West" against Islamism; while it has also been used by Israel against "the Palestinians", particularly Hamas. In any case, the "war on terror" has become, since 9/11, a mantra – a slogan or a symbol that serves a variety of instrumental purposes. In this regard many European societies have been eager participants in, or at least have been drawn into, this discursive game. It has become conceptually a very unhelpful, but nevertheless seemingly unavoidable, point of reference for serious analysis.

In turn, the entire issue of the war against terror has become complexly bound-up with the whole question of the admissibility of Turkey to the European Union. The raising of "the issue of Islam" as a potential or actual challenge to "the West" has resurrected in collective memories the issues of the Christian Crusades of the 11th to the 13th centuries and the formation of the Ottoman Empire; an empire that, at its greatest reach, extended from Vienna in Central Europe all the way round the Mediterranean to Iberia in the west. In fact, another slogan of the period immediately following the attacks of 9/11 was the deployment of the idea that the West (in particular the UK and the USA) would mount its own "crusade" against the perpetrators of 9/11. Enthusiasm for this varied a great deal in Europe. In any case, attacks in London and Madrid were seen by many Europeans as parallels to and/or copies of 9/11. After 9/11 there was controversy, that has lasted until the present day, concerning the Blair–Bush-led invasion of Iraq as well as the somewhat more understandable effort to capture Bin Laden and/or obtain revenge on the Al-Qaeda Movement that he led in Afghanistan.

It is of significance to note that the first Western chartered trading company was the English Levant Company, which was formed in 1581 to trade with the Ottoman Empire. This was the forerunner of the enormously significant East India Company, which was founded at the end of the 1590s, along with other chartered companies that were involved in the opening-up of India and China. The Ottomans posed a great threat to much of Central and Eastern Europe, and only began to be repelled after their defeat at Vienna in 1529. The "defeat" of the Muslims was claimed as "their" victory, on behalf of European civilization, by a number of different East and Central countries. (This could, indeed, be regarded as the glocalization of the overall defeat of the Ottomans.) By the late 19th century the Ottoman Empire – principally in the form of Turkey – was known widely as the sick man of Europe, in spite of it not being regarded as a genuinely European country or region. Even though Turkey, after the fall of the Ottoman Empire, became a fully separate independent republic in 1923, it was to become, primarily for strategic reasons, a member of NATO; an alliance that was established to defend the West against the threat of (Russian) Soviet communism. However, as the European community expanded, the question of Turkey's membership became increasingly controversial and its position geopolitically ambiguous and unstable. (Turkey had been an ally of Germany and what were known as the central powers in Europe during the First World War.)

The defeat of Germany and its Allies, including the Ottomans (Turkey) at the end of the First World War in 1918 led to the fall of three major empires: the Habsburg (Austria- Hungary), the Romanov (Russia), and the Ottoman (Turkish), as well as the overwhelming, if temporary, defeat of the German Reich. The immediate consequence of the fall of the Ottoman Empire facilitated the intensification of the imperial rivalry between the two most prominent imperial Western allies, namely Britain and France. Both of the latter countries had conflicting imperial claims over much of the old Ottoman Empire. This rivalry was particularly acute in the area immediately adjacent to the eastern Mediterranean. In terms of the Paulet–Newcombe Agreements of 1920–1923, mandates or spheres of control were awarded to France with respect to Syria and Lebanon, and to Britain with respect to Palestine. Following the establishment of the state of Israel within the area covered by the British mandate in 1948, and the largely consequent assertion of Arab nationalism led by Gamal Abdel Nasser, the situation in that part of the Middle East became particularly tense. This led to a series of wars and conflicts, the most significant resulting in the nationalization of the Suez Canal in 1956 and the Six-Day War of 1967. Even though the French and the British had long been imperial rivals, they nonetheless collaborated, together with the new state of Israel, in the invasion of Egypt. The Suez Canal was regarded as being vital to both the British and the French since it had been constructed, largely under French control, in order to facilitate much faster access to Asia and the east coast of Africa. It prevented ships having to travel around the Cape of Good Hope and other interested parties having to journey overland to India and China.

In spite of Jihadist Islam appearing to be the greatest challenge or problem to Europe in the recent past it is now, in 2014, the aggression of Russia – or its resistance to the expansion of the West – that seems even more formidable. In fact, it is the challenge to Russia on the part of the former Soviet, Islamic republics that has resulted in this mixture of Russian–Islamic challenges to Europe.

The dominant European colonization of India was undertaken by the British and the French, although the Dutch and the Portuguese played a not insignificant part. In any case, it was undoubtedly the charter trading companies of England/Britain, Holland, France, and Portugal that were of enormous significance in the subjugation and exploitation of India. The (British) East India Company was particularly "successful" in this respect. It regarded the Indians as racially inferior and gained so much power that, in 1813, the British government made serious attempts to mitigate the activities not merely of the Company but also of the Christian missionaries who were unwilling to accept the indigenous religions, notably Hinduism and Islam. By the mid-19th century India was regarded as the jewel in the British crown, and at the century's end Queen Victoria was made Empress of India.

Africa and Latin America have become increasingly prominent in recent years; in large part because of their "penetration" by China, mainly because of the latter's success in obtaining access to raw materials and, to varying degrees, becoming an "ally" of a number of countries in these two parts of the southern hemisphere.

Historically, it has been Latin American countries that have been the most assertive with respect to their attempts to find a prominent place in the contemporary world (Guardiola-Rivera, 2010). This is largely because of the way in which Portugal and Spain decided to colonize the world in the late 15th century, with Portugal taking the East and Spain the West, the principal exceptions being Portugal taking Brazil and Spain the Philippines (Brotton, 2012: 186–217). These developments could be regarded as having constituted the earliest form of "modern" imperialism, and overlapped with the Protestant revolt against the Catholic Church in much of Europe. The Treaty of Tordesillas that divided "the world" between Portugal and Spain was "one of the earliest and most hubristic acts of European global imperial geography, the two crowns [agreeing] that 'a boundary or straight line be determined and drawn north and south, from pole to pole, on the said ocean sea, from the Arctic to the Antarctic pole...'" (Brotton, 2012: 186). Brotton (2012: 187) goes on to say that the world was literally divided in half by the two European kingdoms of Spain and Portugal, "using a map to announce their global ambition". The capture of Latin America by these two Iberian countries was what might be called both "compensation" for the loss of large portions of Europe north of the Mediterranean, as far as the Catholic Church was concerned, and a continuation and further implementation of the spirit that had repelled the Muslims (Robertson, 1986, 1987; McDonagh, 2009).

Catholicism was introduced to Latin America (from Europe) in a basically medieval (pre-Reformational) way and in close, if unequal, alliance with pre-capitalist dominant classes; this having much to do with the present relatively peripheral status of Latin America in relation to transnational Roman Catholicism. (Of course, the recent appointment of an Argentinian Pope and the rapid economic rise of Brazil have changed this substantially.) In fact, it was in the years following the French Revolution and the Napoleonic Wars that the assertiveness of Latin America strengthened greatly. Those were the years of the publication of *The Cosmic Race* (Vasconcelos, 1925) in Mexico not too long after the Mexican Revolution of 1910. This was followed by the Brazilian Fernando Freyre's *Masters and Slaves* (1933) and later by Fernando Ortiz's *Cuban Counterpoint* (1940) as well as Siso Martínez's *Formation of the Venezuelan People* (1941). As Oscar Guardiola-Rivera (2010: 142) remarks, "some of these writers and musicians located this feeling of newness in world history in the genuine nature of the intercultural and multiracial societies of the Americas, born out of early anti-slavery sentiment". He adds, that "it was in Haiti and Colombia, rather than in England or France, that slavery had been abolished for the first time in human history". Strictly speaking, this claim is not entirely accurate, since slavery or the slave trade had been abolished in "pockets" in various places well before that. However, Guardiola-Rivera's claim has to be set against the fact that the slave trade was abolished throughout the British Empire in 1807; and slavery itself was for the most part abolished throughout the British Empire in 1833. However, in the late 20th century these phenomena "reappeared" in most parts of the world in a variety of forms, the usual way of describing these being human trafficking. In fact, the problem of cross-societal prostitution is at present one of Europe's biggest problems.

It should not be overlooked that, in the early years of the 19th century, Argentina was a richer country than the USA. Now, of course, it is Brazil that is "rising" fast and is, in fact, in a problematic relationship with the 19th-century dominance of the USA. Brazil has long had strong intellectual attachments to European culture. This is particularly true with regard to France. In fact, French anthropology, sociology, and philosophy have, for a long time, been very influential. The visual arts, as well as architecture, have also had much impact. With respect to France it should also be noted that the official slogan and guiding principle of Brazil, "Order and Progress", was adapted from French positivism. It should not be thought, however, that the traffic has been all one way. For example, Brazil had a great impact on the work of the major French anthropologist Lévi-Strauss. To a lesser, but still important, extent, Germanic ideas have also been of great consequence in Brazil. Some examples would be: Hegel, Marx, the Frankfurt School, political theology, and recent critical theory, including the work of Jürgen Habermas. It has frequently been remarked how much national identity has been based, particularly in the case of Brazil, upon selective emulation of features of other societies – again notably those in Europe (Schwartz, 1992). This tendency conforms to the oft-noted widespread hybridity of Latin American societies in general (Canclini, 1995). It is also worth mentioning that the seemingly progressive impact of the Protestant religion, notably in Britain, was, at various points, imported into Latin American societies. It was thought, by a number of so-called liberal elites, that bringing the Protestant ethic to Central and South America would enable their societies to prosper economically.

A particularly interesting example of Latin American interpenetration with matters European is the way in which Freyre came to the conclusion that Portuguese imperialism was superior to British imperialism. For instance, he considered miscegenation involving sexual relations between Portuguese-Brazilian men and Afro-Brazilian women led to a superior "race". (This played a large part in the development of the idea that Brazil was a "racial democracy", an idea that was discredited by the United Nations after the Second World War.) It should also be said that other countries of the Southern Cone, notably Chile and

Argentina, were greatly affected by the introduction of British technology and organization – for example railways – towards the end of the 19th century.

Latin American societies are particularly distinctive in the present context because those that gained their independence from the Spanish imperialists during the 19th century were, by virtue of their diplomatic recognition, clearly not as underprivileged as the colonies of Africa and Asia. However, it should not be overlooked that France, Holland, and Britain retained a colonial presence in Central America, and in the north-eastern area of South America, for most of the 20th century. Moreover, Britain in particular retained a neocolonial hold over Brazil and Argentina as well as other countries. One should also add that most countries in the Caribbean (the West Indies) retained their colonial status until well into the second half of the 20th century. Indeed, France still includes some Caribbean islands as part of the mother country – most notably Martinique.

Another example of European impact on Brazil and other Latin American societies was, and, to a much smaller extent still is, *liberation theology* – which played a significant part in the Sandinistan Revolution in Nicaragua in 1979. It should also be noted that different forms of liberation theology developed in many deprived countries, for instance in Africa and Asia, during the same period (Robertson, 1986, 1987, 1988). Here again we find an example of a symbiotic relationship between ex-colonies or "neo-colonies" on the one hand, and European imperialists on the other. Moreover, the ways in which the idea of liberation, at least in religious or politico-religious terms, had different applications in different regions is an excellent example of glocalization on a worldwide scale. An even more clear-cut and well-known case is provided by football (soccer) that first developed in Britain and then spiralled around Europe before landing, so to speak, in Brazil, Argentina, and virtually all other Latin American countries. The same applies to the tango, which started in the slums of Argentina, "travelled" through Europe and Asia – as far as Japan and China – to re-emerge in a modified form in Argentina and to a somewhat enlarged audience. This is, indeed, a classic case of glocalization. It is also (unfortunately) necessary to remark that a number of prominent German Nazis fled to Southern Cone countries, notably Argentina and Paraguay after the Second World War.

At the time of writing, the general relationship between East and West is particularly confused by the more specific relationship between Russia and China concerning the situations in Syria and Ukraine. Russian journalists and politicians have claimed that it is not true, as EU and

USA leaders have said, that Russia is entirely on its own, particularly with respect to Ukraine. To the contrary, Russian commentators quite frequently claim that China, India, and a number of other countries are on their side and are opposed to the West. True or not, there is certainly a Eurasian factor in play, at least with respect to long-standing problems involving China and Russia. (In this connection it should not be overlooked that the Sino-Soviet conflict was one of the most internationally problematic features of the late 1950s.)

These issues only concern us here in so far as they have a definite impact upon or connection with "Europe". The fact that the Sino-Russian relationship cannot be omitted from any consideration of Europe's global presence is well illustrated by the fact that Russia has long regarded itself as a (Slavic) Asian country or empire rather than – or as well as – a European one. In fact, the East-looking versus West-looking tension or cleavage has been the hallmark of much Russian history.

In addition, as Banerjee (2012) has demonstrated, the entire question of Russian modernity and its reliance on Western ideas is crucial to an understanding of the northern hemisphere as a whole. In fact, Banerjee's argument depends much upon European science *and* fiction (Jameson, 2007) and its impact on Russia. Banerjee (2012: 31) invokes Dostoevsky to make the point that "unifying the Oriental and European aspects of Russia's legendary Janus-face was... the vital first step in ending the nation's two-centuries-long struggle for legitimacy". Summarizing Dostoevsky, Banerjee argues that Russia is both Asian and European, and that by synthesizing the two Russia can dispel the fear that Europe will call Russians Asiatic barbarians and, indeed, that Russians will be called more Asiatic than European. They will be released from their tendency to mimic Europeans and would thereby be unencumbered by what Dostoevsky called "the debilitating poison of Europeanisation" (Banerjee, 2012: 31).

Russia – or the old USSR – presents a particular challenge in the present context, although I am here referring to an analytical rather than a geopolitical one. Needless to say, however, these two sets of challenges overlap considerably. As Banerjee has again demonstrated, the Slavic aspect of Russia is very relevant to the condition of Europe, not least because the discourses of "fascism" and anti-Semitism have been so widely employed and used very arbitrarily for political gain. It is also appropriate here to mention the projected formation of the Eurasian Union, that is destined to come into being in January 2015. The Eurasian Union will be very unlike the European Union in so far as it will not be based on the principles of equality and democracy of member states, the rule of law, or of human rights. In fact, Snyder (2014: 16) states that "any democracy within the Eurasian Union would pose a threat to Putin's Russia". To again quote Snyder (2014: 16), "the ethnic purification of the communist legacy is precisely the logic of National Bolshevism, which is the foundational ideology of Eurasia today. Putin himself is an admirer of the philosopher Ivan Ilin, who wanted Russia to be a nationalist dictatorship."

Turning to China, this is almost certainly the greater challenge to Europe and the West as a whole. The impact of the Opium Wars of 1839–1842 and 1856–1860, have long constituted the basis of Chinese mistrust of Europe and, in fact, are still commonly invoked as the major manifestations of European imperialism. As early as 1820 there was enough opium forced upon China to keep a million people addicted (Mishra, 2012: 27). The opening of China by the intrusion occasioned by the wars increased and spread the use of opium, and led to even more addiction. The standard of living, which before 1800 had been superior to that of much of Europe, was drastically lowered by the growth of massive foreign debts and indemnities. This led to the opening of large parts of China to foreign troops (Frank, 1998; Mishra, 2012: 161; Frank and Gills, 2013). The 1900 Boxer Rising by the Chinese was a result of a long-simmering wave of hostility against westerners, notably European missionaries and Chinese converts to Christianity.

The significance of trading companies, particularly the East India Company, cannot be exaggerated as far as the general expansion of imperial power into India and China was concerned. British and French imperialism were by far the most important factors in this respect, although the Dutch, and to a much lesser extent the Portuguese, played important roles as well. The general result was the Europeanization, and, to an extent, the Americanization of the central parts of the east coast of China. The establishment of separate European enclaves on the east coast of China was "legitimated" by the principle of extraterritoriality. This involved the claim that specific overseas territories were subject to the intruders' laws and not to the laws of the indigenous populations. (Here again, we have a case of what can best be regarded as glocalization – each intruder having its own way of intruding.)

Since the most well-known proponents of the subaltern or postcolonial perspectives have been Indian, rather than African, it is not easy to disentangle the connection between African and Indian conceptions of Europe. In any case, there have been some extremely significant African proponents of what is usually called subalternism. Among these is Kwame Appiah (e.g. 1992, 2007). His major contributions include the dismissal of the old European idea that all Africans are ethnically homogenous, that "race" is a European fabrication, and that cosmopolitanism is not a phenomenon that is confined to Europe (cf. Robertson, 2014).

There is no doubt that, in the European mind, Africa has, so to speak, been the recent "home" of European imperialism, notwithstanding the great importance of India as "the jewel" of the British Empire. In fact, Africa is undoubtedly a major site of *glocalization* in the sense that the so-called scramble for Africa involved most "great" European powers, particularly Britain, France, Germany, Belgium, Italy, Spain, and Portugal. This "scramble" is particularly illustrative of different styles of imperialism. Each individual, national imperial project had its own content and form. In other words, individual imperial projects can be regarded as "local" versions of the overall "global" scramble. This stance enables us to reverse the "normal" manner of considering what has almost always been referred to by such terms as modernization or, nowadays, multiple modernizations or multiple modernities. That is, in the context of considering the provincialization of Europe – or at least placing Europe in a global context – it is equally plausible and empirically suitable to think of change, in what used to be called the Third World, as a matter of imperial penetration as opposed to modernization after penetration has occurred. In fact, this is a kind of variation on the epistemological tack adopted by world-systems theorists and a number of theorists of globalization (including the present author) who insist on putting the global context first, rather than making the latter a kind of outcome of societal change. (Indeed, this is a major weakness of the multiple modernities school of thought.)

Turning now to Australia, the first thing to be noted, as far as consideration of Europe is concerned, is the White Australia Policy that kept many thousands of potential Asian immigrants from entering Australia. In fact, the White Australia Policy was once an article of faith that few politicians dared question (Walker, 2005: 64), even though many Australian leaders fully recognized, as long ago as the 1890s, that Australia's proximity to Asia would inevitably lead to close connections between the two continents. However, Japan's defeat of Russia in 1905 intensified the racial prejudice that Australians had concerning Asia. Until the 1890s Australia had had a relatively benign view of Asia's proximity, but the victory of Japan in the Russo-Japanese War in 1905 – the first triumph of an Asian country over a European one – greatly changed this. Moreover, the suspicious, indeed hostile, attitude towards Asia – summed up in the well-known phrase, "the yellow peril" – consolidated this increasingly negative view. In fact, Sax Rohmer's character, Dr Fu Manchu, began his fictional career in 1913. The influence of this character was extremely effective in various parts of the world in making Asians more despised and distrusted. To quote Walker (2005: 69), "the ideal of a white Australia won overwhelming support and was applauded on several grounds, not least that Australia had to be kept free from what was considered Asian contamination. A fear of 'Asian' dirt and contamination informed the conceptualization of Australia's future."

Of course, the anti-Asian policy rested heavily upon the fact that Australia was a British colony and that its major immigrants were British, Irish, and other Europeans. Even though the White Australia Policy largely died away in the later part of the 20th century and was eventually abolished in 1972, Australia presently faces an Asian challenge of another kind. This consists of the rapid expansion of Chinese investment in and purchase of Australian services and goods. According to recent estimates, between 2007 and 2014 Chinese companies bought approximately A$24 billion-worth of property, even though foreigners are only legally allowed to buy new homes (Delaney: 2014).

Cross-cutting the issue of the relationships between and among nation-states, regions, and civilizations is the somewhat overlooked fact of the *Kulturkampf* – or culture clash – syndrome that appears to be affecting the world as a whole. *Intra*-societal tensions and conflicts between those who are for abortion and those who are against it; those who are religious and those who are atheistic; and those who approve or disapprove of same-sex marriage and same-sex relationships, are to be witnessed across much of the contemporary world. Numerous tensions and conflicts are facilitated by extremist, strongly right-wing, movements. One particular recent example: Putin has joined the wave of anti-gay sentiment that is to be found in countries such as Africa, India, and Malaysia. If this kind of conflict intensifies it may well be that civil wars become increasingly common and widespread.

Brendan Simms (2013) concludes his sweeping history of Europe by briefly confronting the question of Europe's future. Among the crucial questions he raises is the significance of Germany, invoking the maxim that Germany is too small for the world and too large for Europe. He convincingly states that Europe has only experienced unity when it had to confront a great external challenge; the major initial case of this being the declaration that Europe was the centre of Christendom as the former attempted to meet the Ottoman challenge in the mid-15th century. However, subsequent threats came as much from within as from without, as was the case with Louis XIV, Napoleon, Hitler, and

Stalin. Simms maintains, somewhat optimistically, that "only a major external threat will unite Europeans today" (Simms, 2013: 533–534). Among the external threats he mentions are Putin's Russia, the Islamist Caliphate, and China. He also raises the question as to whether what he calls the "lands between" – that is, Ukraine and Belarus – will be absorbed by Russia. He may well also have had Moldova and the Baltic states in mind. Indeed, this is common speculation among many students of international relations. However, Simms's impressive analysis has the disadvantage of being nowhere near as genuinely global as that of Osterhammel (2014).

Whither the nation-state in Europe and its future?

It is essential that this book should approach its conclusion with a comment on the nation-state and its relationship to globalization. The main reason for this is that the issue of the relationship between individual nation-states and the European Union as a whole has been very problematic, particularly with the expansion of the latter. The major analytic mistake is that many contributors to the overall debate about globalization, and, not least, the condition and future of the EU, are plagued by the sense that globalization (or globalism) inevitably clashes with the nation-state and assertions of nationalism (e.g. Halikiopoulou and Vasilopoulou, 2011). However, numerous writers on what is variously called global society, world society, and other similar concepts, have adamantly insisted that the nation-state is *part of*, rather than being outside of, the processes of globalization. Indeed, one seriously wonders how it could be otherwise (Robertson, 1990, 1992, 1998, 2001; Krucken and Drori, 2009: 3–66, 173–205; Holton, 2011).

"Mapping" the global arena is most definitely a prerequisite for any plausible consideration of any region in the world (Robertson, 1992: 49–60). Neglect of such an exercise has been a major deficiency of European studies as well as, apparently, European policy. When reference is made to the subject of globalization, more often than not the relevant authors seem to be unembarrassed to claim that there is no widely accepted definition of globalization. Many of them do not even take the time to offer alternatives or justifications for not so doing. However, even though there may not be *total* consensus as to what is meant by globalization, there is surely much more consensus than we are often led to believe. The major difficulty with this claim is that it is made in defiance of major schools of globalization theory. In view of these considerations it is necessary to state, yet again, one approach which many find very plausible. However, before proceeding I cannot resist the temptation to cite, somewhat arbitrarily, one example of what I have in mind. Cooper (2005: 96) claims that:

> Globalisation is itself a term whose meaning is not clear and over which substantial disagreements exist among those who use it. It can be used so broadly that it embraces everything and therefore means nothing, but for most writers, it carries a powerful set of images, if not a precise definition.
>
> (cited in Suny, 2011:115)

Cooper goes on to say that the term should be questioned, "since the processes of integration have not been as global and total as its proponents claim and because the claims of newness of the process are belied by earlier episodes of integration and transnational exchanges" (cited in Suny, 2011:115).

Cooper's identification of integration with globalization is, to say the least, peculiar. Although some writers use such phrases as a "globalized world", the perspective entailed in such a formulation makes no sense. In other words, what does "globalized" mean? If the world were to be globalized surely that would mean that the world had, so to speak, come to an entropic stop! Globalization is a continuous *process* – with no judgement, in its general use, as to whether this process is complete or not. Much more important, however, are the ways in which the nation-state can be rendered *as part of* the process of globalization. This cannot be the place to justify in any detail the genesis of the nation-state. My argument is that globalization has "proceeded" in terms of the following fundamental conceptual components: *the nation-state*; *the system of nation-states* (i.e. international relations); *individual selves*; and *humanity*. Approaching the nation-state in this manner enables us to recognize that not merely can the nation-state itself be explicitly *included* in what I tend to call *the global field* (or the global arena), it can also be viewed as a phenomenon that changes over time. The failure to recognize that the nation-state itself may change, as part of the ongoing process of globalization, is the most egregious lacuna in studies, not merely of the nation-state, but more generally of nationalism and national identity.

The basic principle underlying the present author's claim as to changes in the "shape" of the nation-state is that the relationships between the four individual components listed become more complex and, in a sense, fragile. As far as the nation-state is concerned it is apparent that there has been a definite shift in the direction of (problematic) multiculturality (Bootle, 2014). *Each processual change in any given component affects the other components and the complexity of the relations between them all.* (For elaboration see, inter alia, Robertson, 1992: 25–31, 49–64.)

In applying these considerations to the European Union it can be seen that, with the large and apparently increasing number of member nation-states, each one is subject at any point in time to a number of differing "pressures". Given this, it would seem likely that breakdowns of one kind or another are more or less inevitable. However, another significant consideration is that, in the face of this great variety of pressures, nation-states may well become *stronger*, rather than weaker – as a matter of self-defence or self-protection.

Conclusion

In view of the scope and range of issues raised in this book, and the respects in which Europe influences, and is influenced by, the rest of the planet, it is essential that students, young and old, should immerse themselves in *global* education. In fact, it is encouraging to note that a recent survey of 7 to 14-year-olds undertaken in the UK discovered that they wished to learn more about global issues than any other subject apart from mathematics and English (Finlayson, 2014). Such educational reach is particularly necessary in view of the dangers produced by the stress on, and "retreat" to, "the local" and highly specialized. As has been seen, there is a sense in which the local has been globalized. However, without strong educational efforts the danger is that, far from becoming more global, systems of education will concentrate on what can only be called the parochial, whereas what is being proposed here are forms and styles of education that definitely bear the stamp of the *glocal*.

I have, in this epilogue, considered the place of Europe within the world from four main angles. First, I have looked at the situation in Europe *from within*. Second, I have discussed Europe *from the perspective of and through its relationship with "others"* (Eurasia, East Asia, the Middle East, Africa, Latin America, India, and, to much lesser extent, ex-white-settler colonies). Third, I have considered briefly the *subaltern–post-colonial perspective* on Europe, mainly in a phenomenological manner. Fourth, I have specified a few examples of the ways in which non-European regions were more "advanced" than Europe, and the ways in which European powers have capitalized on the advantages thereby made available to them.

In the introduction to their edited book, *The French Revolution in Global Perspective*, Desan, Hunt, and Nelson (2013) argue that there are three main ways in which the "international" dimensions of the French Revolution can be discussed: the relationship with the Atlantic world; the global imperial crisis of the 18th century; and, the one that they favour, a global approach, emphasizing France's participation in what they call early modern globalization. Broadly speaking, without being specifically concerned with the French Revolution per se, I have adopted a global approach that does not involve choosing between culture, ideology, and politics, on the one hand, and social structures and economic trends, on the other. In other words, I have used the same approach as Desan, Hunt, and Nelson but only very loosely. I have, of course, said relatively little about the colonization of the New World (save for the Spanish and Portuguese ventures) and very little indeed about the USA and Canada. Nonetheless, the imperial rivalry between France and Britain played an enormous role in the American "revolution" (which is not to deny entirely the significance of the Dutch in the latter).

This book has consisted largely of an attempt to alter our thinking about Europe, mainly by applying what used to be thought of as the neologism *glocalization*. In a major sense my premise has been that words have the power to make worlds (Gluck and Tsing, 2009).

References

Abu-Lughod, J. (1989) *Before European Hegemony: The World System A.D. 1250–1350*, New York: Oxford University Press.

Appiah, K. A. (1992) *In My Father's House: Africa in the Philosophy of Culture*, Oxford: Oxford University Press.

Appiah, K. A. (2007) *Cosmopolitanism: Ethics in a World of Strangers*, London: Allen Lane.

Arutunyan, A. (2014) *The Putin Mystique*, London: Skyscraper.

Banerjee, A. (2012) *We Modern People: Science Fiction and the Making of Russian Modernity*, Middletown, CT: Wesleyan University Press.

Bhambra, G. K. (2007) *Rethinking Modernity: Postcolonialism and the Sociological Imagination*, London: Palgrave Macmillan.

Bootle, R. (2014) *The Trouble with Europe*, London: Brealey.

Brotton, J. (2012) *A History of the World in Twelve Maps*, London: Allen Lane.

Buruma, I. and A. Margalit. (2004) *Occidentalism: The West in the Eyes of Its Enemies*, New York: Penguin Press.

Canclini, N. G. (1995) *Hybrid Cultures: Strategies for Entering and Leaving Modernity*, Minneapolis: University of Minnesota Press.

Chakrabarty, D. (2000) *Provincializing Europe: Postcolonial Thought and Historical Difference*, Princeton NJ: Princeton University Press.

Colley, L. (2013) "Wide-Angled: Global History," *London Review of Books*, 26 September, 25 (18): 18–19.

Cooper, F. (2005) *Colonialism in Question:Theory, Knowledge, and History*, Berkeley: University of California Press.

Delaney, E. (2014) "Australia startled by foreign investment", *International New York Times* April 25, p. 8.

Desan, S., L. Hunt and W. M. Nelson. (eds.) (2013) *The French Revolution in Global Perspective*, London: Cornell University Press.

Drori, G. S. and G. Krucken. (2009) "World Society: A Theory and a Research Program in Context", in G. Krucken and G. S, Drori (eds.) *World Society: Writings of John W. Meyer*, Oxford: Oxford University Press, pp. 3–35.

Dyer, G. (2014) *The Contest of the Century: The New Era of Competition with China*, London: Allen Lane.

Fenby, J. (2014) "Forget the Chinese 21st Century?" *The Guardian Review*, 26 May, p. 9.

Finlayson, A. (2014) "A Sustainable School Succeeds", *Education Guardian*, p. 7.

Frank, A. G. (1998) *ReOrient: Global Economy in the Asian Age*, London: University of California Press.

Frank, A. G. and B. Gills. (2013) *ReOrient: Global Economy in the Asian Age*, New York: Paradigm Press.

Gluck, C. and A. L. Tsing (eds.) (2009) *Words in Motion: Toward a Global Lexicon*, Durham, NC: Duke University Press.

Guardiola-Rivera, O. (2010) *What If Latin America Ruled the World? How the South Will Take the North into the 22nd Century*, London: Bloomsbury.

Guenoun, D. (2013) *About Europe: Philosophical Hypotheses*, Stanford, CA: Stanford University Press.

Guthrie, D. (2012) *China and Globalization: The Social, Economic and Political Transformation of Chinese Society*, (3rd edn.) London: Routledge.

Halikiopoulou, D. and S. Vasilopoulou (eds.) (2011) *Nationalism and Globalisation: Conflicting or Complementary?* London: Routledge.

Hall, S. (1982) *The Empire Strikes Back: Race and Racism in 70s Britain*, London: Hutchinson.

Hannerz, U. (2009) "Geocultural Scenarios", in P. Hedstrom and B. Wittrock (eds.) *Frontiers of Sociology*, Leiden: Brill.

Hodges, R. and D. Whitehouse (1983) *Mohammed, Charlemagne & the Origins of Europe: Archaeology and the Pirenne Thesis*, Ithaca, NY: Cornell University Press.

Holton, R. J. (2011) *Globalization and the Nation-State*, 2nd edn. London: Palgrave Macmillan.

Hutton, W. (2007) *The Writing on the Wall: China and the West in the 21st Century*, New York: Little, Brown.

Jameson, F. (2007) *Archeologies of the Future: The Desire Called Utopia and Other Science Fictions*, London: Verso.

Judt, T. (2006) "Anti-Americans abroad", in B. O'Connor and M. Griffiths (eds.) *The Rise of Anti-Americanism*, New York: Routledge pp. 203–212.

Kane, J. (2006) "Ambivalent anti-Americanism", in B. O'Connor and M. Griffiths (eds.) *The Rise of Anti-Americanism*, New York: Routledge, pp. 48–67.

Kohn, H. (1962) *The Age of Nationalism: The First Era of Global History*, New York: Harper.

Lyon, D. (1998) "Wheels within Wheels: Glocalization and Contemporary Religion", in M. Hutchinson and O. Kalu (eds.) *A Global Faith: Essays on Evangelicalism and Globalization*, Sydney: Centre for the Study of Australian Christianity, pp. 47–68.

McDonagh, G. W. (2009) *Iberian Worlds*, New York: Routledge.

Marquand, D. (2011) *The End of the West: The Once and Future Europe*, Princeton NJ: Princeton University Press.

Mishra, P. (2012) *From the Ruins of Empire: The Revolt Against the West and the Remaking of Asia*, London: Allen Lane.

Moyo, D. (2011) *How the West was Lost: Fifty Years of Economic Folly – And the Stark Choices Ahead*, London: Penguin.

Moyn, S. (2013) "On the Nonglobalization of Ideas", in S. Moyn and A. Sartori (eds.) *Global Intellectual History*, New York: Columbia University Press, pp. 187–204.

Neumann, I. (1996) *Russia and the Idea of Europe*, London: Routledge.

Neumann, I. (1999) *Uses of the Other: "The East" in European Identity Formation*, Minneapolis: University of Minnesota Press.

Osterhammel, J. (2014) *The Transformation of the World: A Global History of the Nineteenth Century*, Princeton, NJ: Princeton University Press.

Outhwaite, W. (2008) *European Society*, Cambridge: Polity Press.

Pirenne, H. (1925) *Medieval Cities*, Princeton, NJ: Princeton University Press.

Pirenne, H. (1939) *Mohammed and Charlemagne*, New York: W. W. Norton.:

Robertson, R. (1986) "Liberation Theology in Latin America: Sociological Problems of Interpretation and Explanation", in J. Hadden and A. Shupe (eds.) *Prophetic Religion and Politics*, New York: Paragon Books, pp.107–139.

Robertson, R. (1987) "Latin America and Liberation Theology", in T. Robbins and R. Robertson (eds.) *Church- State Relations: Tensions and Transitions*, New Brunswick, NJ: Transaction Books, pp. 205–220.

Robertson, R. (1988) "Liberation Theology, Latin America and Third World Underdevelopment", R. Rubenstein and J. Roth (eds.) *The Politics of Latin American Liberation Theology*, Washington, DC: Washington Institute Press, pp. 17–134.

Robertson, R. (1990) "Japan and the USA: The Interpenetration of National Identities and the Debate about Orientalism", in N. Abercrombie, S. Hill and B. S. Turner (eds.) *Dominant Ideologies*, London: Unwin Hyman, pp. 182–198.

Robertson, R. (1992) *Globalization: Social Theory and Global Culture*, London: Sage.

Robertson, R. (1997) "Comments on the 'global triad' and 'glocalization'", in Nobutaka Inoue (ed.) *Globalization and Indigenous Culture*, Tokyo: Institute for Japanese Culture and Classics, pp. 217–225.

Robertson, R. (1998) "Identidad Nacional y Globalizacion: Falacias Contemporaneas", *Revista Mexicana de Sociologia*, 1 (January – March): 3–19.

Robertson, R. (2011) "Global Connectivity and Global Consciousness", *American Behavioral Scientist*, 55 (10):1336–1345.

Robertson, R. (2014) "Civilization(s), Ethnoracism, Antisemitism, Sociology", in M. Stoetzler (ed.) *Antisemitism and the Constitution of Sociology*, Omaha NB: University of Nebraska Press, pp. 206–245.

Schwartz, R. (1992) *Misplaced Ideas: Essays on Brazilian Culture*, London: Verso.

Sen, A. (2005) *The Argumentative Indian: Writings on Indian Culture, History and Identity*, London: Allen Lane.

Shambaugh, D. (2013) *China Goes Global: The Partial Power*, New York: Oxford University Press.

Simms, B. (2013) *Europe: The Struggle for Supremacy,* 1453 to the present, London: Allen Lane.

Snyder, T. (2014) "Fascism, Russia and Ukraine", *New York Review of Books*, 20 March: 16–17.

Spivak, G. C. (1999) *A Critique of Post-Colonial Reason: Toward a History of the Vanishing Present*, Cambridge, MA: Harvard University Press.

Suny, R. G. (2011) "Globalisation and the Nation-State: The future of failures," in D. Halikiopoulou and S. Vasilopoulou (eds.) *Nationalism and Globalisation:Conflicting or complementary?* New York: Routledge.

Tsing, A. L. (1993) *In the Realm of the Diamond Queen*, Princeton, NJ: Princeton University Press.

Tsing, A. L. (2005) *Friction: An Ethnogrophy of Global Connection*, Princeton, NJ: Princeton University Press.

Tsytankov, A. (2006) *Russia's Foreign Policy: Change and Continuity in National Identity,* Lanham, MA: Rowman & Littlefield.

Vasconcelos, J. (1925) *The Cosmic Race*, Baltimore, MD: Johns Hopkins University Press.

Walker, D. (2005) "Australia's Asian Futures", in M. Lyons and P. Russell (eds.) *Australia's History: Themes and Debates*, Sydney: University of New South Wales Press, pp. 63–80.

Index

Note: Locators followed by the letters '*f*', 'n' and '*t*' refers to figures, notes, and tables respectively.

Printed and bound by CPI Group (UK) Ltd, Croydon, CR0 4YY